WRITING PROGRAM ADMINISTRATION
AND THE COMMUNITY COLLEGE

Writing Program Administration
Series Editors: Susan H. McLeod and Margot Soven

The Writing Program Administration series provides a venue for scholarly monographs and projects that are research- or theory-based and that provide insights into important issues in the field. We encourage submissions that examine the work of writing program administration, broadly defined (e.g., not just administration of first-year composition programs). Possible topics include but are not limited to 1) historical studies of writing program administration or administrators (archival work is particularly encouraged); 2) studies evaluating the relevance of theories developed in other fields (e.g., management, sustainability, organizational theory); 3) studies of particular personnel issues (e.g., unionization, use of adjunct faculty); 4) research on developing and articulating curricula; 5) studies of assessment and accountability issues for WPAs; and 6) examinations of the politics of writing program administration work at the community college.

Books in the Series

A Rhetoric for Writing Program Administrators edited by Rita Malenczyk (2013)

Writing Program Administration and the Community College by Heather Ostman (2013)

The WPA Outcomes Statement—A Decade Later, edited by Nicholas N. Behm, Gregory R. Glau, Deborah H. Holdstein, Duane Roen, and Edward M. White (2012)

Writing Program Administration at Small Liberal Arts Colleges by Jill M. Gladstein and Dara Rossman Regaignon (2012)

GenAdmin: Theorizing WPA Identities in the 21st Century by Colin Charlton, Jonikka Charlton, Tarez Samra Graban, Kathleen J. Ryan, and Amy Ferdinandt Stolley (2011).

WRITING PROGRAM ADMINISTRATION AND THE COMMUNITY COLLEGE

Heather Ostman

Parlor Press
Anderson, South Carolina
www.parlorpress.com

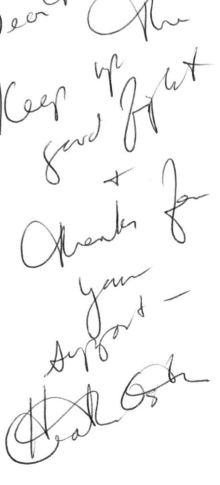

Dear Alexandra

Keep up the good fight + thanks for your support —

Heather Ostman

Parlor Press LLC, Anderson, South Carolina, USA
© 2013 by Parlor Press
All rights reserved.
Printed in the United States of America
S A N: 2 5 4 - 8 8 7 9

The use of the following charts is permitted by the National Center for Educational
Statistics (NCES). Source: NCES website.
Percentage Distribution of Risk Factors for 1995-96 Beginning Postsecondary
Students by Sector of First Institution Attended and by School Activity (table)
Percentage Distribution of Students Beginning at Public 2-year institutions
in1995-96 by initial degree goal and student characteristics, etc. (table)
Main Fields in Which Associate Degrees Were Conferred 2003-4 (table)

Library of Congress Cataloging-in-Publication Data

Ostman, Heather.
  Writing program administration and the community college / Heather Ostman.
    pages cm. -- (Writing program administration)
  Includes bibliographical references and index.
  ISBN 978-1-60235-359-6 (pbk. : alk. paper) -- ISBN 978-1-60235-360-2
(hardcover : alk. paper) -- ISBN 978-1-60235-361-9 (adobe ebook) -- ISBN 978-1-
60235-362-6 (epub)
  1. Writing centers--United States--Administration. 2. Basic writing (Remedial
education)--United States. 3. English language--Rhetoric--Study and teaching
(Higher)--United States. 4. Community colleges--United States--Curricula. I.
Title.
  PE1405.U6O78 2013
  808'.042071173--dc23
                            2013031678
1 2 3 4 5

Cover photo: © 2009 by CEFutcher. Used by permission.
Cover design by David Blakesley
Printed on acid-free paper.

Parlor Press, LLC is an independent publisher of scholarly and trade titles in print
and multimedia formats. This book is available in paper, cloth and eBook formats
from Parlor Press on the World Wide Web at http://www.parlorpress.com or through
online and brick-and-mortar bookstores. For submission information or to find out
about Parlor Press publications, write to Parlor Press, 3015 Brackenberry Drive,
Anderson, South Carolina, 29621, or email editor@parlorpress.com.

For my parents, Grace Wood and Randolph Ostman

Contents

Acknowledgments   *xi*

Introduction   *3*

1 Community College Students   *13*

Open Admissions   *14*

Diversity   *23*

Adult Learning   *36*

Race and Ethnicity   *41*

English as a Second Language (ESL)   *44*

Working Students   *45*

Working-Class Students   *46*

Developmental Students   *48*

Learning Disabilities   *52*

Emotional Needs   *52*

Reframing Assumptions   *54*

2 Writing Program Administration at the Community
College: A History and Overview   *57*

English Departments   *77*

Faculty   *81*

Decision-Making   *98*

The Role of the Writing Program Administrator (WPA)   *100*

3 The General Responsibilities of Community College WPAs   *103*

Curricular Development   *105*

Introduction to Outcomes   *109*

Writing Across the Curriculum   *115*

Developmental Writing   *117*

Reading   *120*

English as a Second Language (ESL)
and Generation 1.5   *121*

Articulation   *122*

Scheduling Courses   *124*

Hiring Contingent Faculty   *126*

Faculty Development   *131*

Writing Centers   *134*

Placement   *135*

Assessment   *137*
Budgets   *139*
Representing Writing Faculty   *143*
Responding to Complaints and Needs   *145*
Managing It All   *147*

4 WPA Work in the New Era of Community Colleges   *150*
American Graduation Initiative   *152*
The Present and Future of Developmental Studies   *156*
Plurality and Inclusivity   *162*
Multiple Literacies in a New Global Context   *164*
Shaping the Identity of the WPA and Envisioning
    the Writing Program   *167*
Pedagogy   *173*
Program Assessment   *174*
Politics   *177*

5 Conclusion: Community College WPAs
    as Educational Leaders   *180*

6 Continuing the Conversation: A Selective
    List for Further Reading   *188*
Writing Program Administration   *188*
Related Community College Information   *190*
Curriculum and Pedagogy   *191*
Developmental Writing Issues   *193*
ESL Issues   *194*
Assessment   *195*
Class and the Community College   *196*
Diversity Education   *197*
Adult Learning   *197*
Writing Centers   *198*

Appendix A: "The Portland Resolution:" Guidelines for
    Writing Program Administrator Positions   *199*

Appendix B: WPA Outcomes Statement for
    First-Year Composition   *206*

Notes   *211*
Works Cited   *217*
Index   *227*
About the Author   *231*

Acknowledgments

This book is the culmination of many long conversations about writing programs and community colleges, in particular those among my colleagues in the Westchester Community College (WCC) English Department's English Studies Committee—not to mention the assistance, encouragement, and advice of several of my colleagues and friends, including Negar Farakish, Frank Madden, Carol Passariello-Smith, Noelle Ostman, Una Shih, Kent Trickel, Sally Linehan, Ed Hengel, Leonore Rodrigues, Elise Martucci, Liz Fritz, Walter Kroczak, Terry Haynes, Heidi Johnsen, and Jason Evans. I would especially like to thank Patti Sehulster, David Blakesley, Susan McLeod, Margot Soven, Joyce Neff, and Jeff Ludwig for their attentive reading and subsequent guidance on the entire manuscript. In addition, Kathleen McCormick's shared wisdom shed much needed light on WPA work in public institutions. I would also like to thank my husband, Ralph Spafford, for his encouragement and wisdom. Most of all, I owe the greatest debt to the students of WCC, who teach me more than I could ever hope to teach them in a classroom.

Writing Program Administration and the Community College

Introduction

The early twentieth century saw the establishment of the first junior college, an institution that became one of the greatest democratic initiatives in American history—as well as one of the most socially, politically, and economically complex enterprises.[1] Like other ambitious democratic enterprises, it emerged through time as one of the most socially, politically, and economically complex institutions. Still, the community college continues to thrive into the twenty-first century, especially as recent economic crises have made attending—and working at—a publictwo-year institution more appealing. If 1901 introduced the United States to the mission of the two-year public institution and invited millions to fulfill their dreams of higher education, then the early 2000s made sure the college became a permanent figure in the future of the nation. The Obama Administration's 2009 call to raise the number of American college graduates brought community colleges into the national spotlight, formalizing the institution's place in the global era of the twenty-first century. If ever there was a time for educators to participate in a great national enterprise, to contribute to the advancement of literacy in the United States, and to enable millions of citizens to realize their educational potential, the time is now for community college writing program administrators.

Even before the national attention and the downturn of global economies, the community college offered writing program administrators (WPAs) a special attraction: students. Because students come from a wide range of backgrounds and bring an equally wide range of competencies, students require WPAs to be responsive to their multiplicity of cultures, literacies, and knowledges. According to the American Association of Community Colleges (AACC), as of 2008, the over 1,000 community colleges across the United States enrolled almost half of all American undergraduates,[2] including 44% of all black students, 55% of all Native American students, and 52% of all Latino students ("Fast Facts"). Many community college students are employed full or part time; many have children;and many are the first in their families to receive a college education ("Fast Facts"). Further, not only does the student body present a complexly diverse population; the same might also be said about writing faculty at two-year colleges, who come from a variety of educational backgrounds and bring similarly varied approaches to teaching. Hence, the WPA in the two-year institution holds a unique responsibility: to administer a writing program, or a core of writing courses, that meets the literacy needs of every student who walks through the college's doors; to simultaneously engage a faculty and an administration who may or may not have the time, energy, or background to support such a program fully; and to learn from and respond to the ever-changing environment of the community college. In these ways, the diversity of students and instructors, coupled with a heavy course load and the task of creating, developing, and/or sustaining a viable writing program, usually with few resources, make WPA work at the community college among the most challenging and rewarding jobs in academia.

Responsible for providing writing instruction for nearly half of the nation's undergraduates (Raines 151), community college WPAs constantly negotiate different professional roles, and these roles are always shifting. WPAs are part instructor and part administrator—if they formally identify as WPAs at all. At many community colleges, the WPA is simply the full-time instructor—or even a committee of instructors—who manages the business of the writing courses. For the purposes here, the term "WPA" refers to any individual or committee directly engaged with the administration of the writing program or writing courses at a given community college. Like many of their counterparts at four-year institutions, these WPAs have authority but no power—and often no budget. Unlike their counterparts, though, they coordinate the program among faculty peers, including legions of adjunct instructors, but never "subordinate" TAs and graduate students who leave the institution after a few years. If they have time—for some there are no course reductions to accommodate this work—WPAs may keep up with developments in the fields of composition and writing program administration, but the challenge becomes disseminating that information to their colleagues, many of whom are not engaged or cannot engage in their field or have backgrounds other than in English (for example, creative arts or education). WPAs also may have to explain information from their field to administrators who do not understand or who assume that "anyone can teach writing."

The roles shift as the WPA's audience shifts daily, depending on context. They interact with any number of community college constituents on a given day: students, faculty, administrators, the union, the academy, the college, and the supporting community. As a WPA in a two-year institution, Victoria Holmsten explains that her position requires her to view her work through multiple perspectives, including those from outside the college:

> In short, my role at the college requires that I look beyond the boundaries of the English department or the writing program. It is my strong suspicion that this is true for my colleagues who work in community college roles. The complications of our institutions require us to live complicated, and constantly shifting lives, in order to require us to respond to the needs of our communities and to construct our roles as WPAs in our local contexts. (436)

The benefits of multiple perspectives—those within and outside of the institution—serve the program, the students, the faculty, and the WPAs. The connections and dialogues beyond one's institution, as Holmsten asserts, enables the WPA to continue bringing new ideas to the college, and even more importantly, continue developing a dynamic program.

In addition to the multiple audiences and contexts WPAs engage, recent years have brought community colleges into nationwide dialogues about literacy and education, making the relevance of WPA work at two-year institutions more apparent to colleagues in other institutions as well as to politicians and the American public. Several factors contribute to this growing recognition; among them is the recent surge in community college enrollment, a result of the national economic crisis that began in 2008, as well as President Obama's 2009 community college initiatives that included: a call to raise the number of college graduates by five million within the next decade (Jenkins and Bailey); the designation of $2 billion in competitive grants for community colleges (Moltz); and the subsequent philanthropic gifts for these institutions (Ashburn). Most important, in the last ten years, educators such as Mike Rose, Kathleen Blake Yancey, Linda Adler-Kassner, and others have called attention to the multiple literacies and competencies students bring to all writing classrooms, but which emerge very clearly in community college writing classrooms, consequently making the experience in the two-year institution essential to national and disciplinary discussions about student literacy. Their work, as well as the work of others, signaled a change in the way educators, specifically writing faculty, have begun thinking about student composition, thus broadening its definition beyond written, essayistic forms. Indicative of this change, in 2008, the Executive Committee of the National Council of Teachers of English (NCTE) adopted The NCTE Definition of 21st Century Literacies, which emphasizes the influence of new technologies on the ways writers compose texts:

> Because technology has increased the intensity and complexity of literate environments, the twenty-first century demands that a literate person possess a wide range of abilities and competencies, many literacies. These literacies—from reading online newspapers to participating in virtual classrooms—are multiple, dynamic, and malleable. As in the past, they are inextricably linked with particular histories, life possibilities and social trajectories of individuals and groups.

Reflecting NCTE's definition of literacies, compositionists continue to explore the multiplicity and complexity of student composing. Many WPAs and writing instructors in the two-year institution have long been engaged in these types of explorations, often out of necessity more than mere personal interest.[3] Mark Reynolds underscores the relevance of two-year college faculty's experience to current dialogues on literacy:

> No one is more knowledgeable about what is needed to expand knowledge in English studies than two-year college faculty members. They have been at the forefront of teaching writing at all levels to diverse populations. Their knowledge about literacy production and transmission is especially valuable. (11)

Also indicative of the community college's relevance to current literary dialogues is the March 2010 special issue of NCTE's journal, *Teaching English in the Two-Year College*, which focused on emergent literacies, featuring topics such as multimodal composition, visual rhetoric, and student proficiencies in Internet-based research in the community college context. Current work on such literacies reflects the rising aware-ness of the multiple competencies and knowledge students bring to all writing courses, so it is highly significant that community col-leges teach writing to almost one out of two American undergradu-ates (Raines 151). The experience of WPAs and instructors at two-year institutions *must be* central to current dialogues about student writing; without their experience, these dialogues only provide a partial picture of literacy instruction in the United States.

In light of current trends in writing pedagogy, as well as recent economic changes, WPAs at two-year institutions hold a unique so-ciopolitical and ethical responsibility, especially given the numbers of enrolled students for whom community college may not be the last resort, but the only resort. For many students, enrolling in the community college is far less about academic ability and much more about access. A college education—or even enrolling in a select few college courses—can open socioeconomic doors otherwise locked to many students. In a 2011 review of twenty studies, Clive Belfield and Thomas Bailey conclude that enrolling in a community college has far-reaching benefits for students, including increased earnings, bet-ter health, less criminal involvement, and less dependence on welfare than their counterparts who never proceed to further education after high school (57). The authors claim that the benefits "appear to be in-creasing over time," as well (60). Between 2007 and 2008, community colleges awarded 609,016 associate's degrees and 323,649 certificates ("Fast Facts")—in other words, in a single year, nearly a million people benefited in many tangible, life-changing ways by enrolling in a com-munity college.

Table A1. Annual Earnings Gains Over High School, by Gender and by Credential Earned or Years Enrolled Without a Credential. Source: Marcotte et al. (164–165, 170–171)

	Annual earnings gain (%)	
	Males	Females
Bachelor's degree	46	92
Associate's degree	17	40
Certificate	8	20
Any number of years enrolled, no credential earned	17	25

	Annual earnings gain (%)	
	Males	Females
1.5 years enrolled, no credential earned	13	17
1 year enrolled, no credential	8	9
0.5 years enrolled, no credential	0	7

Given the socioeconomic stakes for students, the administration of a community college writing program, then, must make necessary the awareness of what short-term and long-term effects a writing course can have on a student, keeping in mind (and keeping an open mind about) the myriad of competencies, possible goals, and complex histories he or she may bring to the classroom. It also requires awareness of sociopolitical and economic forces that limit educational access from outside the institution, but also advocacy in sometimes hostile circumstances.

With these political, social, and pedagogical responsibilities in mind, *Writing Program Administration and the Community College* is organized into six chapters to guide individuals unfamiliar with or new to WPA work in this context. Chapter One, "Community College Students," begins with a description of the diverse students who arrive at the doors of colleges. Since student needs have historically shaped English instruction in this context—forcing instructors to long ago abandon lecture formats and embrace collaborative learning techniques, technology, and media—students are central to the discussion of WPA work. Another reason to place them first, though, is to dispel common assumptions of students, such as all such students are less prepared than their peers enrolled at four-year institutions, or that they are only prepared for vocational training. This chapter offers a general description of the community college's extremely diversified students, who differ in terms of class, ethnicity, race, physical ability, age, family status, sexual orientation, religion, creed, academic abilities, developmental needs, ESL (L2) needs, Generation 1.5, learning disabilities, and other categories. Additionally, their multiplicity of literacies and knowledges cuts across all demographic categories, presenting WPAs with a student population demonstrating a myriad of competencies. Since most of these students have little choice about taking composition courses, WPAs oversee what has essentially become the college's (and for some students, higher education's) gate-keeping course(s).

This has, naturally, enormous social, political, and economic consequences, especially in light of the fact that the desired final destination
of many students is either transfer to a four-year institution or a job.
Since programs in composition and rhetoric within English offer little
training on sensitivity to class and protected categories, as well as to
developmental, ESL, Generation 1.5, and learning disabled students
through to graduate students and new hires, this chapter introduces
the reader to some of the unique needs and considerations of community college students.

To offer a contextual perspective on WPA work at the community
college, Chapter Two, "Writing Program Administration at the Community College: a History and an Overview," outlines WPA work
within the context of the community college's history and compares
this work to its counterparts in four-year institutions, from which
most of the WPA research emerges (and consequently often ignores
the realities and prevalence of community college work). [4] There are
some similarities among the various institutions. For example, a writing program frequently develops in response to the specific needs of an
institution; hence, each one is slightly or terrifically different from the
next (McLeod 7). This is certainly true at a community college, where,
traditionally, the writing program is not separate from the English department but is rather the main focus of the department (Holmsten
432). In fact, many community colleges do not have a writing program
per se, but offer a core of composition-based classes. Consequently,
this book uses the term "program" interchangeably for the administrative work of organizing, overseeing, and/or developing writing courses
within the two-year institution, whether a single individual or a committee addresses the work, as either of these possibilities exist at the
community college. And just as two-year colleges do not always have
a designated writing program, but may have instead a collection of
composition courses, they also do not always have an English department. A broader division or another department may offer the writing
program or writing courses. Whatever the particular organization of
the writing program is, most make the English department—or its
equivalent—a paradox at the community college: It is usually one of
the largest departments on campus, but it can be viewed as a "service"
department, since very few community colleges offer English degrees,
and writing instruction exists to "support" the work of other departments and programs. In light of these circumstances, this chapter ex-

amines the development of writing program administration within the specific context of the community college's history and academic environment.

Chapter Three, "Community College WPAs' General Responsibilities," identifies the most common large and small responsibilities of the WPA and discusses how to prepare for the many challenges encountered in the course of a day or a career. Individuals in this role identify by a variety of terms—such as "Writing Coordinator" and "Lead Instructor," among others—or their work is part of a broader responsibility—such as that of the department chair or an associate dean. In general, these responsibilities include scheduling classes; enrollment management; recruiting, hiring, and training contingent faculty; coordinating placement and assessment; hiring and training of placement readers; overseeing a writing tutorial center; fielding student and instructor complaints; representing writing faculty on committees and to administrators; and, in general, being responsible for everything related to student writing. This chapter outlines the different functions the WPA can fulfill in the community college and how many manage in light of the democratic mission of the institution.

Chapter Four, "WPA Work in the New Era of the Community College," considers the ways WPAs in two-year institutions address continuous change within an era of racing technological advancement, federal and philanthropic attention, developmental studies, and urgent diversity issues. While no single method for navigating change on such a grand scale exists, community college WPAs inhabit an ideal position as professionals whose role at the institution enables them to envision how a dynamic writing program can meet the needs of an ever-changing student population that brings multiple literacies and engages multimodal composing, often with greater ease than their instructors. This chapter identifies the current, major forces shaping WPA work. Within the context of these forces, it explores how advancing communication technologies challenge and compliment WPA work and how program assessment and knowledge of politics may facilitate the development of a program appropriately designed to accommodate and build upon the literacies and competencies today's students demonstrate.

Chapter Five, the conclusive chapter, "Community College WPAs as Educational Leaders," outlines the contributions WPAs at two-year institutions make to national and disciplinary discussions about student literacy. Given the culminating moment of high student enroll-ment, and the rise of emergent communication technologies, these WPAs have the experience and knowledge from working within a di-verse environment to lead dialogues on multi-literate student popula-tions. As a result, they not only have much to contribute to literacy dialogues, they may also be able to shift predominant and hierarchical thinking about literacy instruction in the United States.

Finally, Chapter Six, "Continuing the Conversation: Recom-mended Further Reading," offers a selective bibliography for further research, thought, and dialogue on WPA work and the community college. Despite the constantly developing nature of the work, the lit-erature on writing program administration at the two-year institution has been slower in its development, scope, and breadth. A review of re-lated literature reveals that to date, there are no other books dedicated to the specific work of the WPA in the community college. Several shorter works, though, offer important insights and particular politi-cal views of this work, including articles by Ana Maria Preto-Bay and Kristine Hansen, Victoria Holmsten, Jeffrey Klausman, Patrick Sul-livan, Tim Taylor, and Howard Tinberg, among others. This final chapter offers relevant readings on aspects of WPA work at the com-munity college, in addition to important online materials.

Writing Program Administration and the Community College con-tinues the dialogue already begun by the educators noted above, and others. This dialogue is essential to the developing understanding of writing pedagogy in the two-year institution, especially as community college writing programs are as varied as the students enrolled in them. The students offer opportunities to educators for learning in a myriad of ways. They require their WPAs to remain vigilant and focused on sustaining a writing program based on the democratic principles of an open-access institution. They challenge their WPAs and instruc-tors to continually find new ways of meeting them where they are, educationally speaking. As these students challenge conventional and traditional ways of teaching writing, they sometimes show their teach-ers how little they know about composing in this new age of emergent media technologies and multiple literacies, and how they have as much or more to teach their WPAs and instructors as these professionals have to teach them.

1 Community College Students

Writing programs develop in direct relationship to their institutions, whether they are two-year or four-year schools. Consequently, as Susan McLeod notes, "[B]ecause writing programs are site-specific, they differ from one another, meaning the work also differs widely from campus to campus" (7). Writing programs and WPA work in most types of institutions thus resist oversimplified generalizations. Such resistance is especially evident in community colleges, where the student body in almost any two-year college is as varied and changeable as the over 1,000 institutions themselves (Kort 181). In 1996, Cohen and Brawer observed the mutability that characterizes the nature of community college work: "[Community colleges] change frequently, seeking new programs and new clients" (qtd. in Coley 31). The changing needs of the surrounding community and businesses often affect the development of the college's programs. As a result, trends in student enrollments shift year to year, and WPAs engage in a continual process of change and revision. Cohen and Brawer argue that the writing program at the two-year college cannot remain static for a long period of time: "Never satisfied with resting on what has been done before, [community colleges] try new approaches to old problems" (qtd. in Coley 31). Describing the dynamics of the program at his institution, Klausman explains that "[t]he makeup of the student body at [his] college challenges the creation of a writing program that is inflexible and unresponsive to student perspectives on education" (246). Therefore, the dynamics of the two-year institution fosters an environment of necessary innovation. The community college's continual metamorphosis defies traditional notions of higher education and challenges its WPAs, its instructors, and its administrators to always search for new pedagogies, new technologies, and new ways to address student needs (Cohen and Brawer, qtd. in Coley 31).

Within this context of change, the students present a range of goals, several of which are unique to community college students and not ordinarily found in a four-year institution. They include transferring to a university, fulfilling a requirement for a vocational certificate, or simply taking a course or two without a desire for a degree—to name a few. Regardless of their intentions, students remain a steady, central concern, and a community college WPA must have a general sense of the educational objectives of the students in his or her own institution. Open admissions policies directly shape WPAs' considerations of these objectives and illuminate the requirements of a diverse student population that demonstrates widely ranging levels and types of literacies, who may shoulder multiple responsibilities in addition to school, and who may have complex emotional needs. This chapter first addresses the effects of an open admissions policy on writing program administration, and then its focus shifts to several general factors for consideration in the development of a community college writing program, including: diversity, adult learning, race and ethnicity; and students who present ESL needs, work demands, class-related issues, developmental needs, learning disabilities, and emotional needs. Whether WPAs come to their work with knowledge of these factors, or acquire knowledge about them through experience; these considerations serve as reminders that in the two-year institution, students are always and only the first priority—the center of any writing program.

Open Admissions

Community colleges' open admissions policies, which offer few limiting criteria for access, foster wide-ranging diversity among students. Not surprisingly, open admissions, in addition to the community college's relatively low tuition, precipitate some of the greatest challenges to WPA work in this context. [1] Addressing the needs of such a diverse student population requires understanding and skills not usually acquired or even emphasized in four-year or research institutions, where WPAs complete their graduate work. Further, instead of viewing the open admissions policies as a democratizing initiative, many academics—particularly those outside of the two-year institution—misread the purpose of the policies, subsequently reifying long-held assumptions about community colleges as inferior institutions.

Richard Coley's 2000 ETS report, "The American Community College Turns 100," articulates some of the justification for this unfavorable view. He links the access open-admissions institutions provide to a lack of motivation among high school students, but he views this link within the broader context of comprehensive public education:

> Unfortunately, many graduating high school students come to the community college door unprepared for college. On one hand, community colleges allow students a "second chance." As a result, much community college curriculum is remedial in nature. On the other hand, the availability of such a "second chance" sends the wrong message to students—many believe that they can attain their goals for higher education without doing any work in high school. It is clear that our educational system needs better alignment and articulation, kindergarten through college. Each part of the system needs to do a better job of informing students of what is required and expected of them. (30)

Similary, Thomas R. Bailey, Katherine L. Hughes, and David Thornton Moore, in their 2004 text, *Working Knowledge: Work-Based Learning and Education Reform* assert a view of public education that links the lack of motivation in students to the availability of post-secondary education. While their project maps the effectiveness of work-based learning as a viable area of development for educational reform, they reiterate Coley's claims in their opening chapter, noting the deficiency in student preparedness for college-level work, based on U.S. Department of Education statistics from 1999:

> [M]any high school graduates did not have high school level skills—hundreds of thousands of students entering post-secondary schools had to take remedial instruction to prepare them for college-level work. Beyond these well-known problems, researchers found that most high school students were not engaged in their schooling and made an effort only so that they could get into college (Johnson, Farkas, & Bers, 1997). Learning was often far down their list of priorities. Yet almost all students who finish high school can gain access to some post-secondary institution. Therefore, many students do not see strong incentives for working hard in high school (Rosenbaum, 1997). (1)

Given Bailey, Hughes, and Moore's picture of unmotivated American high school students, assumptions about open-access institutions as inferior may seem a logical conclusion. Like Coley, the authors view the opportunity for open-access secondary education as a safety net that inadvertently reduces incentives to prepare for it, and completes the cycle of an overall failing educational system.

As part of a larger discussion, taken up further in the final chapters of this book, this unfavorable view of the public educational system parallels the current criticisms of the progressive pragmatic jeremiad of education Linda Adler-Kassner describes in *The Activist WPA*. She traces the development of the public educational system to its roots in the Progressive Era ideology that shaped American education and defined the early twentieth century in the United States. "Long-entrenched assumptions and approaches," Adler-Kassner writes, directly affect the work of the WPA in today's bureaucratic institutions:

> This is especially true of the "grammar" of American education, a version of the American jeremiad formulated during the Progressive Era, the period between 1898 and 1920. As it has been explained by historian Sacvan Bercovitch, the American jeremiad posits that America—as a nation of chosen people endowed (by God) with a mission of exceptionalism—is always progressing toward the achievement of a virtuous democracy. This is the nation's errand. However, the wilderness into which that errand is pursued is rife with potential for declension—individuals or groups who do not embrace the values of the virtuous democracy, or impediments like disease and poverty. (37–38)

One result of the jeremiad is its "porous" nature, argues Adler-Kassner, enabling anyone with a particular agenda to adopt a rhetorical stance that appears to prioritize the educated individual within a democratic society, such as early Progressive Era educational theorists like John Dewey and Jane Addams advocated. Adler-Kassner explains that "the 'evasion of philosophy' in this narrative—that is, pragmatism's emphasis on generalizable methods, solutions, and applications rather than its focus on particular challenges stemming from particular temporal and spatial contexts—makes it available for a variety of purposes" (52). As a result, criticism of the public educational system appears to legitimately cut at its foundation—at institutions, teachers, and administrators. Summarizing a column by the conservative George Will, Adler-Kassner explains how critics of public education use rhetoric that echoes progressive sentiments as it simultaneously undermines the public system:

> Embedded in Will's column are elements of the progressive counternarrative that is now being turned against educators through the lens of progressivism. It goes like this: the purpose of school is to prepare students for participation in the democracy, and teachers (and school systems) have long been granted the expertise, within the progressive frame, to tend to this preparation. However, in the last X years (the number of years depends on the argument being advanced), teachers and school systems have begun to fail in their appointed mission; they are not preparing students because they do not understand the nature of the *new* democracy. (54)

The centrality of individual intellectual development within the progressive pragmatic jeremiad enables it to be used to foment conservative arguments, as Adler-Kassner notes, even as it is the same jeremiad that enabled the creation of social services, programs, and agencies offering assistance to American citizens in need (55–56).

Adler-Kassner's argument sheds light on the critical view of open-access institutions shared by Coley, Bailey, Hughes, and Moore. Based on the premise that public schools are failing, the authors share the perspective that secondary, open-access institutions complete the cycle of diminished preparation and motivation. Their collective criticism extends from the more pervasive conservative educational argument Adler-Kassner critiques, and takes the perspective of looking at public education as a closed, static system. Further, it ignores the possibility of open-access secondary institutions as providers of a multiplicity of educational possibilities, and not the ending to a singular, mostly unproductive educational journey.

The view of the community college as an end in a closed system, one that reinforces a cohort of citizens unprepared for democratic engagement, also views the two-year institution through a traditional educational lens, where students progress from kindergarten to Grade 12 in a vertical line, which can extend to a linear progression through college: freshman year to sophomore year and junior year to senior year. Community colleges do not restrict students' educational objectives to the traditional expectation of achieving of a degree, nor do they assume that students enroll directly after high school, after earning a diploma. Students bring to the college an array of educational goals and prior educational experiences that thwart the limits of traditional and conventional education. In fact, Cohen and Brawer suggest that the definition of two-year institutions begs reconsideration because of this array of possibilities:

> Perhaps community colleges should merely be described as untraditional. They do not follow the tradition of higher education as it developed from the colonial colleges through the universities . . . . Community colleges do not even follow their own traditions. . . . They maintain open channels for individuals, enhancing the social mobility that has characterized America; and they accept the idea that society can be better, just as individuals can better their lot within it. (qtd. in Coley 30–31)

Cohen and Brawer's claim that community colleges "maintain open channels" for students offers a more accurate view of the two-year institution and how an open-access policy functions within it. Resistant to the limits of convention, the college enables students an opportunity to define for themselves how they wish their education to be shaped, given their educational goals and prior educational experiences.

Table A2. Transfers from Community Colleges to Four-Year Institutions. Source: NCES: Table 19–1. Percentage distribution of students beginning at public, two-year institutions in 1995–96 by initial degree goal and student characteristics; percentage who transferred to a four-year institution; percentage of transfers who completed an associate's degree first; and percentage of transfers who persisted through June 2001.

Student Characteristics	Percentage distribution of beginning students	Percentage who transferred to a four-year institution	Percentage of transfers who completed an associate's degree first	Percentage of transfers who persisted through June 2001
			All beginning students	
Total	100.0	28.9	33.3	78.9
Initial degree goal in 1995–1996				
Bachelor's degree	24.8	50.8	18.8	82.3
Associate's degree	48.9	26.5	50.6	78.6
Certificate*	10.8	1.0		

Student Characteristics	Percentage distribution of beginning students	Percentage who trans- ferred to a four-year institution	Percentage of transfers who completed an associate's degree first	Percentage of transfers who persisted through June 2001
No degree*	15.6	21.1	19.4	22.8
Total	100.0	34.6	34.9	80.4
		Beginning students with associate's degree or bachelor's degree goals		
Initial degree goal in 1995–1996				
Bachelor's degree	33.6	50.8	18.8	82.3
Associate's degree	66.4	26.5	50.6	78.6
Enrollment after high school graduation				
Started college the same year	60.7	43.4	35.0	79.6
Delayed starting college	39.4	21.9	36.9	81.6
Attendance pattern through 2001				
Always attended full-time	28.3	44.6	41.7	78.9
Did not always attend full-time	71.7	30.7	31.0	81.3
Parents' education				
Bachelor's degree or higher	31.1	52.5	29.5	84.3
No Bachelor's degree	68.9	27.6	40.5	76.6
Sex				
Male	49.3	41.2	32.3	78.0
Female	50.7	28.3	38.5	83.8
Dependency				
Independent	27.4	18.7	24.6	85.3
Dependent	72.4	41.3	36.8	79.9
Family income of dependent students				
Low quartile	28.7	35.3	46.1	77.9
Middle quartile	50.1	41.3	36.7	79.2
High quartile	21.2	49.7	28.0	83.1

* Interpret data with caution; estimates are unstable.

Furthermore, Cohen and Brawer dispute findings such as those of Coley and Bailey, Hughes, and Moore. They argue instead that the assumption of community college students as less motivated than their counterparts in four-year colleges is only partly substantiated by research:

> The conventional belief is that community college students—in contrast to students in four-year colleges—are less interested in academic studies and in learning for its own sake; instead, they are interested primarily in the practical, which to them means earning more money. Although some research evidence supports that belief, the perception that higher education is to be used particularly for occupational training seems pervasive among students in all types of institutions. (60)

Whether one views the impact of open-access institutions on the comprehensive, public educational system this way or not, students unaccustomed to, or unenthusiastic about, academic vigor exist in the two-year college setting, just as they do in the four-year college. Their existence does not mean that WPAs must submit to the single narrative view of community colleges as an inferior institution. On the contrary, one of the greatest and most necessary challenges for community college WPAs is to reframe this narrative based on the rich diversity of abilities, competencies, and experiences students bring to the two-year institution.

WPAs and instructors new to the community college context quickly come to understand that many external assumptions portray an inaccurate picture of the student body. For example, writing about the moment of realization when their experiences at Santa Barbara City College (SBCC) contradicted earlier presumptions, Jody Millward, Sandra Starkey, and David Starkey collectively assert: "At SBCC, I saw immediately that what I had been told about CC students' low 'skill level' was not true" (40). To dispel assumptions linked to open admissions policies, Glen Gabert has said that such policies "[have] been one of the most misunderstood characteristics of community colleges. . . . It is more accurate to say that community colleges admit anyone who demonstrates reasonable potential for success in the program to which they seek admission" (qtd. in Reynolds 4).

Only institutions themselves can define what "reasonable potential" means. For many, the minimum requirement is a high school diploma or GED equivalency certificate. At Florence-Darling Technical College in South Carolina, for instance, open admissions is defined similarly to Gabert's definition:

> In order to promote achievement by individuals with varied potential, open admissions is defined as a practice which (1) admits to the College all citizens who can benefit from available learning opportunities, and (2) places into specific programs of study those students whose potential for success is commensurate with program admission standards.

Other two-year colleges more loosely define open admissions, such as the Community College of Vermont, which claims to simply "enroll all students who can benefit from our courses." Explicit in both colleges' criteria is the expectation for students' "reasonable" success at the institution. Further, implicit in both criteria for enrollment is the institution's expectation to assess student competencies, which has implications for the WPA—a point addressed in Chapter Three. Whether the open admissions policy is outlined with fairly specific criteria or with general guidelines, the ideological shift away from the perspective of "no standards" is essential to the writing program. Frank Madden reframes discussions about open access policies by arguing for the transformative experience these institutions offer: "Our open admissions students and our emphasis on the introductory elements of what we teach define our mission as transformative and different" (722). Seen through this lens, the perception of community colleges having few or no standards, then, is entirely inaccurate, especially in light of its accountability to multiple constituents, including students, the institution, the community, the state, an accreditation agency, and four-year institutions with which it shares articulation agreements. None of these constituents could otherwise accept the legitimacy of the college.

However, establishing and articulating standard criteria can present formidable difficulties, as well. An open admissions policy challenges efforts to standardize how writing is taught from within an institution because of the wide range of literacies and competencies students bring to the college. In addition, as Daphne Desser argues, the range of programs the college offers complicates these efforts:

> Open-admissions policies make it more difficult to create regularized, effective, and suitable curricula. The community college is attempting to cover too many bases right now; it of-

fers vocational education, a cheaper, easier alternative to the university and a catch-all support system for minorities, the disabled, working adults, and other nontraditional students. (110)

While Desser's perspective is somewhat critical of the community college, she points to difficulties shared by all open-admissions institutions. Attempting to meet the needs of all students presents several challenges—some are surmountable, and some insurmountable. The diversity of the students necessitates greater attention to individual learning styles, and the most effective way to keep up with students' literacy needs is to perform continual assessment. Referring to her own institution, St. Petersburg College (formerly St. Petersburg Junior College), Sylvia Holladay links open admissions to programmatic evaluation, and subsequently to programmatic innovation:

> Because of open admissions at SPJC, we have a history of curricular innovation. If we admit a student, we believe it is our responsibility to provide the appropriate courses and instructional techniques. In our constant search for better methods to help all students succeed in expressing themselves more effectively, we continually review and revise our courses and our methods of assessment. (31)

As Holladay explains, continual assessment of student competencies, as well as of writing courses and assessment methodologies, provides the feedback needed to maintain the development of a democratic and dynamic writing program. Through assessment, the WPA can find a balance between maintaining the appropriate standard criteria and providing instruction for a range of different kinds of learners, which is a point returned to in Chapters Three and Four.

Ongoing assessment requires WPAs to be cognizant of preparing students for their possible next steps. While community college students are not necessarily "tracked," WPAs benefit from knowing the following:

- How many students intend to transfer to four-year institutions?
- How many students enroll in certificate programs versus enrolling in associate degree programs?

- How many students are employees enrolled in corporate college programs, or are in partnerships with the college to fulfill job-related requirements?
- How many students place into developmental writing courses and then intend to continue in the sequence of writing courses?
- How many students are individuals for whom a degree or a certificate is not in their immediate plans, but take courses here and there?

The above considerations represent only a few possible student objectives, and are exclusive of scores of other possibilities, but they point to some common student scenarios.

Additionally, community college WPAs—like WPAs at other institutions—must consider the social, political, and economic effects the writing program can, and will later, have on students. For example, what are the educational, social, and financial effects for students who enroll into mandatory developmental courses? Furthermore, how does not passing a developmental course the first time affect a student? In an example compositionists have long debated, for what does a credit-bearing writing course prepare the students? Work? Other courses? How is this goal different in the community college setting than the four-year college setting? Or is it the same? These questions are context-specific, but they point to some immediate issues the community college WPA encounters. Answers begin to emerge by taking into account, to a certain extent, the collective identity of the students in one's institution, including where they intend to go as well as where they have been. Open admissions policies directly impact the student population, and how the WPA views such policies also directly impacts the development of the writing program.

DIVERSITY

The college's diverse student body is a direct result of open admissions and forms the most important factor for consideration by the WPA: an extremely diverse student body. In fact, a general portrait of the students' diversity becomes nearly impossible. What parallels exist between the middle-aged woman with two children and the Iraq War vet? The twenty-five year old man who has been in and out of three different colleges before now, and the Russian immigrant, who just arrived in the United States six months ago, and wishes to achieve the

"American Dream"? The ex-convict and the twenty-year veteran of the phone company? The urban students, the suburban students, and the rural students? What do all of these students have in common besides that they—and millions of others—enroll in community college writing courses? They probably have very little in common, except that they entrusted the college, and by extension, its WPA and instructors, with their education. Importantly, each student comes to the community college with his or her own individual history—sometimes a complex one—and those histories easily become wellknown to the WPA and instructors. In fact, as Patrick Sullivan points out, community college writing faculty "become invested in [their] students' successes and failures in ways that are significantly different from those of [their] colleagues" in four-year institutions ("What Is?" 378). He notes that the relationships between faculty and students transcend traditional and more rigid boundaries between faculty and students, sometimes resulting in "heavy emotional burdens to shoulder for those of us who function in the classroom as 'coaches'" ("What Is?" 379). Sullivan's comments specifically address underprepared students, but they extend to any student expressing his or her educational needs to a sympathetic and proactive faculty member. Students' personal stories can be as present and memorable in their writing, as the students are themselves in the classroom.

The individual knowledge that WPAs and instructors have of their students becomes doubly impressive in light of high enrollments in the two-year institution. The MLA Committee on Community Colleges reports:

> [S]tudents in the typical community college class have a wide range of ages and life experiences and varying degrees of academic preparation. Students' ages may run from 16 to 80. Some are still in high school, some are ready to transfer to a university, and some hold advanced degrees. While this diversity is exciting, it also makes community college teaching more challenging.

Of all U.S. college students, 44% are enrolled in community colleges, with most of those students enrolling in writing courses ("Fast Facts"). According to the AACC, of these enrolled students, 43% are first-time students, and 7.4 million are enrolled in credit-bearing courses.[2] Full-time students make up 40% of the student body, and part-time students make up 60% ("Fast Facts"). Comparatively, community colleges have the lowest number of full-time student enrollments among all types of institutions in the country (Bailey, Jenkins, and Leinbach 15). One of the most significant characteristics of this student population is its diversity and relative maturity. At 61%, women make up the majority of the student population across the country. In addition, during the academic year 2007–2008, community colleges enrolled a student population that was 13% Black, 16% Hispanic, 6% Asian/Pacific Islander, and 1% Native American—the highest percentages among all colleges and universities.[3] Of all community college students during this academic year, 13% were single parents, and 42% were first-generation college students ("Fast Facts"). Last, the average age of the community college student is twenty-eight years old, with 15% over forty years of age ("Fast Facts").

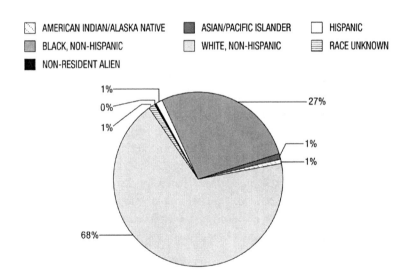

Figure 1. Enrollment by Ethnicity. Source: American Association of Community Colleges

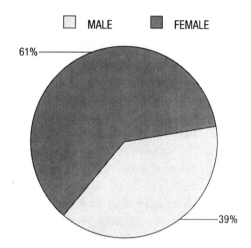

Figure 2 Enrollment by Gender. Source: American Association of Community Colleges

From the perspectives of class and educational preparation, community college students are just as diverse. Students come from all socioeconomic classes in nearly equal proportions, with slightly greater representation in the lower income categories (Bailey, Jenkins, and Leinbach 28), and nearly half of enrolled students are financial aid recipients of some kind ("Students at the Community Colleges").[4] Similarly, community college students reflect the full range of educational preparedness. While the proportion of developmental students tends to be higher in community colleges, students who demonstrate exceptional competencies also enroll in two-year institutions. Thus, the literacies, knowledges, and competencies of community college students are as diverse as the student body.

Reflective of this diversity, ninety percent of this student population fulfills at least one subset of the nontraditional student category (Millward, Starkey, and Starkey 38). Even though community college students make up nearly half of all undergraduates nationwide, and thus are far more representative of a "diverse" norm, the bias in academia continues to favor the traditional student, which is unrealistic, since this student is neither the norm nor the majority anywhere. The picture of the traditional student is that of an individual who enrolls full-time in a four-year college directly after high school. He or she does not work, does not support other people, is not married, and is between the ages of eighteen and twenty-two. A closer look at the traditional student quickly gives way to a more complex picture of American college students, of whom, 43% *start* their postsecondary education at a community college (Cohen and Brawer 50). At the community college itself, 41% are first-time students ("Students at the Community College"), implying that 59% of students are not enrolling for the first time, indicating further that they bring a myriad of educational experiences with them: transfers from other institutions, GED recipients, successful and unsuccessful encounters with learning institutions, and other educational experiences. Certainly many of these statistics comprise the profile of a student "at-risk." The U.S. Department of Education, NCES, compares the risk factors between community college students and their counterparts at four-year institutions (see Table A3).

By far, community college students shoulder far more external commitments than their counterparts at four-year institutions. Clearly, their commitments present a risk to the completion of their educational goals. As a result, community college students are less involved in on-campus activities than students enrolled in four-year institutions. Given their high level of external commitments, their lesser involvement presents little surprise. However, student participation presents a conventional marker of student retention; lesser involvement in college-related activities also reflects their elevated risk status.

Both sets of statistics (Tables A3 and A4)—for at-risk factors and for school activity—identify the heavy and varied commitments community college students engage with outside of school. They point to the risk many of these students face as they try to remain in college to attain their educational goals. What both tables omit are overlapping categories, for example, a single parent who also works, or a part-time student who works fulltime and has a GED certificate instead of a high school diploma.

Table A3. Percentage Distribution of Risk Factors for 1995–96 Beginning Postsecondary Students, by Sector of First Institution Attended. Source: U.S. Department of Education, National Center for Education Statistics, 1995–1996.

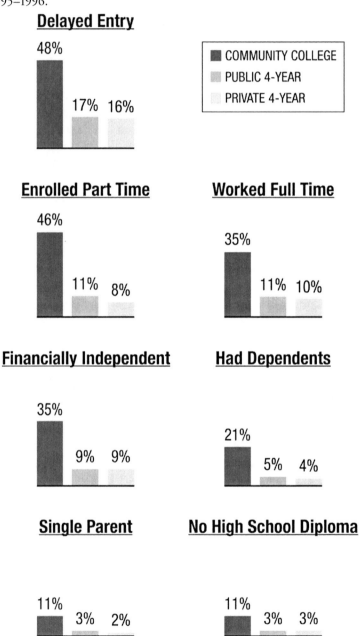

Table A4. Percentage Distribution of 1995–1996 Beginning Postsecondary Students, by School Activity and Sector of First Institution Attended. Source: U.S. Department of Education, National Center for Education Statistics, 1995–1996.

Participate in Study Groups

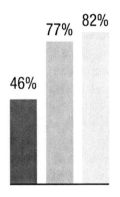

- ■ COMMUNITY COLLEGE
- PUBLIC 4-YEAR
- PRIVATE 4-YEAR

Speak with Faculty Outside of Class

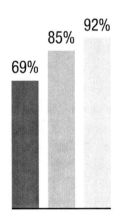

Participate in School Clubs

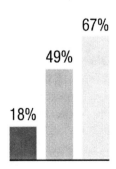

The complex lives of community college students cannot be articulated or distilled into simple terms. More typical of the community college student are the complex personal narratives, journeys, and circumstances that led to his or her arrival at the institution's doors. A few autobiographical student narratives demonstrate this complexity:

Arlinda

I arrived at community college simply because it was close to home and since I am still unsure of what I am going to major in. I figured community college was a good place to start. Growing up in a family that emigrated from Europe and didn't have the educational opportunities that America presents, I was expected to attend college and earn a degree. Therefore, I am in college to earn a degree and create a bright, successful future for myself. Other than school, I have many other obligations. Some of those obligations include my job and baby-sitting my little sister. Although I now have a slightly more optimistic attitude concerning school, I wasn't so ready to face it a few years ago. I never liked school, and I still don't. It wasn't that school was hard. I was always a good student; I just didn't agree with the conformity that the public school administration forced onto the students. My favorite teachers were always the ones that encouraged students to think outside the box and contribute their own ideas to the class. I didn't like learning from a textbook. Life isn't a book. Learning about history from a textbook ultimately isn't going to teach students anything if teachers don't apply it to society today. In addition to that, I always found it difficult to sit still for long periods of time. But throughout my experience attending school, I have realized that it is a lot easier to create a successful life for yourself and your family when you have an education.

Joseph

I received a Regents Diploma from high school in 2010. I also graduated from Putnam-Northern Westchester BOCES [Board of Cooperative Educational Services] with honors. My honor society's name is the National Technical Honor Society. I was an average student; BOCES was the place that helped me get honors. I took a class called "Microcomputer Technology" for two years. I like working with my hands and working with electronics. My mother does not have a college degree, only a basic diploma, and my father dropped out of the eighth grade. When I was in high school, I went to school then worked after school. Still today, I go to school and work for almost eight hours. I don't have time for a social life. After high school, I made a decision to go to St. Thomas Aquinas College in Sparkill, NY. I was not doing so well living away from home. Now, I live with my aunt and uncle. They want me to go to college. They were the push that led me to this point. I got into community college. My aunt and uncle help me with my homework if I don't understand what the textbook says or what the professor has asked. They are an inspiration to me.

Leo

I was always dreaming of becoming a zoologist when I grew up. I wanted to become, like Steve Irwin, "The Crocodile Hunter." When I came [to this area], I hated everyone because I was looked at like a gangster. I was far from all of that. But I eventually hung out with the bad kids who just smoked weed and drank a lot. For some reason, I clicked more with them than the jocks or any other crew in high school. From there I went downhill fast. I started to skip classes, played hooky, smoked before and after school, never did homework, and just started picking fights. My grades dropped drastically from what I began with. I started to get suspended all the time for almost everything I did. . . .

I eventually pushed my parents to the point where they put me into an inpatient rehab. I served nine months of my life in there. While I was there I realized I was in danger of failing my junior year and being held back. When I was discharged from rehab, I came back as a brand new kid. I changed a lot of my ways and saw things differently. In my family, I am the first to graduate high school with a diploma and that is a big thing.

I now have two jobs and am a full-time student here at the community college. I have changed my major to accounting and I expect to graduate next semester after three summer courses. It's pretty difficult to handle schoolwork with two jobs. I usually run on a tight schedule that leaves me with no time for homework and deprives me from sleep. When I'm not working at Pizza Hut as a shift manager, I'm delivering sodas. If I am not doing either, then I am at school or sleeping. I really need the money because of the amount of bills I have.

My parents are both immigrants to this country, but are now citizens. They never finished school, but encourage their kids to do so.

They worked all their lives and continue to break their backs to support our family. My parents don't want us to follow in their shoes, but to learn from their mistakes. I have two brothers and I'm the middle child. So far, I've got the strongest head on my shoulders and have decided to strive for a degree. My older brother had to drop out, because of baby mama drama. As for my little brother, he doesn't completely understand that school's important yet. He's more into girls, booze, and weight lifting. But I am determined to finish community college with an associate's degree in accounting. I am going to transfer. I'm not sure how life's going to be when I start to dorm, but one thing's for sure: I'm not going to mess up my opportunity.

Thomas

A lot has happened since I was in school last (forty years ago). I am a full-time student presently. I lost my job in a mass layoff about two years ago. I worked in the same position for nearly twenty years. I found out I had not updated my skills to the level of the twenty-first century. I bought many computers, but did not get my own until 2009. Never thinking I would have to use one, I really thought that I could get away with it. My biggest fear besides school right now is trying to get the hang of this computer. My educational goal today is not what it was in the past. When I get my degree, I will be the first of my brothers. My youngest brother asked why I went back to school. He said I should retire and get a part-time job. My kids love the idea of me being in school. They think it's great and so do I. I would love to have my degree, just to say it's mine.

Leslie

I came to the U.S. at age twelve. I started seventh grade at Port Chester Middle School as an English as a Second Language student. I was mainstreamed the following year and enrolled in the Honor Society. Then I went to White Plains High School. When I got to community college, I paid the first year through different scholarships from high school, and the second year I received the Kathryn W. Davis scholarship. Through my time earning my associate's degree, I have worked in restaurants and volunteered.

Noelle

College was something I grew up knowing I should attend, but wasn't exactly primed for during high school. When I graduated, I didn't know how to apply to schools or where I wanted to go, and on top of that were my less-than-stellar grades. The reality was I was a terrible, disinterested student. I didn't find the work difficult. I found sitting in class, surrounded by my "peers" difficult. But I made an attempt at college anyway.

I enrolled in the local community college in September of 1991, when I was 18 years old. But I was completely unprepared for what college would ask of me, which was, mainly, to be an adult, do my work, and go to class. I left feeling like a failure. Then, when I was 22, I moved to Virginia, and by 24, finding I was qualified for working in bars and waffle houses and little else, I enrolled at Tidewater Community College (TCC). I took classes here and there, and switched my focus from English to nutrition to social sciences. I was serious about my classes and determined to do well, but I wouldn't commit to more than one or two classes at a time, and I couldn't make a decision about what I actually wanted out of school. I dropped out when I found out I had to take two non-credit math classes to catch up enough to take college algebra.

After being married for a few years, I had a son, and then, a month after finding out I was pregnant with my second son, in 2006, I enrolled again as a full-time student at TCC for an Associate's of Science in social sciences. I liked online classes because I had two young children, and my husband, being in the Navy, was deployed often. Finding a sitter I trusted who could be relied on wasn't easy or affordable.

When my youngest son was two, I got divorced. I finished my associate's degree and graduated TCC with a 4.0 GPA (I didn't use any of my previous college grades). I have since transferred to a four-year school, and will be applying to a doctoral program for psychology when I am finished. Overall, my community college experience was a positive one.

Ed

My father was a high school dropout who got his GED in the Army. When he was discharged, he got a job digging graves, and later got a job with the NYC Sanitation Department. My mother finished high school with a diploma in secretarial skills. As for me, after enrolling at a four-year, private, Catholic college for three semesters, I had to quit school and get a job because my mother had gotten very ill with cancer, and the money ran out. I married soon after, and then became a night student for nine years, six of which were spent at a community college, where I took courses in electrical technology, electrical engineering, and then business courses, usually one at a time. It was for my business courses where, for the first time, I actually studied for an exam, took notes, did my assignments, and got my first (non-technical related) "A" since elementary school. Eventually I earned a BBA in management, graduating summa cum laude, from a four-year institution. My wife and children all earned graduate degrees, and after a while I decided to round out my education with a Master's in English Literature.

Sally

I am a 58-year-old Caucasian woman. I have been married for twenty-four-and-a-half years. I have two children, one of each gender, aged eighteen and twenty. Both are college students. I have an AAS from Nassau Community College ('72), and a BS in communications from SUNY Oneonta. I have also attended FIT and Pace University for graduate work. I have worked as a waitress, bartender, make-up artist, wardrobe/personal shopper, and broadcast sales account executive. I am currently employed as a permanent substitute teacher at in a high school. I have taken English classes at the community college. I am required by New York State to be pursuing my teaching certificate in order to substitute for more than forty days per school year. I have declared secondary-level English to be my area of concentration and need additional undergraduate English credit.

Edward

The reason I went to community college is because, yet again, my parents told me that they couldn't afford school, and I wanted to get an education so badly. I attended the college for one year, until I was rudely awakened by my parents' divorce. Needless to say, I was devastated and dropped out of school for three years. At this point, I was following in the footsteps of my parents who both did not attend college, and I didn't want to struggle like they did. I finally realized that I must graduate and prove to myself that I can. This is my last chance at furthering my education even more, and I will not give up until I achieve my goal of graduating and doing something above and beyond my own expectations. While trying to do my own schoolwork, I work in a public school with fifth through eighth graders. I love working with the kids because I feel like I am bettering their lives by teaching them things I wish I knew as a child.

* * *

Many community college students embody the characteristics of the traditional college student—enroll after high school, do not work, and complete an associate's degree by taking consecutive semesters of full course loads. Far more have complex stories, like the stories of the students above, match the definition of a nontraditional college student. For instance, while Leslie is no longer a "traditional" ESL student, she is one of the "Generation 1.5" students who have earned high school diplomas in the United States; not only has she earned a diploma but she has also earned full scholarships. In other examples, Thomas, Noelle, and Ed enrolled to complete their degrees long after high school, and all had raised families. Several students overcame great difficulties before enrolling, such as Leo, when he worked through addiction as a teenager, while others encountered personal difficulties that interrupted their studies, like Edward, whose emotional response to his parents' divorce halted his college career. Sally already had a degree and returned to fulfill requirements for her role as a permanent substitute teacher, but in the meantime, she raised a family and continues to work through school. The life experiences of these students categorize them as nontraditional students, but more importantly, they demonstrate the range of learning experiences—both formal and informal—they brought *to* the community college. Arlinda and Leslie were bilingual and bicultural before enrolling. By Noelle's second enrollment in community college, she had knowledge of childrearing and managing household finances. Even more important, several of these students note that they found their earlier educational experiences unsatisfactory. Arlinda, for instance, explicitly critiques her early education when she writes: "It wasn't that school was hard. I was always a good student; I just didn't agree with the conformity that the public school administration forced onto the students. . . . I didn't like learning from a textbook. Life isn't a book." In this statement, she articulates her understanding of the difference between experiential knowledge and knowledge traditionally taught. Clearly, she values the former, which supports why she favored teachers that allowed her to take some responsibility for her own learning: "My favorite teachers were always the ones that encouraged students to think outside the box and contribute their own ideas to the class." Although Arlinda verbalizes the distinction between ways of knowing, her comments illuminate the depth of experiential and situated knowledge that all of these students brought with them to their enrollments. And through the snapshots of their autobiographical narratives, they demonstrate the range of competencies and the complexity of knowledge all community college students bring to the writing classroom.

Regardless of race, ethnicity, class, gender, age, religion, creed, and sexual orientation, students enter community colleges with a range of prior learning experiences. For as many who have had positive, prior interactions in classrooms, there are many who had negative prior interactions in classrooms. Subsequently, their attitudes toward education and even toward their own learning and knowledge, is complex and at times difficult to decipher. Given that the national average age of the community college student body is twenty-eight, many students enroll—or return to— college with knowledge and literacies acquired in adulthood and outside the classroom. WPAs must be cognizant of (or at least open-minded to) the myriad of possible learning styles and inclusive of less "conventional" types of knowledge, such as various subjugated or situated knowledges. Now, well into the twenty-first century, WPAs encounter a multi-literate student body; community college students of all ages and demographics demonstrate a wide range of literacy proficiencies. For example, they are bi- or multilingual, or they are competent and comfortable using various media and technologies: social networks, online resources, text messaging systems, and more. The range of student knowledges and literacies directly affects the development of the writing program and its articulated criteria, a point discussed further in Chapter Four. Even though it may not always be possible to ensure that every single student receives what he or she needs, an open mind, continual assessment, and dialogue with students and faculty helps to increase the chances they get enough attention to their knowledge and literacy requirements.[5]

ADULT LEARNING

As a subset within the category of the nontraditional student, adult learners present a substantial area of consideration for the WPA, given the average maturity of the community college student. As noted earlier, the American Association of Community Colleges places the median age of community college students at twenty-eight years old. The concerns of the adult student vary from individual to individual, but adult learning theory provides a lens through which to view the general needs of community college students, of whom forty-five percent are between the ages of twenty-two and thirty-nine, and fifteen percent are forty years or older ("Fast Facts"). Age places such students immediately into a nontraditional student category, and with age very often comes additional external commitments, such as work and family, as seen in a few of the biographical sketches above, notably those of students Noelle and Ed, who worked their education in and around their familial obligations. Like most adult students, their experiences shaped how they learned in the classroom.

To demonstrate the proportion of older students at the community college, the following chart compares age of students by institution type:

Table A5. Percentage Distribution of Undergraduates, by Level of Institution. Source: U.S. Department of Education, National Center for Educational Statistics, 1999–2000 National Postsecondary Student Aid Study

Age as of 12/31/99	Level of institution		
	Less than 2-year	2-year	4-year
18 years or younger	2.0	40.2	52.7
19–23 years	1.9	34.6	56.2
24–29 years	4.0	49.5	40.7
30–39 years	4.0	58.6	32.3
50 years or older	3.2	65.0	27.4

In their comprehensive guide, *Learning in Adulthood,* Sharan Merriam, Rosemary Caffarella, and Lisa Baumgartner emphasize the primacy of the social context in adult learning experiences. In particular, they point to the influence of three factors shaping adult learning today: demographics, globalization, and technology (21–26). Among these factors, the authors also reaffirm one of the major premises of adult learning theory, which underscores the prior knowledge and experiential learning acquired before adult learners enroll in higher education. This emphasis points to how prior knowledge and experiential learning affirms the cognitive abilities of adult learners. The authors provide the following example:

> In working with welfare recipients, for example, instructors might recognize that parents on welfare have had to learn how to take care of their children on very constrained budgets, keep their families safe and healthy under difficult living conditions and in general make do with very little. Rather than asking questions about how they have learned to do this successfully, what is focused on most often is their lack of formal education and skills training. Formal schooling and skills training are important, but so are the ways they have informally learned about life skills that have kept them and their families fed and clothed. (27–28)

Typical of adult learning theorists, Merriam, Caffarella, and Baumgartner legitimize these students' cognitive abilities by identifying the areas where they gain situated knowledge, such as in the context of providing for a family under difficult financial circumstances. Their recognition of this example not only legitimizes situated knowledge, but it raises the status of the subordinated learner, someone who has lacked "formal schooling and skills training." In so doing, Merriam, Caffarella, and Baumgartner challenge the assumptions of formal education. Further, they identify three kinds of locations where learning can occur: formal institutional settings, non-formal settings, and informal contexts. The authors include a fourth category for online learning, but note that it overlaps with the other three. Most relevant among their delineations are the areas of non-formal settings and informal contexts for learning, as opposed to formal institutional settings—including community colleges themselves—that are typically bureaucracies, organized around curriculums, and "formally recognized with grades, diplomas, and certificates" (29). Non-formal education generally refers to "organized learning opportunities outside the formal education system," such as community-based learning and indigenous learning (30). P.H. Coombs defines informal learning as "the spontaneous, unstructured learning that goes on daily in the home and neighborhood, behind the school and on the playing field, in the workplace, marketplace, library and museum, and through the various mass media" (qtd. in Merriam, Caffarella, and Baumgartner 35). The authors claim that it is "by far the most prevalent form of adult learning," the nature of which "makes it so difficult for adults to recognize" as learning, even as studies of adult education trends show that nearly ninety percent of adults spend hundreds of hours in informal learning (Merriam, Caffarella, and Baumgartner 35).

Contrary to the field of adult learning, predominant trends in higher educational research tend to ignore the abilities, competencies, and knowledges that adult learners bring to their formal studies. As a result, the Lumina Foundation for Education Report on "Returning to Learning" claims: "Millions of adult students are seeking degrees in a system built largely for—and around—traditional students" (Pusser et al. 3). In other words, many institutions of formal education—both two-year and four-year institutions—are underprepared to serve the adult learner. Drawing the parallels between adult learners and non-traditional students generally, Cathy Leaker and Heather Ostman write:

> And more often than not, that [educational] system—and the status and economic pressures that sustain it—works against students who don't meet the traditional profile and don't de-limit their learning within its boundaries; perhaps the most disturbing NCES statistic is that nontraditional degree-seeking students are more likely than their traditional counter-parts to leave without having met their objective. The reasons for such a discrepancy are complex, but when the classroom is reified as a contained space of intellectual formation and rhetorical-material preparation, what gets overlooked are the "rhetorical-economic-material" needs of those students who shuttle, often precariously, between the overlapping learning spaces of study, work, family and community. (694)

With so many students identifying as adult learners, community college WPAs must be cognizant of the resistance adult learners experience within traditional education. Particularly when these students may have had unpleasant educational experiences, or when the economic stakes for their success are very high, they require WPAs to be mindful of their vulnerability, since, as Leaker and Ostman note, they "are more likely than their traditional counterparts to leave without having met their objective" (694).

Another important aspect of the adult learner is the social and emotional significance of their enrollment. For some, the expectations they place upon themselves add enormous pressure to an already complex life. In returning adult student Noelle's autobiographical sketch, the failed attempt at finishing a semester at community college in her late teens contributed to her expectation of herself to not only complete a semester, but to earn an associate's degree with a 4.0 GPA at Tidewater Community College. She writes:

> When I first started college I still had the same immature high school mentality. I didn't take it seriously and when I realized it mattered how I acted, what I said and did, I got scared. I'd already "blown it" in my mind so I left and I felt like I'd failed miserably and irreparably. Going back to school in Virginia my attitude changed, primarily because I wanted to actually do something with my life. I grew up. A bit of a perfectionist in me sprung up, but I felt I had something to prove to the world: that I was good enough and not just a flake or throw away person. So I made it my mission to do really well, even if it took me forever. Having a baby slowed me down a bit; I was only able to take one or two classes a semester until he was a little older, but it was worth it because I could give so much more to both my family and my education than I could have if I'd taken a full course load.

Noelle's perception of her earlier attempt at community college raised the stakes for her second attempt. Her maturity, she asserts, contributed to the awareness of herself as a more accountable figure in other people's lives. Also, it enabled her to make reasonable choices, in terms of her time management, to fulfill her educational goals as an adult. But the internal expectations Noelle felt affected the fundamental sense of herself, as seen in her comment: "I felt I had something to prove to the world: that I was good enough." While not all students who share heightened expectations for their academic success are equally able to manage their time effectively, Noelle's account demonstrates some of the emotional significance placed upon her enrollment in a community college as an adult. Furthermore, students in Noelle's situation might also have to simultaneously contend with unpredictable factors of life that occur in the areas of family, jobs, and health. When an event like a serious illness or a death in the family occurs, the already pressured, busy life of the adult student can be further complicated with the emotional strain that accompanies such events, making uninterrupted enrollment in community college challenging. With all of the variables that characterize the lives of adult students, their enrollments are bound to be fraught with outside commitments and complex emotional significance. Nevertheless, because of their rich life experiences, these students challenge traditional assumptions about knowledge and can inspire WPAs to consider new ways of thinking about knowledge production.

RACE AND ETHNICITY

The racially and ethnically diverse undergraduate body forms another of the most important considerations for the WPA in a community college. By 2009, 55% of all Native American students, 46% of all black students, 46% of all Asian/Pacific Islander students, and 55% of all Latino students in the United States enrolled in community colleges, according to the AACC ("Students at the Comm College"). Within community colleges themselves, these racial and ethnic populations made up thirty-five percent of total student enrollments ("Students at the Community College"). While the AACC does not present statistics for white students, these students also present diverse needs, challenges, and competencies as those of their peers. Regardless of the racial makeup of any two-year institution, Cohen and Brawer note that the student demographics very often proportionally represent the community surrounding the institution (55).[6]

Cohen and Brawer's point emerges most clearly in the examples of Hispanic-Serving Institutions (HSI) and tribal community colleges. As the Latino population continues to be the most rapidly increasing population in the United States, 53% of Hispanic-Serving Institutions are two-year colleges. The establishment of HSIs results from the executive order, Educational Excellence for Hispanic Americans, signed by President Clinton in 1994. The act recognizes "accredited, degree granting, public or private, non-profit colleges or universities with 25% or more total undergraduate full-time equivalent (FTE) Hispanic enrollment" (Laden, qtd. in Kirklighter, Wolff Murphy, and Cárdenas 2). Such colleges develop organically over time with the surrounding community. Similarly, tribal community colleges purposefully reflect the ethnic and cultural concerns of the surrounding community. However, while tribal community colleges have similar open admissions policies as other community colleges, they distinguish themselves with a specific mission based on cultural identity. Over thirty tribal community colleges within the boundaries of thirteen states have been established through support from the Tribally Controlled Community College Assistance Act of 1978 as well as Congressional grants, beginning in 1980 (Cohen and Brawer 56). These institutions primarily serve Native American students and preserve the centrality of Native American culture(s) for these students. In addition, tribal community colleges contribute to developing the economic well-being of the local community, offering resources to community members. Tribal community colleges, like the HSIs, reflect the generally shared ethnic backgrounds of the community and are the strongest examples of Cohen and Brawer's point.

Regardless of the student body's racial or ethnic makeup, the community college WPA has a particular responsibility to be cognizant of the literacy histories of the ethnic or racial groups he or she serves. This awareness directly relates to the effectiveness of an open-admissions policy. Specifically, the accessibility provided by open admissions is only as meaningful as the college's ability to retain students long enough to achieve their educational objectives. Sensitivity to the complexity of ethnic literacy histories can help to manifest the democratic intentions of an open admissions policy. Millward, Starkey, and Starkey emphasize the urgency of addressing the needs of underrepresented students, claiming that "school failure among minority groups has much to do with the relation of that group to the 'majority' group. If the minority group is viewed as a low-status one in the larger society, then failure rates, not surprisingly, are much higher" (43). The WPA can shape a program that responds to students' needs in his or her specific institution, but that may mean developing or sustaining the faculty's awareness of the ethnic histories of literary instruction. For example, in African-American history, English literacy functioned as an empowering element in the pursuit of freedom for enslaved blacks:

> The slaveowning South, both the legislative and social power structure, seemed to understand this role that literacy could play in challenging oppression. While it is difficult to imagine, given the reductionist views of literacy today, literacy was at the very center of the debate about slavery in the 1830s. African American slaves and freedmen sought literacy as a means of challenging and transforming their communities

> and the nation. In doing so, they shook the ideological under-
> pinnings of Southern slavery. (Fox 120–21)

In the above passage, Tom Fox demonstrates how slave owners deliberately withheld literacy from slaves, and how literacy played an essential
role for disrupting racial oppression. The example of slavery is an ex-
treme case of oppression in the nation's history, but it helps to illuminate how English literacy in higher education can function as a tool
of empowerment or disempowerment. While writing instruction for
some student populations can echo such an empowering experience,
for other students, literacy instruction is fraught with a destructive
history. In the example of many Native Americans, English literacy
instruction contributed to the control and subsequent destruction of
indigenous people. Scott Richard Lyons identifies this history:

> And although Standing Bear and others would recall multiple
> forms of Indian resistance, from torching schools to running
> away to counting coup on the Western text, the duplicitous
> interrelationships between writing, violence, and colonization
> developed during the nineteenth century—not only in the
> boarding schools but at the signings of hundreds of treaties,
> most of which were dishonored by whites—would set into
> motion a persistent distrust of the written word in English,
> one that resonates in homes and schools and courts of law still
> today. (1129–30)

The experiences of African Americans and Native Americans are only
two examples that demonstrate distinct and complex ethnic literacy
histories. Naturally, there are many other literacy histories. The broader point here underscores the centrality of multicultural sensitivity to
the development of the writing program and the WPA's responsibility
to the needs of the institution's students, a point further discussed
in Chapter Four. Efforts to develop a deeper awareness of multicultural issues and concerns proves more challenging in certain institutions than others, depending on the ethnic makeup of the faculty
themselves and their own starting points, which is addressed more in
Chapters Three and Four.

English as a Second Language (ESL)

Another factor for consideration in the design of a community college writing program is the enrollment of English as a Second Language (ESL) students   or Second Language   Learners (L2). While ESL programs may exist separately from the writing program, very often students enroll in such programs in preparation for credit-bearing composition courses. These students represent a range of cultural and ethnic identities, and additionally possess a range of English literacy skills. In fact, in several institutions, international students represent a major portion of the student population. The AACC reports that nearly 100,000 international students residing in the United States—almost thirty-nine percent—enrolled in community colleges in 2009 ("Students at the Community College").[7] An important distinction to note here is the difference between Generation 1.5 students and ESL students. Generation 1.5 students have lived in the U.S. for longer periods, have transitioned out of ESL programs in high school, and have earned a high school diploma in this country, but at times may exhibit linguistic similarities to ESL students, especially in their writing. While they are not "traditional" ESL students, they also enroll in large numbers and, at times, present similar English literacy concerns.

If the WPA oversees the administration of ESL courses, the preparation of students for mainstream writing courses becomes the central objective. Shepherding ESL students into these courses includes assessment and academic support, such as a writing tutorial center or an academic skills center. Of primary concern is the WPA's awareness of the needs unique to ESL students. For example, many ESL students may write as well as or better than native English speakers, but they also may require longer time than their native English speaking peers for completing assignments. In addition, these students' oral competency is not necessarily an indicator of their written competency. Their simultaneous emergence into American culture presents another example of their particular needs, stemming from their adjustment to the English-literate society of the U.S. Therefore, unlike their American-born peers, ESL students often require cultural and social literacy in the classroom as well.

Still, like all community college students, ESL students learn at different rates and bring different levels of literacy and learning abilities to the college. Within the Latino community alone, many nationalities are represented, and a "one-sized fits all approach to teaching

Latino students does not work, since the category is so varied within itself" (Kirklighter, Murphy, and Cárdenas 8). Cristina Kirklighter, Susan Wolff Murphy, and Diana Cárdenas emphasize the complexities within one ethnic ESL population, but their point extends just as easily to the complexities of all ESL students and even the needs of all community college students: what works for one group does not necessarily work for another group, or is even needed by individual members of any particular group. ESL students, like students in nontraditional categories, present significant challenges to traditional notions of education, literacy, and intelligence. All of these students remind community college WPAs of the need for continual assessment of student competencies and the writing program. They further challenge singular approaches to writing pedagogies that view all students from the lens of a single educational narrative.

WORKING STUDENTS

The great numbers of students who work during their enrollments present another important factor for the WPA's consideration—as seen explicitly in the earlier student self-narratives of Arlinda, Joey, Leo, and Sally. For the majority of community college students, negotiating work, school, and other obligations, such as familial and religious commitments, presents a constant challenge. Many struggle to prioritize the needs of a job against the needs of college work. The AACC reports that of all full-time community college students, 27% work full-time and 50% work part-time; and of all part-time students, 50% work full-time and 33% work part-time ("Students at the Community College"). The WPA must necessarily consider the challenges facing working students, but doing so within a program or set of courses that maintains an appropriate standard. Even though a student may have to juggle thirty hours of work in addition to his or her schoolwork, that student also has a reasonable expectation for access to an adequate education, one that does not compromise quality and preparedness for convenience. In light of this challenge, the WPA may need to engage the writing faculty on issues with working students, particularly insofar as student schoolwork may be late or come intermittently. Some discussion about how to address this and related issues, such as attendance and tardiness, may be necessary, particularly if faculty come from other institutions with students who generally work less.

Even though the work lives of students can present formidable challenges, WPAs and instructors can teach students how to best manage their time and balance the demands of work, school, and family life. Referring to working community college students in their own institution, Millward, Starkey, and Starkey write:

> Our students come to campus, drive to a job, go and pick up a child or a sibling, and rarely have a "room of one's own" for thought and reflection. Our two-year college libraries and labs have limited hours. While it is difficult to bring these benefits to students through classroom assignments, in conjunction with teaching critical thinking, computer literacy, reading, writing, and research, students give high marks to those types of assignments in course evaluations. In a sense, we are giving them the tools they need to decode academia. (41)

Of course, the skill set a student enters college with can determine his or her success, or the enrollment in a college "success" course, which teaches students basic college skills, such as time management, note taking, and organization, may also help. Managing the demands on his or her time, working students often find themselves in constant negotiation between two powerful commitments in their lives. Sometimes the dual commitments enable students to become very organized and reduce the significance of other priorities, such as a social life. As the student Joseph writes in his autobiographical narrative, after school and eight hours of work each day, "I don't have time for a social life." Still, working students face formidable challenges. The choice to make work the first priority may result in a decline in performance at school, risking failure. The choice to make school a priority could risk missing rent for a month. The potential risk in either choice presents a daunting challenge for a large proportion of community college students.

WORKING-CLASS STUDENTS

While community college students come from a range of socioeconomic backgrounds, working-class students present another important consideration for the WPA. Many of these students find themselves negotiating identities at home and at school, sometimes with little support from either environment. Many grow up with a value placed on tangible results from manual labor as work, and consequently, they may find that their "work" in school does not measure up to familial standards. As Ann Penrose notes, "By virtue of their decision to attend college, these students have not only entered alien territory but distanced themselves from the understanding of family and friends" (qtd. in Millward, Starkey, and Starkey 44). This alienation may exist for a few reasons. One cause certainly is the family expectation for work, and another possibility is a resulting sense of betrayal of family values for social and economic advancement. For example, a parent may want his or her children to go further with their education than the parent did, but that desire also instills a sense of betrayal, in that the children reject the family and become "better" than they are. Mike Rose, in *The Mind at Work*, makes this point in his portrait of worker/laborer Joe Meraglio, whose child had gone to college:

> And, like so many, [Joe] sees education as the springboard for opportunity. It's a belief that for some time has led the nation to support public education: education as engine of mobility. In sending his kid to college, though, Joe Meraglio locates himself in a tension familiar to many Americans: on the one hand, a belief in advancement through education and a pride in making it possible, but, on the other, worry that more advanced education will change things, make kids grow distant, put on airs, at the worst, regard the lives of their parents with disdain. (163)

The tension Rose describes can emerge in a variety of ways for working-class students at home. How they process tension depends on how they respond to their family's explicit and implicit criticisms—if they even exist. Still, even if a working-class student experiences no difficulty at home, society assumes that a priority for formal education and learning can reinforce feelings of alienation from collegiate life. This other tension, Rose points out, is the tension in American society "between practical life, experience, and common sense versus schooling, book learning, and intellectual pursuits," with the latter more highly valued in society than the former (*Mind* 163). The composition classroom is the location where students can first encounter this tension, as they encounter a new academic discourse. The sensitivity to issues related to the working class for WPAs and instructors can strengthen the bridge to academia for these students.

The discipline of writing program administration generally would benefit from further study of working with this student population, but for community college WPAs, the urgency for more research and more effective practices is immediate. As Howard Tinberg claims, "Composition, simply stated, does not know what to do with the working class," even as compositionists have sought out the working class as a student population to empower through writing and to serve "both the community and the academy" ("Are We Good Enough?"). How WPAs work with working-class students depends upon how they reflect on their own roles as administrators of writing programs, as well as how students' needs present themselves.[8]

DEVELOPMENTAL STUDENTS

The needs of developmental writing students also represent a significant consideration for the WPA. Responding to the needs of the underprepared student, all community colleges provide developmental courses. Public two-year institutions enroll the highest rates of developmental students, as compared to their counterparts at four-year institutions. However, enrollment in developmental courses spreads evenly among classifications of race and ethnicity, class, and parents' education (Bailey, Jenkins, and Leinbach 21). One conservative estimate claims that forty-four percent of first-year community college students places into one, two, or three developmental courses (reading, writing, and/or math) (Attewell et al., qtd. in Cohen and Brawer 291), while a 2008 report by the Center for Community College Student Engagement found the number to be much higher: sixty-four percent of incoming students placed into a minimum of one developmental course. Thomas R. Bailey, of the Community College Research Center at Teacher's College, Columbia University, places the number of developmental students at sixty-five percent (Foderaro). For some two-year colleges, the percentage is as high as eighty-eight percent, such as it is at Tennessee's Shelby State Community College (Hobbs, qtd. in Cohen and Brawer 291). Given the range of developmental writing classes offered at many community colleges, a student may take up to five developmental classes within the course of his or her total enrollment (Scordaras 271).

Table A6. Entering Students and Developmental Education. Percentage of Entering Students Who Enroll in Developmental Courses. Source: 2008 SENSE field test data, Survey of Entering Student Engagement, CCCSE

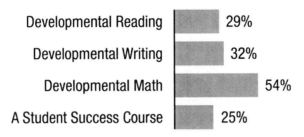

For writing instructors, enrollments in developmental studies make for the reasonable assumption that part of their course loads will inevitably include teaching developmental writing. For WPAs, these enrollments mean the administration of developmental writing courses is not separate from their programmatic responsibilities, or separate, for that matter, from the department or division in which composition is taught.[9] There are, however, community colleges in which developmental courses—writing, math, and reading—are centralized and therefore not part of the English or composition writing program.

Most often, the administration of developmental writing courses parallels or extends the administration of credit-bearing writing courses for the WPA, and therefore includes placement, support, and assessment. The tools of assessment and placement must indicate the competency of students, including their ability to have reasonable success in an appropriate level of writing course. Further discussion of assessment and placement follows in Chapter Three. More relevant to the discussion here is the development of support services. The duties of many community college WPAs include oversight of a writing tutorial center (further discussion of these duties also appears in Chapter Three), because academic support for developmental writing students is as important as appropriate placement into such courses. For some students, it represents the stark difference between success and failure in college, since many come to college without a history of success in their previous English courses. Mina Shaughnessy's observations in her seminal work *Errors and Expectations* regarding basic writing students illuminates this vulnerability, particularly when she points out how many of these students have experienced a history of errors—instead of a history of success—or at least of errors continually pointed out by their instructors (392). Consequently, developmental writing students often have not gained the confidence, however minimal, that their non-developmental peers have gained in the writing classroom. On the contrary, Shaughnessy writes:

> Most damaging of all, they have lost confidence in the very faculties that serve all language learners: their ability to distinguish between essential and redundant features of a language left them logical but wrong; their ability to draw analogies between what they knew of language when they began school and what they had to learn produced mistakes; and such was the quality of their instruction that no one saw the intelligence of their mistakes or thought to harness that intelligence in the service of learning. (394)

Central to the above passage is the acknowledgement of basic writers' intelligence. The damage done by earlier teachers who did not or could not see "the intelligence of their mistakes" can have lasting effects. As a result, the vulnerabilities demonstrated by many developmental students are complex, and efforts to retain these students must address not only knowledge and skills, but also the emotional and academic support needed for academic success—a daunting responsibility, given many students' earlier lack of success.

The task of reversing the damage of earlier critical learning experiences becomes more formidable within a cultural context that links sub-standard academic achievement with the lack of character. For example:

> In the first half of the nineteenth century the poor performer was a "dunce," "shirker," "loafer," "reprobate," or "wrong-do-er" who was "stupid," "vicious," "depraved," "wayward," or "incorrigible." Some of these labels imply that students lacked intelligence, but the majority suggest a flawed character. (Hull et al. 795)

Until recently, our society's regard for such students had not evolved all that much beyond these nineteenth-century sentiments. Even during the 1950s and 1960s, students themselves were still ultimately blamed for their low levels of success: "For almost two centuries the dominant way to think about underachieving students has been to focus on defects in intellect or character or differences in culture or situation that lead to failure, and to locate the causes within the mind and language of the individual" (Hull et al. 798–99). Therefore, providing academic support—in the form of a tutorial center, for instance—is as necessary as providing instructors and tutors who demonstrate emotional intelligence, the ability to respond appropriately to the myriad needs of developmental students, and the ability to see their students' intelligence within their writing.

The challenge for any community college WPA or writing instructor is in comprehending the literacy needs of developmental students in the program or in individual classes. The range of abilities can be astoundingly wide. For instance, in a given non-credit bearing developmental writing class, the student body may have first-time basic writing, first-year students, as well as repeating basic writing students, some of whom, depending on the college's policy, may be caught in a cycle of not passing the course and repeating it over and over. Among these students, academic needs may include literacy instruction in addition to disability support for a wide range of learning and physical disabilities, such as dyslexia, Asperberger's syndrome, and deafness, to name only a few. Notably, the AACC reports that of all community college students, twelve percent have acknowledged disabilities ("Fast Facts").

For developmental writing students, community college courses offer more than writing instruction; they can bolster students' confidence, and, in astute, intelligent hands, they can utilize the competencies and literacies the students *bring* to the classroom. Writing instructors can introduce students to the discourse(s) of the academic world, or—in the worst-case scenario—they can exclude them further from that world. The role of the WPA can be instrumental in developing a supportive environment for these students by also developing an informed and sensitive faculty.[10]

Last, developmental students are aware of the delay a non-credit developmental course causes to the completion of their college education. The delay affects them socially, educationally, and financially. If the institution does not have a policy regarding repeated enrollments in developmental courses, WPAs should address this concern, since continuous enrollment in developmental writing courses can cause financial obstacles to the completion of degrees for some students. While financial reasons do not merit passing students when they have not adequately fulfilled course objectives, they present reasonable considerations to keep in mind during the development and assessment of non-credit bearing writing courses.

Learning Disabilities

Although not all students with learning disabilities enroll in developmental courses, the WPA should be aware of their numbers within the writing program. While the administration of services for students with learning disabilities does not usually fall under the list of the WPA's responsibilities in any institution, a general knowledge of this population and their lawful entitlement to specific services benefits both the student and the program.

The spectrum of learning disabilities appears at community colleges, and while many students who enroll directly after high school may present documentation that enables them to special services, not all students in need have the necessary documentation, especially those not enrolled directly after high school. The WPA must be aware of the services available to students with learning disabilities at the college, and should disseminate this information to writing instructors. The services range from state to state, but students may qualify for extended time for exams or assignments, tutorial support of various kinds (including scribe assistance), and various computer-assisted and other technological services.[11]

Emotional Needs

A final, significant factor for the WPA's consideration is the emotional needs of many community college students, regardless of race, ethnicity, class, gender, or academic ability. With the cumulative pressures of work, family, and school, many students lead very complex lives, as noted earlier. While every WPA, as well as every instructor, must strike their own balance in regards to how involved—or uninvolved—in the concerns of students they want or need to be, awareness of some of the complexities and challenges students face is not only essential—it is often unavoidable. Sylvia Holladay argues that writing instructors (extended here to include WPAs) must work with community college students where they are emotional to help them develop confidence within the academic setting:

> Most of our students are nontraditional and at-risk and are
> locked in chaotic, crisis-driven lives. Usually they feel impo-
> tent when they enter the two-year college; our goal is not to
> give them power but to help them develop the ability to think
> and to write that will give them sufficient self-esteem, confi-
> dence, and authority to free themselves, to change their lives.
> (30)

Not everyone working at a community college would agree with the
generalization about community college students feeling "impotent"
and powerless, but Holladay's point implicitly emphasizes the need
for instructors'—and by extension WPAs'—sensitivity and responses
to students' personal needs and situations, and at times, their unique
circumstances. She recognizes the primary role of writing instructors
to help students "develop the ability to think and to write," but she
considers these abilities as part of a transformative process of the self.
On this point, Holladay correctly links the emotional significance of
a student's enrollment—a significance seen earlier in the examples of
Leo's and Noelle's autobiographical narratives—as their emotional
needs are very much tied into their positions as writers—a point that
will affect writing program development at any college. With a population of students that demonstrates the complexity Holladay suggests,
the WPA must be mindful of how personal experiences translate into
participation in writing classrooms. Although full knowledge of all
students' personal lives is not possible, the mindfulness that this connection exists is useful.

Working within the protocol of their institutions, WPAs may
sometimes have to translate student needs to instructors, and instructor expectations to students. Knowledge of the institution's policies and resources for trauma and emergencies is essential, including
knowledge of on-campus social workers, counselors, medical professionals, and security. If few or no resources are available, WPAs should
compile their own lists of current local resources, such as domestic
violence hotlines, rape crisis centers, and counseling centers.[12] In addition, WPAs, as well as instructors, should be prepared for emergencies
within the classroom. Having access to phone numbers and important
offices (such as security or the school health office) can mean the difference between life and death in certain circumstances. Thus, the
WPA's emotional intelligence, the ability to perceive the needs existing in front of him or her, is as essential as the ability to communicate

those needs to the appropriate professional when a student asks for help.

REFRAMING ASSUMPTIONS

In light of the enormous diversity and complexity of the student population, the community college WPA has a responsibility to not only develop a viable writing program, but to advocate for enrolled students. Misconceptions about students, particularly in terms of race, ethnicity, class, and academic ability feed external assumptions about the community college's academic legitimacy. Economics plays a contributing role in fostering these assumptions. Ira Shor argues that lower tuition functions as an indicator—albeit a false one—of lower status:

> In an unequal society, it seems that schools, colleges, and teachers count only if their students count. Further, students count only if they pay high tuition and come from upper-income homes (the most important indicator of college retention and success). Visibility and status to accompany high tuition and the lushness of your academic address. Teachers or students whose academic address is a community college have a hard time being taken seriously in academe as well as in the political media and professional worlds. (133)

During the academic year 2007–2008, 27% of federal dollars spent on higher education went to community colleges, despite their enrollment of 43% of all college students (AACC, "Doing More with Less"). Interestingly, although tuition tends to be lower for community college students, lower tuition rates do not necessarily mean that the two-year institutions spend less on each student, as compared to their public, four-year counterparts. Most expend amounts similar to four-year institutions; tribal community colleges, are the exception, spending twice the amount of other institutions. However, variations on spending exist among community colleges themselves, and the range can be great, depending on the state (Cohen and Brawer 172).

In addition to open admissions policies, economics only represents one factor among several for the external perception of community colleges as inferior institutions, while another is many two-year institutions' provisions of vocational education. With an academic profile that includes car repair and electrician training, community colleges' struggles with academic legitimacy parallels their students' struggles for intellectual legitimacy within the academy and American society. These struggles might not be overcome by individual WPAs—although they may help shift public attitudes toward the college, a point returned to in later chapters—but community college WPAs can provide support within the classroom by hiring and training faculty who understand the multiple responsibilities that many community college students shoulder and the difficulties many confront. Instructors with contextual knowledge of their students might provide an environment supportive of students struggling with a full range of responsibilities and personal issues. To do this, WPAs and faculty must resist unsupported external assumptions. Sullivan links some common assumptions with the privileges of class and power within a classroom, pointing out the dangers of misreading student performance:

> Still, though, I believe that students from financially disadvantaged families are often misunderstood—or imperfectly understood—by some members of our profession. I have heard colleagues speak scornfully about students who can't muster the requisite enthusiasm or motivation or "get-up-and-go" for their schoolwork. I have heard colleagues refer to their underachieving or undermotivated students with a startling degree of hostility and impatience. ("Cultural Narratives" 149)

Of course, the attitude Sullivan describes depends on the particular situation, the instructors, the institution, and the students themselves, but the more important issue here is that the community college WPA must be mindful of the bias instructors may bring with them into the classroom. The WPA may need to find ways to resolve prejudice, or at least eliminate it as much as possible. How he or she addresses bias depends on the WPA, as no formula exists. However, sensitivity to students requires a certain level of emotional sensitivity and cultural awareness that, if not innate, must be learned. Glynda Hull, Mike Rose, Kay Losey Fraser, and Marisa Castellano identify the importance of recognizing who the students are, both collectively and individually:

> To focus on the possible cultural or class differences of a student . . . can both reveal the logic of her behavior and—given the ways we carry with us to react to difference—blind us to the shared cognitive and linguistic processes she displays . .

> . . [Yet,] to focus on the shared nature of . . . cognitive and
> linguistic processes can blind us to the specifics of her back-
> ground, and, further, can lead us to downplay variability and
> the way difference has been historically embedded in ineq-
> uity. (808)

Implicitly, Hull and her colleagues argue for an awareness of the relationships between culture, class, and cognitive and linguistic processes. For them, these interdependent categories present challenges,
but lead to breakthroughs in the ways instructors and WPAs consider
their students' abilities. When such breakthroughs occur is the time
for WPAs to act, to use the emergent awareness or knowledge about
their students to reframe external and internal discussions about student learning. In fact, they are in the best position to advocate for such
students, because they are well-acquainted with the diverse needs and
abilities of such a complex student body.

The great diversity among community college students presents
unique challenges to the WPA. The notion of diversity at the two-
year college speaks to a full range of demographic differences. Less
visible than other external characteristics, the cognitive and linguistic
abilities of students, the range of educational experiences, and varying expertise with technology and the media all represent significant
factors in the development of a writing program. With each incoming
cohort of students, the community college WPA must decipher the
educational needs of such a complex population. The rewards for such
work are great. Remaining mindful of the history and mission of the
community college, and preparing a solid foundation of administrative tools, are among the best ways to prepare for the new cohort of
students each year.

2 Writing Program Administration at the Community College: A History and Overview

Several characteristics distinguish writing program administration in the community college context from WPA work in four-year institutions. The unique socioeconomic history and development of the community college over the last one hundred and ten years have shaped particular aspects, such as the department that offers writing courses, the writing program itself (or the lack of a program, in some cases), the community college writing faculty, the development of writing pedagogies, the decision-making processes, and the definition of the WPA's role within his or her particular institution. While variations appear from one college to the next, many two-year institutions share more similarities within these distinct categories with each other than they do with four-year institutions, although a greater number of parallels exist with small liberal arts colleges than with large, research institutions. Beginning with a historical context, this chapter outlines these aspects of the community college and how they affect writing programs within them. It also identifies distinctions from four-year institutions where appropriate.

A Brief History of the Community College and English Instruction

One of the paradoxes of the community college has been its origins as a "grand and ongoing democratic enterprise, [which] may well prove to be the public institution best situated to liberate citizens from the privations of poverty and class" (Sullivan, "Cultural Narr." 142). Viewed in a certain light, this democratic vision seems accurate: The open admissions policy offers anyone able to achieve some success at the college through an opportunity for an education and possible social and economic mobility (Reynolds 4). Viewed in another light, one might see the community college as an attempt to fortify the American caste system by limiting access to education beyond the associate's degree, or by providing training suitable for jobs at designated socioeconomic levels. The impact of these views, and the complex history of the public two-year institution, have special relevance to the work of the WPA, especially in terms of providing a context for understanding trends in student enrollments and for understanding current public responses to, and support for, the college. Both have bearing on the development of writing programs within the institution. They influence a curriculum that seeks to address the complex needs of a very diverse student population within an educational hierarchy that places pressure on the two-year college to fill gaps (i.e. developmental education) often overlooked by four-year institutions.

Conceived of as early as the 1850s, the first junior college was founded in Joliet, Illinois, in 1901, after several prestigious university presidents urged its establishment. The expansion of industry and the increasing demand for qualified workers, the extension of adolescent development, and the movement for increased equality among American citizens contributed significantly to the development of the community college over the course of the twentieth century (Cohen and Brawer 1). As a result, these two-year institutions "became the new growth industry in higher education, in part to deal with the sheer numbers of students but also in part because of the growing democratization of higher education, a sense that everyone, not just the elite few, had a right to attend college" (McLeod 69). Further evidence of the community college's role in the democratization of American higher education emerged in 2009, when President Barak Obama called upon public two-year institutions to play a central role in reinvigorating the national economy (Jenkins and Bailey)—a point discussed further in Chapter Four. Due to the recent global economic slowdowns, the right to accessible education has become a lifesaver to thousands of recently unemployed citizens. Because of its low tuition and it local missions, the community college is best situated to address the educational needs of local constituents, particularly those in need of work.

The term "community college" aptly expresses its educational role within a locale. Until the 1940s, the term "junior college" was used synonymously with the term "community college." But by the 1950s and 1960s, the terms began to connote different institutions, including: junior colleges that were two-year institutions associated with private universities' lower divisions; and community colleges, that were associated with public, comprehensive two-year institutions (Cohen and Brawer 4). Now, other terms can equally apply to community colleges, including "city college," "county college," and "branch campus." The missions of community colleges vary somewhat, but, for many, the relationship between the institution and the local community figures most prominently. Anne Breznau emphasizes the connection between the college and its surrounding community:

> The community college is, just as the term implies, an organ of the community, a way for local residents to be educated while remaining within the confines of their families, jobs, and lives. Whether you take a job at El Paso, Kirtland, or KCC [Kellogg Community College], you enter an organization governed by local leaders, often funded by local millage, and existing to serve local people. It is natural for the community to feel ownership of such a college.

Breznau stresses the influence of local leadership and funding to support the surrounding community's interests. Columbus State Community College's (CSCC) mission statement demonstrates further evidence of this relationship within its own local community:

> The mission of Columbus State Community College is to provide quality educational programs that meet the life-long learning needs of its community. Through its dynamic curriculum and commitment to diverse learners, the college will serve as a catalyst for creating and fostering linkages among the community, business and educational institutions. The college will proactively respond to the changing needs of our community and its role in the global economy through the use of instructional and emerging technologies. ("Our Mission")

Columbus State Community College's mission statement codifies the institution's relationship to the community; each sentence refers to the interests of local constituents. San Antonio College's mission statement also emphasizes the institution's relationship with its community, expressed in an explicit statement regarding its commitment to a diverse student population. In the following example, the mission statement identifies very specific ways this commitment manifests, with a focus on students' educational goals, including transfer, job preparation, and skills development:

> San Antonio College is a public community college which provides for and supports the educational and lifelong learning needs of a multicultural community. As a leader in education, San Antonio College is committed to excellence in helping students reach their full potential by developing their academic competencies, critical thinking skills, communication proficiency, civic responsibility, and global awareness. San Antonio College fulfills its mission by offering the following:
>
> - Transfer education designed to provide students with the first two years of a bachelor's degree.
> - General education courses in the liberal arts and science to support all college degree programs.
> - Career preparation provided through a wide range of programs to prepare students for immediate employment.
> - Developmental studies for students needing to bring their basic skills to a level appropriate for college work.
> - Continuing education to offer a variety of training, licensure, and professional programs.
> - Strategic Enrollment Management that includes a uniform strategy to identify, attract, enroll, and retain students who reflect the population of our service area.
> - Academic support services that include a comprehensive learning resource center and basic skills activities that complement instruction.
> - Student support services that include a comprehensive learning resource center and basic skills activities that complement instruction.
> - Student support services to provide assessment, counseling, tutoring, financial assistance, and social and cultural activities for all students, including those with special needs.
> - Promotion of cross-cultural understanding and appreciation through instructional and social activities that contribute to cultural awareness and interaction.

- Involvement of business, industry, and professional groups in planning and revising educational programs to meet workforce needs.
- An environment conducive to learning through an attractive physical campus and wellness oriented programs and services.
- Continuous assessment of programs and services and the utilization of results for improvement.
- Operation of the College within available fiscal resources to provide accountability to taxpayers of the District. ("Mission Statement of San Antonio College")

The San Antonio College mission statement specifies that the institution "provides for and supports the educational and lifelong learning needs of a multicultural community" by identifying the relationships between the college and its constituents and between enrolled students and supporting taxpayers ("Mission Statement"). The mission's first bullet regarding transfer credits also speaks to the institution's awareness of its relationship to the academic community at large. Last, the college very explicitly outlines its commitment to preparing students for work and to "business, industry, and professional groups" with whom it partners "in planning and revising educational programs to meet workforce needs" ("Mission Statement").

Community colleges with less explicit mission statements may still emphasize similar principles, such as the commitment to the local community and the preparation of students for work. Though fairly concise, Tampa's Hillsborough Community College Vision and Mission Statements articulate a broad view of community that includes the global society, with a particular emphasis on the diversity of its constituents:

Vision

Hillsborough Community College will deliver education of the highest standards enabling a diverse community of lifelong learners to achieve their maximum potential in a global society.

Mission

Hillsborough Community College, a public, comprehensive institution of higher education, empowers students to excel through its superior teaching and service in an innovative learning community. ("Vision and Mission")

Certain community colleges may claim specified missions, even as they still qualify as public, comprehensive two-year institutions; these focuses are noted in their names, such as technical college and vocational college (Cohen and Brawer 4–5). Even in these colleges, similarities among their missions emerge, as seen in the example of Springfield Technical Community College's (STCC) mission statement and institutional vision:

STCC Mission Statement

Springfield Technical Community College, a leader in technology and instructional innovation, transforms lives through educational opportunities that promote personal and professional success. To this end, the College is committed to:

- Fostering inquiry
- Embracing diversity
- Respecting an open exchange of ideas
- Encouraging leadership
- Inspiring creativity and serving the future with a caring faculty and staff.

Vision

Springfield Technical Communtiy College will be the leading-edge educational solution for workforce, community, and innovation. ("More about Springfield")

STCC's mission and vision statements demonstrate the institution's commitment to "technological and instructional innovation" for the purpose of providing education for the "workforce" and the "community" ("More about Springfield").

Tribal community colleges of North America also share many similarities with other community colleges; however, the relationship with the supporting tribe or nation tends to be even more explicit than most community colleges' relationships with their surrounding communities. For example, Little Priest Tribal College expresses this relationship simply in its mission statement: "Little Priest Tribal College is established as the educational institution by the Winnebago Tribe of Nebraska to fulfill the goal of its namesake, Chief Little Priest, 'Be strong and educate my children'" ("LPTC Mission Statement"). The college's philosophy statement, though, articulates an awareness of a pluralistic world, one similar to the awareness demonstrated by other community colleges:

> In the Winnebago heritage of respect, integrity and self-reliance, Little Priest Tribal College is chartered by the Winnebago Tribe of Nebraska, a sovereign nation, to provide higher education opportunities. The college will prepare its students to succeed in a multi-cultural world by emphasizing quality education of the highest level, humanistic values, and life skills. ("LPTC Mission Statement")

In another example of a tribal community college's mission statement, Wind River Tribal College emphatically expresses its commitment to the supporting tribes it serves:

> The Wind River Tribal College Board of Regents is dedicated to the preservation, continuation and protection of Tribal self-determination, language and culture. The Wind River Tribal College exists to provide education, innovative programs, services, and activities to create an environment of learning and success.
>
> The Tribal College provides, maintains, and operates a post-secondary institution on the Wind River Indian Reservation that includes educational, vocational, cultural and technical programs.
>
> The Tribal College provides expertise in skilled and knowledgeable personnel.
>
> The Tribal College prepares students to be self-sufficient in a rapidly changing world.
>
> The Tribal College provides an opportunity for people to become productive members within families, communities, and

Tribes through economic development on the Wind River Indian Reservation.

The Tribal College sustains the sovereignty of Northern Arapaho and Eastern Shoshone Tribes.

The Tribal College facilitates language and cultural revitalization. ("Wind River")

Wind River Tribal College offers the same types of opportunities to its constituents as other community colleges in terms of its "educational, vocational, cultural and technical programs." However, it distinguishes itself from other community colleges by specifying "Tribal self-determination, language and culture" as its top priority, with further emphasis on "self-sufficiency" and the sustenance of "the sovereignty of Northern Arapaho and Eastern Shoshone Tribes." Its commitment to its constituents is like the commitments of other community colleges to their own constituents, but because of the institution's specific mission and purpose, the commitment is necessarily political and ethnically focused.

Besides these institutions' relationships to the supporting communities, all of the community colleges noted above share the most basic characteristic of the associate's degrees offered. For the purposes of this book, the definition provided by Cohen and Brawer is used to identify a community college: "any institution regionally accredited to award the associate in arts or the associate in science as its highest degree" (5). A minority of community colleges, however, award bachelor's degrees. Cohen and Brawer report that The Carnegie Foundation reclassification of higher educational institutions in 2006 categorized community colleges that awarded up to ten percent of their degrees as bachelor's degrees, as "baccalaureate/associate colleges." They add that the National Center for Education Statistics (NCES) shifted the definition of such colleges to the category of "four-year public" institutions, which explains why twenty-five community colleges disappeared from the general listing between the years 2004–2005 (4–5). This text will use the Cohen and Brawer's operative definition of community colleges, with a focus on those institutions that concentrate on offering associate's degrees, exclusive of those that are community-supported adult education centers or vocational training centers.

Such community colleges originate from the junior college, which developed as a provider of additional instruction by secondary schools. The development resulted from the desire of several university presidents to separate the first and second years of general education from the years of advanced study at the four-year university level. From the beginning, junior colleges provided general liberal arts education ("Community Colleges Past to Present"). Two different perspectives shaped their establishment, one viewing the college as part of the attempt to model American higher education on the German educational system; the other views the college as a legitimate institution unto itself. Henry Tappan, president of University of Michigan and a supporter of the college's establishment, viewed the community college, for example, as a gymnasium, after the German style, providing students with preparatory courses for advanced study at the university. Whereas University of Chicago president William Rainey Harper, another supporter, saw the college as an institution of higher education and established a junior college within the parameters of the university (Tinberg, "Teaching" 138).

Despite the noble intentions behind its founding, the community college's struggle for legitimacy within higher education originates in its early history as a "junior" or preparatory college. For community college WPAs today, this battle for academic currency permeates all disciplinary, national, and political discussions about student literacy instruction in the two-year college context. Whenever a WPA from a two-year institution enters such discussions, the qualifier "community college" is inevitably used to distinguish the concerns or issues related to the writing program from the dominant discourse of four-year institutions. And not only do external misconceptions about the college abound; they can also exist within the two-year institution. Frank Madden points out that even community college English faculty may subscribe to predominant assumptions, noting the comments of a department chair during his attendance at an ADE seminar:

> It was probably the use of "we" that upset me most. I listened with astonishment as a community college English Department Chair told a gathering of department chairs at an ADE Seminar, most from four-year colleges and universities, that "we" are different. Speaking of graduate education and employment, she declared that two-year college English departments don't need "overtrained" PhDs or faculty members who

> pursue their own scholarship or engage in theoretical debates. In essence, she suggested, two-year colleges want faculty members with just enough academic preparation and intellectual energy to follow the program and teach their classes.
>
> Few two-year college faculty members avoid hearing the negative stereotyping of the public or others in the profession: our institutions are not quite real colleges; we are glorified high school teachers. Few of us avoid being stung by friends at other college or universities who toss out demeaning generalizations about two-year college faculty in our presence—as if they were givens. But this was different. This was the voice of my own two-year college colleague confirming what many in the profession already believe—that two-year college faculty are less than legitimate members of the academy. (721)

While Madden describes how one department chair internalized the external, predominant view of the college, he claims that from his years of community college experience, he learned that most colleagues in the profession "do not share this retrogressive view—a view that may represent what 'we' used to be but not what we are or what we are becoming" (722).

The two-year college's struggle for academic legitimacy is somewhat paradoxical, given its tremendous—and rising—enrollments. From 1909, after the establishment of twenty junior colleges, the institution grew to 170 colleges by 1919. By the 1960s, as many as 457 community colleges had been founded (McLeod 69). With the legislation of affirmative action and the establishment of Educational Opportunity programs, citizens for whom higher education had been out of reach in the past, now had access. The sizes of the colleges tend to be small by university standards, but they are located in a range of regional settings. The MLA Committee on Community Colleges reports that fifty-eight percent of community colleges enroll less than 4,500 students, while seven percent enroll up to 15,000 or more students. The institutions have homes in rural locations (37%), urban locations (39%), and suburban locations (24%). In fall 2008, the total enrollment for community colleges (including public, private, and tribal) was 12.4 million, and 7.4 million of these students were enrolled in credit-bearing courses ("Fast Facts"). The MLA Committee on Community Colleges reports that because of "the sheer number of students they reach, two-year colleges have an enormous impact on American higher education." Further, the MLA Committee points to the California Community College system as an example, which, "alone is composed of 109 colleges, serves more than 2.5 million students, and is the largest system of public higher education in the world." The number of public community colleges continued to grow steadily over the last century, and by 2011, the AACC places the total number of community colleges at 1,167, of which 993 are public and thirty-one are tribal ("Fast Facts").

As evident by rising enrollments, public two-year institutions offer a viable option for students of higher education. Two recent factors also contributed to the increase in enrollment. The global economic crises, which began in the late 2000s, escalated enrollment numbers for community colleges and inspired the Obama administration's commitment to community colleges, which has also contributed to the increase. In 2009, President Barack Obama called to raise the number of college graduates by five million within the next ten years (Jenkins and Bailey), and while the initial funding to support this increase did not materialize, the administration allotted two billion dollars in competitive funding for community colleges (Moltz). In January 2011, the administration released details of the two billion dollar grant program, providing for the creation, expansion, and restructuring of job-training programs at the two-year institution (Gonzalez). Chapter Four addresses the implications of this funding. The economic crisis brought students looking for preparation for new job fields, and students who intended to enroll in more expensive four-year institutions, but found them suddenly out of reach due to changed personal financial situations. These factors represent the sociopolitical and economic significance the community college has always held. Yet, in spite of its formidable enrollment numbers and its enormous contribution to American undergraduate education, the community college still wrestles to assert its academic legitimacy.

Several political perspectives provide insight into the college's struggle for legitimacy. Kevin Dougherty, in his study of the origins of community colleges, *The Contradictory College*, identifies a few class-based views, ranging from the democratic view of the two-year institution as a populist enterprise designed to raise the socioeconomic status of the masses, to a Marxist view of the community college as an institution that codifies the caste system, preventing significant class mobility. Doughtery argues that Functionalist Advocates view the community college democratically, as an institution that fulfills multiple purposes by offering a college education, providing training for workers, and helping universities maintain high standards:

> Community colleges, these advocates claim, democratize college access by being plentiful, nearby, and inexpensive, by offering vocational education and adult education in addition to more traditional college offerings, and by adhering to an "open door" admissions policy that imposes few entry requirements. (17)

Students who attend community college, he adds, have the opportunity to transfer to a four-year institution to continue their education, if they wish (17). In this view, the two-year institution does not limit the possibilities for its students; on the contrary, it offers multiple opportunities for the advancement of education and career/vocation. "Open admissions" equals nondiscriminatory and equal access to educational opportunities.

Another perspective—that of the Instrumental Marxists— according to Dougherty, views the community college as an attempt to fortify the American caste system. As noted earlier, several university presidents collectively called for the establishment of a separate two-year institution: David Starr Jordan (Stanford University), Alexis Lange (who was the Dean at the School of Education, University of California), in addition to Henry Tappan (University of Michigan) and William Rainey Harper (University of Chicago) encouraged the development of the college in the early twentieth century. Ira Shor questions their motives: "Would a society dominated by white, male, and corporate supremacy build 1,200 new community colleges to disturb its old hierarchies of race, gender, and class? Would an unequal system dismantle itself by distributing so many instruments for equality?" (135).[1] Jordan, like Tappan, "wanted to split the first two college years from the rest of the university in order to create a university more akin to its European ancestors, an elite institution focused on research and scholarship" (Reynolds 3). Jordan is also acknowledged as the individual who identified the split with the terms "junior" and "senior" colleges (Reynolds 3). In this way, argues Dougherty, Instrumentalist Marxists claim the establishment of a junior college assuring the primacy of large research universities, despite the surge of student enrollments in two-year institutions (18–19).

Institutional critics, Dougherty suggests, offer a third perspective on the inherent class issues at work during the founding of two-year institutions. They view community colleges as a way to enable students to find a place in a society that does not need an abundance of "overeducated" citizens. In other words, "Community colleges . . . are agencies for the 'management of ambition,' reconciling students' high demand for, and society's limited supply of, college-level positions" (Brint and Karabel, qtd. in Dougherty 20). In this view, associate's degrees, as well as vocational programs offered at the college, reinforce the limitations placed upon educational and socioeconomic advancement through training and degree options. By encouraging and rerouting students to vocational programs—what Dougherty refers to as the "diversion effect"—students have "lower educational attainment" as a result (21). These students do not transfer to four-year institutions; and they—the thinking goes—help preserve the elitism of these institutions by not enrolling in them.[2]

With an emphasis on the local nature of the institution, Cohen and Brawer identify additional views that offer alternative motives for the establishment of the community college. They point to several reasons, including the desire of business owners for trained citizens suitable to the needs of their work, and also the desire of communities across the United States that saw the establishment of a local two-year institution as a way to add prestige and recognition to the community itself (10).

Perhaps most relevant to the discussion is Cohen and Brawer's point that the community college is a uniquely American institution, which, in their view, contributes the most to its proliferation over the last century. Even as European countries experienced similar growth in populations and desire for trained workers, none developed a parallel institution, where students could transfer the earned degree for further baccalaureate study. In contrast, the Association of Canadian Community Colleges (ACCC) claims over 900 community colleges and institute members ("Serving Communities"). While these institutions are beyond the scope of this discussion, the ACCC website provides more information. Even though Canadian community colleges share similar missions, Cohen and Brawer argue that the establishment of the community college reflects the democratic ethos of American culture:

> [S]ince it's founding, the United States has been more dedi-
> cated to the belief that all individuals should have the op-
> portunity to rise to their greatest potential. Accordingly, all
> barriers to individual development should be broken down.
> Institutions that enhance human growth should be created
> and supported. Talent is potentially to be found in every so-
> cial stratum and at any age. People who fail to achieve in their
> youth should be given successive chances. (11)

Reflective of the position of the Functional Advocates, Cohen and
Brawer present an optimistic, democratic view of the community college as an institution situated for educational access and class mobility.

Composition instruction has been similarly perceived as a democratic initiative that either empowers its students or functions as a
class-based, gatekeeping mechanism within higher education. Furthermore, as a discipline itself, composition has had its own struggle
with legitimacy within academia. Composition instruction originated
with Harvard College offering a first-year writing course, English A,
in 1885. Within five years, most colleges and universities in the United
States followed suit. Robert Connors notes that the course was not
intended to hold a permanent place in the curriculum as much as it
was to provide a temporary solution for improving students' writing
skills until the secondary schools could accomplish acceptable student
literacy competencies (48–49).

Composition evolved over the course of the late nineteenth and
twentieth centuries, but scholars never considered it as a professional
area of study. Quoting Edward P.J. Corbett, McLeod traces this history from its origins in English departments: "By 1910, composition
had become almost totally apprentice work, and responsibility for its
oversight became the province not of a scholar or a curriculum expert
but an administrator" (qtd. in McLeod 31). Consequently, as Susan
Miller, in her discussion on the "feminization of composition," points
out, composition occupies a marginalized space in the academy:

> Even discounting the economic or survival needs that are
> often cited to explain composition's importance in the ori-
> gins of English departments, composition conveniently, and
> precisely, contained within English the negative, nonserious
> connotations that the entire field might otherwise have had
> to combat. In mutuality with literary study, it enclosed those

who might not "belong," even as it subsumed the soft, nonse-
rious connotations of vernacular study. It became a place that
the "best men" escape from. . . . (45)

Within the hierarchy of English instruction, the study of literature historically superseded the study of composition in everything
from staffing to funding. Since its establishment, composition, first
as a course and then as a course within a discipline, has undergone
numerous revisions, refutations, and re-establishments, but within the
last thirty years, it has secured its place in American higher education.
Still, because of its labor-intensiveness, most English departments del-
egate composition instruction to their least influential instructors, and
in four-year institutions, instruction has largely fallen to TAs, graduate students, and adjunct instructors. The compositionist's struggle for
legitimacy within their own departments and within the broader discipline of English studies parallels a similar struggle engaged by community colleges.

Fortunately, composition has not experienced the same marginal-
ization in the two-year school. Composition has "long suffered from
a sense of not being respected as a professional field," but in community colleges, the lack of respect "is probably less the case, at least
among our fellow faculty" (Klausman 244). One reason for the higher
regard of composition at the community college is that it comprises
the bulk of the English courses, and full-time faculty, and also legions
of adjunct faculty, teach a range of writing courses. In other words,
composition is the primary focus of English courses at the community
college. Victoria Holmsten reiterates the point that instructors "are
not marginalized members of a department that is primarily focused
on teaching literature to English majors" (432). Helon Howell Raines
makes the distinction that "[i]n two-year colleges, *writing* traditionally
is the center of an undergraduate English or language *program*. This
differs from the situation in which a *program* focuses on a particular
genre or level of *writing*"(154). Referring to her own colleagues in the
English department, Holmsten puts it another way: "we *are* a writing
program" (432). Independent of disciplinary biases, composition instruction continues to thrive at the community college, and very often,
search committees prioritize job candidates whose knowledge and experience includes composition pedagogy—a point discussed later in
this chapter.

In the two-year college, English composition course offerings include developmental writing courses that are generally not separated to another department or program.[3] Full-time and part-time instructors both teach these courses, and the hierarchy regarding these course assignments is minimal. Holmsten points out that the inclusion of developmental writing signifies one of the most important distinctions between writing instruction at two-year and four-year colleges:

> One major difference between community college writing programs and university programs seems to be in the placement of developmental writing programs, perhaps even the existence of developmental courses. In community colleges, developmental education is usually defined as an essential part of our mission to meet community needs. (432)

The mission statement of San Antonio College demonstrates Holmsten's claim in its bullet, stating: "Developmental studies for students needing to bring their basic skills to a level appropriate for college work" ("Mission Statement"). Developmental education forms a central component of the community college English department's identity. In contrast, developmental writing courses in the four-year institution, if they exist at all, occupy marginalized spaces in the department or in a separate department or program altogether.

In addition to composition and developmental writing courses, community college English departments offer a range of English courses, including in some instances English as a Second Language courses and reading courses. Many college catalogs include composition at the entry and advanced levels; various creative, business, and technical writing courses; and literary courses that cover a broad range of areas, such as: British, American, Native American, African American, world, multicultural, women's, mystery, science fiction, and others (Reynolds 5). Faculty members at two-year institutions teach within the range of these courses. The MLA Committee on Community Colleges reports that English faculty may also teach studies in film, cultural studies, humanities, journalism, and others as they fit their experience ("Community College Teaching Career"). The following English course listings from SUNY Westchester Community College, Springfield Technical Community College, and Palomar Community College provide examples of the breadth and specificity of courses taught in a two-year institution:

Westchester Community College English Course Listings (Valhalla, NY)

Eng 91 Basic Writing 1
Eng 92 Basic Writing 2
Eng 101 Composition and Literature 1
Eng 101H Composition and Literature 1-Honors
English 102 Composition and Literature 2
Eng 113 Reading and Writing Poetry
English 113h Reading and Writing Poetry Honors
Eng 115 Creative Writing
English 117 Women in Literature
Eng 124 Professional and Technical Writing
Eng 126 Readings in Human Rights-Honors
Eng 200 American Literature through the 19th Century
Eng 201 Modern American Writers
Eng 202 Children's Literature
Eng 203 African American Literature
Eng 204H Literature of New York-Honors
Eng 205 British Literature 1
Eng 206H Cambridge Literature-Honors
Eng 207 British Literature 2
Eng 208 Literature of the Americas
Eng 209 Short Story
Eng 210H The American Dream-Honors
Eng 211 Modern Drama
Eng 214 Special Topics in Literature
Eng 215 Introduction to Shakespeare
Eng 215H Introduction to Shakespeare-Honors
Eng 216H Cambridge Introduction to Shakespeare-Honors
Eng 217 Perceptions of the Holocaust
Eng 217H Holocaust Studies-Honors
Eng 218 Literature and the Environment
Eng 221 Literature and Society
Eng 222 Writing Projects Seminar
Eng 224H Great Books-Honors
Eng 225 World Literature 1
Eng 226 Leadership and the Humanities
Eng 227 Contemporary Global Literature
Eng 239 Modern American Poetry
Eng 241 Latin-American Literature
Eng 298 Women Writers
Eng 298H Women Writers-Honors
Eng 299 Caribbean Literature

Eng 300 Life Writing
Film 125 Writing for Film
Film 125H Writing for Film-Honors
Film 220 Fiction into Film
Film 220H Fiction into Film-Honors

While the English course listing for Springfield Technical Community College (STCC) demonstrate comparable breadth as Westchester Community College's course offerings, STCC places greater emphasis on business and technical writing courses, indicative of its mission. The business and technical writing courses appear high on this course offering list, following the core composition courses, and preceding most of the literature courses:

Springfield Technical Community College (Springfield, MA)

ENGL-100 English Composition 1
ENGL-101 College English
ENGL-110 Honors English Composition 1
ENGL-200 English Composition 2: An Introduction to Literature
ENGL-201 Business English
ENGL-202 Technical Report Writing
ENGL-203 Fundamentals of Oral Communication
ENGL-210 Honors English Composition 2
ENGL-300 Literature of the Western World 1
ENGL-301 English Literature: Anglo-Saxon to Neoclassical Periods
ENGL-302 American Literature: 1620–1860
ENGL-304 Introduction to African-American Literature 1
ENGL-305 Children's Literature
ENGL-308 Women in Literature
ENGL-309 Sex and Sexualities in Western Literature
ENGL-319 Introduction to Journalism
ENGL-321 Introduction to Creative Writing: Poetry
ENGL-329 Latino Writers in the U.S.
ENGL-345 The American and European Short Story
ENGL 350 Early Non-Western Literature
ENGL 351 Non-Western Literary Voices
ENGL-361 Introduction to Theater
ENGL-380 Literature in Society
ENGL-400 Literature of the Western World 1
ENGL-401 English Literature 2: Romanticism to Modernism
ENGL-402 American Literature: 1860-Present

ENGL-404 Introduction to African-American Literature 2
ENGL-408 Women in Literature 2
ENGL-421 Introduction to Creative Writing: Fiction
ENGL-900 Directed Study in English (individual study)
JOUR-900 Directed Study in Journalism (individual study)
THTR-110 Fundamentals of Acting
THTR-310 College Theater Workshop 1
THTR-311 College Theater Workshop 2
THTR-312 College Theater Workshop 3 ("STCC Course Descriptions")

Few community colleges offer a specific Associate of Arts degree in English, but at Palomar Community College in San Marcos, California, such a program of study exists. The college emphasizes the degree's relevance to possible jobs and describes it as providing "the background for students to succeed in diverse fields, such as advertising and marketing, teaching, journalism and telecommunications, law, technical writing, and business administration," as well as preparing "students for upper division course work in English" (*Palomar College 2010–2011 Catalog*). The Palomar Community College AA Degree Major in English follows:

Program Requirements   Units

ENG 205 and Introduction to Literature 3
ENG 202 or Critical Thinking/Composition 4
ENG 203 Critical Thinking/Composition Through Literature

Literature Surveys (Select 9 Units) Of these nine units, students must take either a two-semester survey of British literature or a semester each of British and United States literature.

ENG 210 Survey of British Literature I 3
ENG 211 Survey of British Literature II 3
ENG 220 Survey of World Literature I 3
ENG 221 Survey of World Literature II 3
ENG 225 Literature of the United States I 3
ENG 226 Literature of the United States II 3

Elective Courses (Select 2 courses) Any of the above courses not previously taken or pick from the following:

ENG 135 Introduction to Creative Writing 4
ENG 136 Intermediate Creative Writing 4
ENG 137 The Literary Magazine: History/Production 4

ENG 215 Introduction to the British Novel 3
ENG 230 Introduction to the American Novel 3
ENG 240 Introduction to Classical Mythology 3
ENG 250 Introduction to Shakespeare 3
ENG 260 Literature through Film 3
ENG 265 Science Fiction 3
ENG 270 Popular Literature 3
ENG 280 Women and Literature 3

TOTAL UNITS 22–24 (Palomar College 2010–2011 Catalog)

The breadth of the English course offerings indicates that instructors teach various subjects within the discipline:

> Contrast, for instance, a graduate creative writing program, or even a freshman writing program in a university, to the operative context of a two-year college English department. In the two-year school, the creative writing instructor may also teach technical writing, composition, and literature, all of these at the freshman or sophomore level. (Raines 153)

As a result, faculty members tend to be generalists, even as composition emerges as the primary course taught.

While English departments in four-year institutions prioritize specialists with training in specific literary genres, movements, time periods, or geographic locations, two-year colleges do not often seek such specificity. The following community college job description for an Instructor in Humanities, Fine Arts at Heartland Community College demonstrates a more common preference for generalist applicants:

Tenure-Track Faculty: English Composition/Humanities

Instruction—Humanities, Fine Arts

We seek applicants for a tenure-track position anticipated to begin in the Fall 2011 semester. Will teach Composition and Humanities courses with a specialization in Dual Credit/ Dual Enrollment Instruction and will participate in College P-20 initiatives. A minimum of an M.A. or M.S. in English is preferred. A broad base in English Studies is preferred. This position serves a Writing Program with outcomes that are grounded in social and cultural theory as well as a general Humanities Program. Duties will include main campus and

Dual Credit/Dual Enrollment teaching assignments at district high schools. ("Employment")

Here, the institution makes explicit its desire for a generalist by stating: "A broad base in English Studies is preferred." The MLA Committee on Community Colleges reports that job applicants with a wide range of knowledge have an advantage during the search process. The Committee refers to the comments of a search committee chair who suggests that generalists may best address the academic needs of a diverse student classroom: "As an English instructor chairing a hiring committee commented in an interview, two-year colleges need experienced teachers 'who [can] go into the classroom with a bunch of twenty-five people with twenty-five different interests all going in different directions and get them focused and keep them focused'" (qtd. in Twombly 432). In addition to possibly anticipating the needs of "twenty-five people" in a classroom, generalist candidates also offer the flexibility needed to teach different courses at introductory levels that community college English departments offer.

ENGLISH DEPARTMENTS

Because composition is a requirement for matriculated students, departments of English—or their equivalent (i.e. a Humanities Department)—are usually the largest departments in the community college, perhaps second only to math in some cases. Community college English departments tend to have the highest number of full-time student equivalents (FTSEs, or FTEs), courses, and faculty members (Nist and Raines 59). The greater representation is not so different from their four-year counterparts, since the history of English departments includes subsuming college composition into its course offerings: "By gaining control of the teaching of writing, English departments gained control of the only universally required course, and therefore largest enrollments, making it one of the biggest (and in some cases most powerful) departments in the university" (McLeod 27). This development in English instruction extends to community college English departments that focus on instruction on the levels of first- and second-year curricula.

Even as English departments are among the largest departments, most two-year institutions do not offer English as a major. As the table from the 2005 *NCES Digest* indicates, the majority of associate's degrees went to students in the broad fields of "Liberal arts, general studies, [and] humanities":

Table A7. Main Fields Associate's Degrees Were Conferred, 2003–2004. Source: National Center for Educational Statistics Digest, 2005.

Main Fields	Associate's Degrees	Percentage of Total
Liberal arts, general studies, and humanities	227,650	34
Health professions and related sciences	106,208	16
Business, management, and marketing	92,065	14
Computer and information science	41,845	6
Engineering and engineering-related technologies	39,652	6
Visual and performing arts	23,573	4
Security and protective services	20,573	3
Mechanics and repairers	12,553	2

Most of these areas of study prepare students for distinct work fields. Although an English degree can prepare a student for work, some of the possibilities tend to be either less obvious or less lucrative to those enrolling for work-related goals. Consequently, disciplines outside English frequently view courses as lacking "content," and English departments as "service" departments, supportive of the work of other disciplines—a view well known to English instructors in four-year institutions, and a view that ignores the relationships between writing and knowledge-building.[4]

Several implications for the WPA result from this external disciplinary view, some more favorable than others. For instance, faculty from other disciplines may offer input into the development of writing courses. Howard Tinberg demonstrates in *Border Talk* how faculty in several disciplines collaborated at Bristol Community College to develop the college's writing center. In the book's introduction, he explains:

> The work that follows is an attempt at translation, a translation of the work and talk that teachers do. I intend to report

what I observed when several colleagues from a variety of disciplines at my community college, along with a group of peer tutors, came together in the summer of 1994 to talk about writing, reading, and knowing. . . .

. . . As I struggle along the borders, I see myself as occupying a "contact zone," the place where, according to Pratt, cultures interact and influence each other. The language that emerges from such a zone "interlock[s] understandings and practices" (1992, 7).

Looking back at our summer workshop, I now see that we were straining to produce that very kind of language ourselves. It was not simply that we were looking to find a common language with which to talk about writing and knowing (as generalists, we felt quite comfortable with the notion). We were also attempting to see whether we could translate to one another the differences that defined us as teachers of psychology, nursing, dental hygiene, literature, history, business, mathematics, and ESL. In my mind, that was the greater challenge. (ix-xii)

Unified in their common objective of talking about "writing and knowing," Tinberg and his colleagues demonstrate an interdisciplinary commitment to supporting and contributing to writing initiatives.

Other implications may also present themselves. Non-writing faculty members may make specific requests, such as the creation of business writing or technical writing courses that meet the needs of the students in their disciplines, and team-teaching among writing instructors and instructors in other disciplines may occur. Another possible implication is that because of the influence of other disciplines or the nature of the college, the WPA may recommend teaching APA style of documentation in a composition or other writing course.

Still, some writing faculty view their work in terms of the broader academic community, beyond the disciplines represented at the community college. Referring to the "behemoth" English department at his two-year institution, Klausman writes:

Our sense of service, then, is less to our "more powerful Other" on campus and more to the academic community as a whole: I suspect that at two-year colleges, composition courses serve the vague aim of helping students to write "in the academy"

or "in the professional world," and not "in their majors," for
which courses do not exist on our campus, nor for other disciplines, which are disparate and relatively small. (242)

In Klausman's example, writing courses aim to prepare students for
their interdisciplinary work beyond the college.

Just as an English major may not exist at a community college, not
all of these institutions even house an English department or an autonomous writing program. Raines's 1990 study of community college
writing programs points out that two-year schools sometimes lack a
distinct writing program, but also English instructors may form

an unofficial department with a de facto chair and even
may be part of a larger division of related disciplines, such
as philosophy, foreign languages, or communications. These
divisions are designated by various titles such as General Education, Liberal Arts, or Language Arts, terms which indicate a
crossing of disciplines common in community colleges. (154)

In the twenty years since Raines's study, little has changed. In a 2009
study, Tim Taylor reports that there are few recognizable trends for
locating where English courses are taught in community colleges:

There is no predictable pattern of where "English" tends to
be housed. Of the twenty-one responses, three two-year colleges grouped these disciplines as a department—composition, creative writing, ESL, and literature—which is a pretty
traditional grouping. In some cases, there were variations on
that grouping with other disciplines like journalism, philosophy, women's studies, reading, or folklore included. In some
instances, however, writing courses were part of a larger communication division that included speech communication,
drama, art, music, and mass communication. (127)

Taylor's findings suggest that the organization of English courses varies with the institution offering the courses. One typical organization
for writing instruction in the community college context does not necessarily exist.

FACULTY

While many writing faculty at community colleges have conventional educational backgrounds and pedagogical training, many do not share "typical" educational backgrounds. Like the students, faculty can be an equally diverse population. Prior to the 1960s, instructors usually had experience teaching in secondary schools (around eighty percent in 1920). By the 1970s, this number declined significantly, and more instructors arrived from graduate schools, trade schools, and other two-year institutions (Cohen and Brawer 85–86). Today, faculty come to the college with a range of degrees, such as the Master of Fine Arts, Master of Arts in Imaginative Literature, Master of Arts in English, Master of Education, PhD in Literature, in addition to Doctor of Arts and PhD in English (Klausman 243). Klausman points out that the diversity in degrees attained by the faculty at his college parallels the diversity among the approaches to teaching writing (243). Instructors demonstrate a range of aptitudes, knowledges, and attitudes regarding writing pedagogy. Faculty also employ a range of pedagogical training. Some have knowledge of composition studies, and some have none at all. Both points, the variation of degrees and the range of competencies demonstrated by the faculty, underscore the preference community colleges place on generalists who can teach English courses. A diverse faculty with far-reaching abilities best suits a diverse and complex student population. As Tinberg states: "In a certain sense, we community college faculty are quintessentially postmodern. We possess no single identity, but rather have shifting and blurred identities. Like the subject of postmodern anthropology, we move in a variety of worlds" (x-xi).

The following autobiographical narratives of writing faculty from several community colleges shows the "variety of worlds" the instructors inhabit, and the breadth of experience and knowledge they bring to the composition classroom. For some instructors, simply the love of language and writing led them to the community college composition classroom.

Patricia, Full-Time Instructor

My mother taught us early the power of the written word and a love of language. I began practicing the use of that power by writing for school newspapers and literary magazines, publishing letters to the editor, and keeping journal upon journal of ideas, stories, poems, and letters I never mailed, but that served as catharsis. I worked my way through undergraduate school not only by working in the cafeteria and at a hot dog stand, but also by teaching others to write. I worked my way through two levels of graduate school by teaching in the public schools and working at a customer service public relations department, at summer camps, and at doughnut shops, as well as by freelancing as a writer and editor for magazines and newsletters. Eventually I wrote novels and children's books, too, and during the last few years, I have added scholarly publications to my repertoire. Writing continues to serve as one way I breathe. But I combine that way of breathing with actually earning a living. I have taught English—writing and literature—since 1977, initially in grades seven through twelve, and then as an adjunct in a couple of four-year schools, before landing a tenure-track job at a community college.

Like Patricia's autobiographical narrative, the following self-narrative depicts a love of language that includes foreign languages, leading to a deeper understanding of immigrant students' experiences.

Leonore, Adjunct Instructor

I've gone through various career permutations, but my main focus has always been on language. It started at the University of Florida, where I took my first course in linguistics and became instantly hooked. I got a B.A. and went on to study applied linguistics at the University of Pittsburgh. Along the way, I began to focus my attention on language acquisition, especially in deaf children. It was also in Pittsburgh that I started teaching English as a Second Language. I developed a love of teaching people how to expand their linguistic skills, whether it was through learning a new language or developing the control over their own native language. Eventually my academic focus shifted to deaf education and Teaching English to Speakers of Other Languages (TESOL), and I eventually earned a Master's in Education as well a certificate in TESOL in 1997. In fulfilling a long-held desire to travel, I embarked on the challenge of teaching English abroad. My first position was in a private school in Istanbul, Turkey, teaching reading and literature to students in middle and high school. At the end of that year, with the Ozel Yildiz Lisesi, I got a job with International House Language School, also in Istanbul. At the same time, I was learning Turkish and gaining a much deeper appreciation of what it must feel like for my ESL students back in the States as they navigated living in a new country while learning a new language. In 2001, I had the opportunity to transfer to another IH school, and so I moved to Braga, Portugal, a decision partly based on having family in the area. It was a new, exciting challenge, and a chance to further expand my own understanding of teaching, of English, and of another foreign language. In 2003, I made the decision to return to the United States. I was able to apply the knowledge gained from my own experience of being an immigrant to my teaching, which also applied after I started teaching credit classes at the community college in September, 2007. Since then, I've found that my experiences in teaching such a wide range of students and in various situations were relevant to the college's student population, as I see it diversify more with each passing year. My lifelong study of language is now focused on writing, not only how to help students improve their own skills, but on how I can channel my ideas and experiences and express them in my own writing.

Leonore's love of teaching and language stems from her interest in multiple languages and cultures, as well as her appreciation for and deep empathy with her students. The next faculty narrative demonstrates how a love of language that developed from creative writing translates into teaching.

Elizabeth, Full-Time Instructor

I am a poet, and I came to the two-year college out of curiosity and the need to find a real teaching job. I fell in love with the work and haven't looked back.

I never know what will happen in the classroom each day. Community college students are amazingly diverse in cultures, backgrounds, ages, and experiences. Most of my knowledge about teaching comes from my colleagues, who are generous in sharing. The rest I learned—and I am still learning—from being a parent.

In twenty-one years at the college, I have seen many changes, but the one constant is our commitment to students. This makes the work a service to others. Teaching here has shaped me in social and political ways, and opened my eyes to inequalities in education.

Teaching at the community college offers freedom, too. We are free to follow our passions in writing, to research and to study what we desire, and we are encouraged to keep growing. At present, I am writing new poems, trying to find a publisher for my first book of poetry, and learning new ways to teach Shakespeare's plays through acting.

While the love of writing links the following faculty member's self-narrative, her route to teaching was less conventional than some. As a result, the instructor developed an identification with her students that has proven invaluable:

Heather, Full-Time Instructor

I wish I could say I had a straight path to the academic life, but it wasn't that way. When I was younger, I wanted to be a writer, and I wound up working all kinds of jobs to support myself. For a while I worked at an automotive garage, then in balloon store and a deli. I cleaned houses and I worked in a couple of offices. Eventually, I went back to school and earned a PhD in English. I started teaching after getting a position as a TA at the university, even as I worked part-time at a construction company. Still, I kept writing and then later, publishing. And as it turned out, I loved teaching. It felt like a natural fit, and seemed to link well with my intellectual and creative interests. Now I see how my circuitous route to teaching helps me to identify with a lot of my students who took similar routes to college. I especially identify with students who are working through school—I remember all too well what that was like, and have the worry lines to prove it!

Sometimes, the work backgrounds enable faculty to connect to their students. The following self-narrative demonstrates the instructor's application of his degrees in English to his work life, and now in his return to teaching.

Walter, Adjunct Instructor

After earning Bachelor's and Master's degrees from Fordham University, I taught English for nine years in private and public high schools. Then I wrote feature stories for the Gannett newspapers. After a year of newspaper work, I worked as a free-lance editor for various trade and educational publishers, among them Random House, Scholastic, Inc., the Academic Press, Grosset & Dunlap, and Macmillan, Inc. I was later a full-time editor for the Globe Book Company and for Prentice Hall. As an editor for educational publishers, my work largely consisted of rewriting manuscripts and writing original material as requested. Now I am teaching composition and literature courses at [a community college] to an increasingly diverse student population, whose widely varying levels of academic preparedness, differing language backgrounds, disparate personal circumstances, and individual career goals make designing an effective writing course a challenging undertaking for me. I try to inculcate the idea that the art of writing is the art of rewriting.

With increasing regularity, community college writing instructors bring knowledge of composition pedagogy to the classroom, as seen in the following self-narrative.

Heidi, Full-Time Instructor

I had solid training on the teaching of writing in both my Master's program at Brigham Young University and the PhD program at the State University of New York at Stony Brook, with not only a multiple-day orientation before the semester began, but also semester-long seminars for all composition teachers. The focus of my doctoral degree was early American literature, but I've always taught some composition in my eighteen years of teaching. It wasn't until I joined LaGuardia Community College's faculty in 2003 that I began working with basic skills writers. My publications have so far been evenly split between American literature and rhetoric and composition.

The faculty self-narratives demonstrate different pathways to the community college. Each has a slightly different focus, although there are some shared threads. For some, like Patricia, Elizabeth, and Heather, the love of language and writing led to a teaching career. For Leonore, the love of language led to teaching international students, and her own experiences abroad enabled her to appreciate her students' educational struggles more. Heather and Walter see the relevance of practical work experience in the classroom, and Elizabeth enjoys the links between her creative writing life and the creative life in the classroom. One of the most common threads among these faculty self-narratives is an appreciation of the students, particularly their inherent diversity. Several faculty members express an awareness of a student body that is "amazingly diverse in cultures, backgrounds, ages, and experiences." Their appreciation for their students extends, in many ways, to other aspects of their work, including the freedom to write and to create. Taken together, their narrative accounts of the work at the community college suggest that the institution has much to offer individuals who love to teach.

To effectively teach such a student population, many community college instructors have abandoned outmoded teaching methods because of the complexity and intensity of their teaching experience. Reynolds claims, for example:

> The majority [of community college instructors] long ago eschewed the lecture as the primary means of conveying material. They have long been knowledgeable about collaborative learning and the social construction of meaning. They long ago embraced the use of media in teaching, and they have been pioneers in the use of technology in the classroom. . . . They have also been pioneers in the development of writing centers, locales where they have addressed the needs not just of underprepared students, but also in all disciplines across their institutions. (8)

Many instructors have engaged in innovative teaching strategies within the community college writing classrooms for years. Anne Breznau, formerly the Chair of the Kellogg Community College English Department, also emphasizes pedagogical innovation. "Innovation in teaching, however, garners both respect and support. Pioneers in pedagogies that increase students' sense of community or make effective use of technology or software often receive release time to develop their own courses." The MLA Committee on Community Colleges reiterates Breznau's point in its 2006 report: "Instructors must be flexible and creative to meet these students' needs. A one-size-fits-all pedagogy simply does not work at the community college" ("Community College Teaching Career"). Holladay reiterates this point as well, connecting innovative teaching with the diverse and dynamic student population at the community college:

> Our curriculum and instruction have been shaped, not by practices or theoretical models, but by the students' needs. Before the returning student gained nationwide attention, we had developed techniques for working effectively with adult students. . . . Before K. Patricia Cross wrote about the needs of the nontraditional student, we were using conferences, self-pacing, student tutors, writing labs, and collaborative learning to help underprepared students write more effectively. . . . Before rhetoricians advocated the process approach, we were out of necessity working with students on the parts of the process, intervening at strategic points so that they could experience success instead of more failure. (31–32)

While not all community college faculty members engage in innovative teaching, Holladay identifies a significant trend in teaching at the two-year college. Out of need, many instructors are at the forefront of experimentation and innovation. The ever-changing student population requires faculty to continue finding new ways of addressing each class when it arrives at the college (Kort 181).

The value placed on pedagogical innovation stems from the centrality of teaching at the college. Therefore, most job descriptions for instructors at the two-year college prioritize teaching experience. Note the emphasis on teaching in following excerpts from posted 2011 job openings:

Prairie State College

Assistant Professor, English
Preferred Qualification:
1. Experience teaching English, especially at a community college.
2. Interest in and experience working with developmental writers.
3. Course work in the theory and practice ofteaching writing.
4. Broad background in literature.
5. Familiarity with inquiry-based learning.
6. Experience working with culturally and intellectually diverse students.
7. Ability to use technology to enhance teaching and learning.
8. Interest in pedagogy and familiarity with outcomes assessment. ("Posting Details")

Community College of Allegheny County

English Faculty (Reg FT 10 month with benefits)
General Summary
The primary responsibilities of the faculty are to teach and to develop the curriculum. To meet these responsibilities, faculty must remain knowledgeable about advances in their disciplines, in learning theory, and in pedagogy. . . .

Job Duties
1.　The primary responsibilities of faculty are to teach and develop the curriculum. Prepare and provide students with course outlines that support learning objectives set forth in the course syllabus. . . .
2.　Create an effective learning environment through the use of a variety of instructional methods. . . .

Job Specifications

. . . Applicants for teaching assignments are expected to have strong communication skills. Applicants are expected to have post-secondary teaching experiences; work experiences in the discipline to be taught; and knowledge of industry-related software and systems, including industry certifications, where appropriate. ("Job Details")

The job descriptions from Prairie State College and from Community College of Allegheny County both prioritize teaching experience within the community college context. Further, Prairie State College purposefully invites generalists "Broad background in literature"—and experienced professionals who have worked with a diverse student population—"Experience working with culturally and intellectually diverse students." Both faculty searches prioritize applicants with technological competence. Prairie State College includes the desirable "[a]bility to use technology to enhance teaching and learning," and Community College of Allegheny County specifies a desire for applicants with "knowledge of industry-related software and systems." In addition to emphasizing the ability to teach writing, both colleges—typical of most—emphasize the central role of educational technology.

Reflective of the two-year institution's general interest in recruiting individuals with teaching experience, the MLA Committee on Community Colleges provides a list of commonly asked questions at community college job interviews. The majority of the questions center on teaching, including inquiries into applicant's knowledge of developmental students, technology, and distance learning:

General Questions

Why are you interested in teaching at a community college?

What is your understanding of the mission of a community college?

What are the greatest challenges for higher education in the next ten years? For community colleges and their missions?

What service contributions can you make to this college?

What contributions can you make to your profession through your work at this college?

Describe your experiences with developmental education or with meeting the needs of students with disabilities.

Describe your experiences incorporating technology into your teaching.

Explain specifically how you incorporate the concept of diversity into your classes.

What are your experiences with distance learning?

What have you done in your courses to maximize students' success in learning?

How do you identify students' needs and how do you meet them in and out of class? Give specific examples.

What do you know about our college or student population?

What experiences have you had with defining student learning outcomes and assessing them?

What's your greatest teaching success? Why? What's your greatest teaching failure? How did you handle it? What have you learned from it? (MLA Committee on Community Colleges)

The priority placed on teaching during the hiring process extends to the criteria for evaluation throughout the course of a faculty member's career. The evaluation processes for reappointment, promotion, and tenure place the most value on the instructor's teaching performance. The MLA Committee on Community Colleges reports:

Evidence of teaching excellence, not research, is the means by which most community colleges award tenure and promote faculty members, at institutions where tenure and promotion are available. Research is viewed as an add-on after success in teaching except for two-year colleges that are incorporated into four-year university systems, which usually do require research and publication. Faculty members at public community colleges report spending 70.8% of their time teaching but only 3.5% on research, compared with public doctoral university faculty members, who report spending 50.8% of their time teaching and 28.2% on research (Cataldi, Bradburn, and Fahimi 29).

The 2004 National Study of Postsecondary Faculty translates the percentages into contact hours: community college English instructors devote 18.1 hours on average each week to teaching—and average of 431 contact hours. In comparison, instructors at public doctoral institutions commit 8.1 hours to teaching on average, and have 287 contact hours per week ("Community College Teaching Career").

Cohen and Brawer argue that the professionalization of community college faculty supports innovative teaching, particularly as it evolves in response to students' needs, and, they write, "In a few colleges, the faculty have developed their own projects to modify institutional practices in testing and placing new students" (108). Cohen and Brawer make the distinction, too, that this professionalization does not have to parallel that of faculty in a four-year institution. On the contrary, they write:

> It more likely would develop in a different direction entirely, tending toward neither the esoterica of the disciplines nor research and scholarship on disciplinary concerns. . . . A professionalized community college faculty organized around the discipline of instruction might well suit the community college. The faculty are already engaged in course modification, the production of reproducible teaching media, and a variety of related activities centered on translating knowledge into more understandable forms. A profession that supports its members in these activities would be ideal. Teaching has always been the hallmark of the colleges; a corps of professionalized instructors could do nothing but enhance it. (107)

The TYCA ad hoc Committee on Research and Scholarship in the Two-Year College also supports this view: "At two-year colleges, good teaching matters most, but this committee views scholarship as a prerequisite and a corequisite for good teaching—because teachers' scholarship legitimizes their expertise, informs their classroom practice, and provides their students with models for intellectual inquiry" ("Research" 3).

Many instructors are theoretically informed, and this is increasingly true in today's academic market. They can have training in composition studies as the beneficiaries of graduate programs offering guidance to their English graduate students, or are the recipients of graduate degrees in composition and rhetoric. Likewise, many instructors maintain an active research agenda. Faculty members can be active in professional associations; they attend conferences and publish articles and books. Journals such as *Teaching English in the Two-Year College (TETYC)* and *Journal of Basic Writing,* as well as *College English* and *College Composition and Communication (CCC),* have encouraged community college instructors to submit and publish their work. Many instructors have authored textbooks (Reynolds 6).

Yet, with few exceptions, the community college as an institution generally places little significance on faculty scholarship; it is not an explicit part of most tenure or promotion procedures, making faculty research and writing voluntary endeavors. Also, the WPA Portland Resolution, offering a broad view of WPA work, is relevant to two-year colleges mostly because of its outline of role responsibilities. Its secondary purpose in providing the basis for scholarship, and the CWPA statement, "Evaluating the Intellectual Work of Writing Administration," have less relevance for individuals in community colleges than at four-year institutions. At two-year colleges, WPA work is usually considered to be service. It falls into one of the two primary areas of faculty evaluation—service and teaching—for promotion and tenure.

Still, the publication of more research on WPA work and composition at the community college benefits WPAs in two-year and four-year institutions. Increasingly, instructors in two-year institutions are researching and publishing—a significant shift, since composition theory and research has been conducted by and for four-year college practitioners, and have tended to ignore composition in the two-year college context. Barry Alford expounds on this oversight and its consequences: "Teaching in the two-year college has been invisible intellectual work, usually driven by theories and practices generated from university campuses a long way from the students and faculty at two-year institutions. Two-year college faculty often end up being gatekeepers for standards they did not create and do not control" (v). In addition, as Alford notes, two-year college WPAs find themselves holding their students and faculty peers to standards created by different types of institutions that do not serve the particular needs and goals of two-year college students: "The fact of the matter is that too few community college teachers are writing about the work that they do. Too often we and our work are constructed by others rather than by ourselves. It is indeed time for more of us who teach at the two-year college level to write about our work; to present papers and to publish" (Tinberg, *Border Talk* 72).

The 2004 Two-Year College English Association (TYCA) report on Research and Scholarship in the Two-Year College, and its 2011 followup report, support Madden's view of community college faculty. Contrary to Madden's colleague's comments at the ADE Seminar, the TYCA report underscores the faculty's—and by extension the college's—legitimacy by stressing the relationship between good teaching and scholarly activity:

> At two-year colleges, good teaching matters most, but this committee views scholarship as a prerequisite and a corequisite for good teaching—because teachers' scholarship legitimizes their expertise, informs their classroom practice, and provides their students with models for intellectual inquiry. . . . The committee understands scholarly renewal as a continuing dialogue. The scholarship-teaching connection we envision benefits not only the scholar, but that scholar's students, institution, and professional associations. (3)

The TYCA report stresses the benefits of scholarship on teaching effectiveness in the community college context. But more relevant to the discussion here is the report's claim that faculty at the two-year institution can and should engage in scholarly activity—and that many already do. The report emphasizes the need for more engagement, despite institutional pressures to increase faculty productivity. Both the TYCA report and Madden argue that the community college's legitimacy depends on faculty's scholarly engagement and the value of its situated knowledge of community college writing pedagogy. Faculty gain external "legitimacy" "when two-year college faculty are perceived and respected as 'genuine knowledge-makers as well as conveyors and translators of knowledge'" (Tinberg qtd. in Madden 722).

A few academic journals have faithfully published research in composition studies within the community college context, representing some of the scholarly and innovative work of two-year college writing faculty. A cursory look at general areas of research in the community college context, published in the last few years of *TETYC*, include the following topics:

Composition:

- Reflective writing practice;
- Contributions creative writing can make to composition; and
- Critical language awareness.
- Developmental Writing:
- Transfer issues for developmental students;
- Developmental writing and rhetoric;
- Developmental writing and knowledge production; and
- Accelerated composition and other topics for ESL studies.
- Assessment:
- Assessing collaborative writing;
- Assessment of English programs;
- Assessment and material conditions of students; and
- Assessment of learning communities.
- Approaches to Multimodal Teaching:
- Online teaching strategies and pedagogies;
- Multimodal composing;
- Multimedia composing;
- Peer review and digitally supported classroom practice; and
- Peer review and gender.
- Diversity Concerns and Writing Pedagogies:
- Teaching writing to students of trauma (and war);
- Addressing issues of race and disability in writing pedagogy; and
- Adult learners and academic discourse.

What prevents this knowledge from being shared more freely with the discipline at large is in part a due to the general disregard of community college work. Community college instructors also lack time and opportunities to write and publish, contributing to this limitation. As more professionalized graduates from English departments enter the job market, though, the contributions of community college faculty members in the discipline also grows.

Increasingly, institutions hire candidates with doctoral degrees in hand, whereas in the past, community colleges hired candidates with Master's degrees and no expectations for further graduate study. In 2011, the American Association of Community Colleges (AACC) reported that most faculty members hold a Master's degree, but a significant portion of them hold doctoral degrees. The broad distribution follows: two-thirds of full-time faculty members have earned Master's degrees, one-fifth have earned a doctoral degree, one-eighth have earned a Bachelor's degree, and fewer than one-tenth have earned professional degrees (Rifkin). Echoing the colleague overheard by Madden at an ADE seminar, in 1998, Breznau explained that a PhD did not necessarily help a candidate's prospects at Kellogg Community College:

> One hiring requirement is a master's degree in English or in composition and rhetoric. We have not opened our searches to MFAs despite Western Michigan University's fine program. We are not sure what animal MFA programs produce nationwide. A PhD is not an asset; in fact, we would be cautious about hiring a PhD, lest the cultural gap between KCC and the PhD's expectations be too great. Perhaps tellingly, the one person we did not tenure in the last seven years was the only PhD we hired.

Madden suggests a divergent view from Breznau's regarding the value of a terminal degree. He argues that doctoral degrees hold value in the community college setting, as long as job candidates also demonstrate "extensive preparation in both content and pedagogy—preparation that takes into account the nature of introductory courses and open admission/general education students" (725). He claims that graduate students who desire working with college students benefit most from "programs that can expand the parameters of traditional textual, theoretical, and historical research to include ethnographic research and the scholarship of teaching. There is reason to believe this is the kind of research [that is] most productive at the two-year college" (725).

The large numbers of part-time faculty compound the range of experience and knowledge of the full-time faculty. According to Cohen and Brawer, community colleges hire more part-time instructors than four-year institutions. They indicate that in 1953, the number of full-time instructors to part-time instructors was 12,473 (52%) to 11,289 (48%), but by 2003, the number of full-time instructors to part-time instructors was 138,300 (37%) to 240,000 (63%) (94–95). They also argue that the increased use of part-time instructors negatively affects the profession of teaching at the community college: "Nothing deprofessionalizes an occupation faster and more thoroughly than the transformation of full-time posts into part-time labor" (Clark, qtd. in Cohen and Brawer 98). The authors add that this trend reflects the reliance on part-time workers as a broader, national trend in labor practices (98). While the minimal requirements for an adjunct position usually parallel those for a full-time position, the great difference lies in wages ("Community College Teaching Career"). As the MLA Committee on Community Colleges reports: "the pay per course is often only a fraction of what the full-time faculty member receives. . . . This limited pay from any single institution leads many adjuncts to teach part-time at two or three colleges to earn a living wage, yielding the phenomenon of the 'freeway flyer'" ("Community College Teaching Career"). In other words, adjunct instructors contract with multiple institutions and spend great portions of their days commuting between them.

As a result of these hiring trends, most community college WPAs find themselves in a difficult position, since they work with and often hire part-time instructors. The difficulty of this position stems from a paradox: In an institution established with the purpose of providing open access and class mobility, its existence depends on the exploitation of contingent labor—an unprotected class of instructors with little job security, and nearly always no pension or health benefits. For instructors, though, part-time work offers some advantages, depending on individual situations. Understanding these possibilities benefits the WPA with knowledge of the workforce. In a hiring guide for new job candidates, the MLA Committee on Community Colleges notes the following reasons making adjunct work in the two-year college appealing:

- Teaching at a community college for a semester or two is the best way to determine if this kind of work suits you.
- Having teaching experience at the community college will often make a difference between getting or not getting an interview when a full-time position opens up and may be important for being offered the position as well. Two-year colleges often favor the candidate with teaching experience at a community college over the candidate with a higher degree and university teaching experience. The interview questions themselves will resonate differently with each candidate. The answers of candidates who have

already taught at the community college will tend to ring more true, especially as to their commitment to teaching at this level.

- Successful adjunct instructors may have a better chance to obtain a full-time position at the institution where they have been teaching, if that experience has been successful. Although many community college administrators view good part-time faculty members as a pool of potential tenure-track hires (Twombly 441), adjunct experience does not guarantee that you will be interviewed for a tenure-track position, which often leads to hurt feelings among the part-time staff.

- If your search is limited to one geographic area because of family commitments or continuing work with your graduate institution as you complete your doctorate, it may make sense to interview for a part-time position at a neighboring college and begin being known by the faculty in the institutions of your area.

According to the MLA Committee on Community Colleges, one advantage this type of adjunct work is it offers solid teaching experience. A second advantage is the attraction it offers to instructors who must remain in a certain region. For the instructor who lives in the area, the community college may provide reasonable teaching work locally, and for the two-year institution, the same instructor offers knowledge of the local community and its students.

Helena Worthen notes the apparent advantage of such hiring practices for the college's administration: "[T]he threefold logic for relying on contingents continues to grind inexorably forward: Part-timers bring expertise, save money, and increase management discretion, an unbeatable combination" (54). She warns that the dangers of hiring a mostly part-time faculty prevents open dialogue about pedagogy "because the conditions of contingent teaching silence debate about disciplinary concerns: to disagree fundamentally about how to do your job with someone who has power over your job is to risk losing your job" (45). Despite objections from faculty, unions, and faculty discipline associations, the practice of hiring adjunct faculty has escalated over the last fifty years. Working with a faculty largely rendered powerless by the terms of their employment, the community college WPA occupies a unique position. He or she becomes the chief communicator, a go-between for administrators and part-time faculty who teach writing. One advantage of this position is that the WPA can also become the chief advocate for a faculty cohort that largely has no voice in the institution.

Yet, the lack of expertise among a large number of part-time instructors presents another challenge to WPAs, and contradicts Reynolds's and others's earlier claims that faculty are on the forefront of teaching innovation. One of the difficulties of relying so heavily on contingent faculty is that many part-time instructors may have very little related experience, or experience that has not prepared them for teaching writing. Klausman claims that often in hiring so many part-time instructors—some at the last minute, days before the semester begins—the WPA cannot know the abilities of all of the instructors: "In many places, my college included, there simply are not enough well-qualified, theoretically informed adjunct faculty to staff all of our classes" (245). For some instructors—and some full-time instructors—complacency is sufficient. These are instructors who teach only what they know, without striving to learn more or to reach the myriad of students in their classes. They exist at nearly all institutions. Klausman argues that this kind of complacency begs for WPA intervention; in fact, without a WPA, writing courses at the community college never find the coherency of a writing program:

> I think it is reasonable to believe that without the support and substructure a WPA provides, many two-year college faculty even in English will teach "only what they already know about writing" and in their own peculiar ways, and that writing classes will never quite become a writing program but something else entirely. (239)

Klausman's perspective does not necessarily apply to all two-year institutions, but he points to an important role the WPA can have in organizing faculty and writing courses, and in providing faculty development. Hiring contingent faculty creates regularly changing cohorts of instructors year to year; sometimes the alterations to the faculty are greater one year from another. Either way, the WPA should remain cognizant of the needs and abilities of part-time faculty.

Fortunately, and regardless of aptitude, many instructors—full-time and part-time—who teach in a two-year school have historically shared one steady characteristic: a commitment to serving the underserved. In keeping with the Functionalist Advocate point of view, most community college instructors are likewise committed to a "non-elitist, non-hierarchical philosophy of education [that] drives the mission of two-year colleges" (Nist and Raines 59). Perhaps, as a result, the MLA Committee on Community Colleges reports that "[m]ost two-year-college faculty members find their work deeply satisfying" ("Community College Teaching Careers"). Instructors may see their work as part of a broader civic engagement; a sense of mission is embedded in the work for many. "For most of us at two-year colleges," Madden states, the role of the faculty "is defined by the needs of our students and vision of ourselves as transformative educators" (727). Further, the majority of instructors share an interest in cross-cultural issues, and did so "long before it became fashionable to discuss them" (Reynolds 9). Thus, the faculty's commitment to students can ease difficulties facing WPAs and help foster an openness to faculty development initiatives.

DECISION-MAKING

One of the most significant differences between WPA work at the two-year college and at the four-year institution is the decision-making process. Since community college WPAs work with their peers, including part-time instructors, they reach decisions often by consensus and through collaborative processes. Recent job announcements articulate the preference for applicants who can work collaboratively with peers. The following excerpts demonstrate this priority:

Mountain View College, Dallas County Community College District

- Must be a team player and work cooperatively with faculty, students, colleagues, and local teachers. ("Search Jobs")
- Prairie State College:
- Our highly collaborative department is currently working on a number of important initiatives, including assessment and a realignment of our composition curriculum. ("Posting Details")

Both Mountain View College and Prairie State College specify the desire for applicants who can work "cooperatively" and collaboratively with college constituents.

The collaborative approach to decision-making can manifest in different ways. WPAs solicit their colleague's input, or a committee collectively carries out the WPA work. Frequently, community colleges develop "decentered" WPAs, a model in which there is not one person solely responsible for the administrative work, but several individuals with specific, assigned roles. Taylor explains that in some cases, a centralized approach is impractical for economic or personnel reasons at the two-year college. Further, a de-centered, collaborative approach can reflect the commitment of instructors to their students and to their subjects:

> Instead, counter to two-year colleges that have the luxury of an officially designated WPA, collaboration might offer coherence, sanity, and respect for pedagogical difference. In some cases, collaboration through very influential committees and/or lead faculty members in charge of specific course offerings reflect that instructors are quite invested in the writing courses that they teach almost every semester—whether developmental, basic, ESL, composition, or professional writing. (Taylor 129)

Taylor found that thirty-eight percent of survey respondents worked within a structured collaboration processes for making decisions about writing courses. For example, Westchester Community College's English Department engaged in several group-writing exercises to collectively brainstorm, discuss, and develop its English Studies Program in 2008–2009, when it sought to revamp its course offerings. Members of the department participated in this collaborative work with respect and mutuality—such a process enabled all members equal say in the development of the program, and hence, equal ownership. Collaborative decisionmaking, or what Taylor refers to as "postmasculinist," points to Hildy Miller's notion for the synthesis of masculine and feminine approaches to decision making: "[l]eadership is therefore characterized as relational. Personal authority may appear as being receptive, willing to promote discussion, listen to divergent views, and look for common interests" (qtd. in Taylor 131). Jeanne Gunner also identifies this collaborative approach to WPA work, calling it "collaborative administration," entailing "ideological critique, a restructuring of institutional power, and, in practice, a sharing of authority" (254). For many WPAs who encounter resistance to programmatic changes, Gunner's approach offers reasonable and satisfying success since it is inclusive of divergent opinions. The principles of such an approach are based in communication and mutual respect. Additionally, collaborative administration spreads the responsibility for the writing program among all of the collaborators and makes each not only accountable for the work and its results, but also equally invested in its success.

For WPAs in community colleges who depend on collaborative support to forge change in their programs or courses, disengaged faculty have a burdensome effect. Their lack of participation in programmatic business that requires input or buy-in may require further effort by the WPA, ranging from activities such as informal hallway conversations to connect with faculty, to formal faculty development. Klausman writes:

> My guess is that we, as WPAs in two-year colleges, must face the challenge of forging a theoretical center from which to work, encouraging all faculty to participate, but finding ways of working with or replacing faculty who are theoretically opposed or merely indifferent. Undoubtedly, coming from an egalitarian perspective as we in the community college like to believe we do, this may be an unsettling realization. (245)

However, the presence of a WPA might motivate faculty members in such a situation. A truly collaborative and egalitarian department (or division) simplifies this work.

THE ROLE OF THE WRITING PROGRAM ADMINISTRATOR (WPA)

Just as writing programs, students, and faculty vary from community college to community college, the role of the WPA also varies. In some two-year institutions, as noted earlier, more than one person performs the work of the WPA, and specific tasks are delegated to different members of the faculty or administration. At others, "WPA structures could likely be a collection of practitioners and administrators" who do not have a designated title (Taylor 123–24). On the other hand, individuals coordinating centralized programs might hold any of the following titles: department chair, assessment coordinator, assistant dean, writing administrator, lead instructor, associate dean, assistant chair, or writing coordinator (Holmsten 430). Several titles reflect writing program work as the primary responsibilities of the WPA, and several simply reflect a general distinction for the administration of writing courses under the umbrella of other administrative duties. No matter what the role is called, there is often little office support, and certainly no TAs or graduate students, to help with the workload. With several different tasks to manage, the WPA does not necessarily fit into a single, defined academic role.

Until very recently, the role of the WPA in the community college was relatively undocumented. Holmsten observes:

> The written record of the WPA in the community college appears to be virtually nonexistent. We do not have a long-standing tradition of writing program administration or writing programs in which to place our work. It is probable that this kind of work has not existed much in the relatively short history of the community college in this country. (430)

WPA work in the two-year institution may also be undocumented because scholarship in general tends to be produced by four-year institutions, though community college WPAs—and writing instructors—have published more research of late, as noted earlier.

Regardless of titles and how the role is documented, one challenge for community college WPAs, like all WPAs, is to define the work themselves. They may find they have more leeway to define their roles than their colleagues in four-year institutions. Homsten suggests that the relative youth of the college partly explains the greater freedom:

> In this newer institution that still seems to be in the process of defining itself, it is no surprise that as WPAs we are working to define our positions. In spite of the lack of a written record, it is possible that this work has existed, but has taken on different names and forms in the contexts of different institutions. (430)

On the other hand, when the position is not predetermined, as McLeod notes, the lack of definition may leave the position open to definition by those not serving in it: "Without a clear definition of the work, WPAs sometimes find themselves in positions that others define for them in unrealistic ways" (9). Swiftly assessing what a particular institution and its specific students need will help the WPA shape the role in ways that are manageable and meaningful.

To aid this assessment, the following chapter explores the multiple responsibilities of most community college WPAs. How any WPA shapes his or her role depends on every aspect of the writing program's administration, including the nature of the department or division, teaching practices, and the decision-making processes—all within the context of a complex history that places them with unique sociopolitical responsibility. None of these aspects of WPA work remains static, either. Especially at the community college, all aspects, like incoming students each year, shift; the greatest challenge for the WPA may be to stay continually cognizant of the dynamics of the institution, its faculty, and its students.

3 The General Responsibilities of Community College WPAs

Despite the variety of job titles, the community college WPA is perhaps most simply understood as the individual or individuals associated with everything related to student writing at the college. To support the principles of democratic educational access, the writing program must be dynamic, particularly given rapidly changing student populations (Kort 181). To plan for or anticipate changes in the program is ideal; however, WPA work is often reactive, more crises-driven than reactive, as McCleod suggests (4). Community college WPAs, like their four-year institutional counterparts, often "spend their work days responding to emergencies rather than planning for the future" (Crowley 220). Beyond the crises, WPAs in two-year colleges share many responsibilities with those in four-year institutions. With a few major exceptions, the 1992 Portland Resolution, developed and adopted by the Council of Writing Program Administrators, outlines many of these day-to-day tasks. Section II of the Resolution identifies several points of overlap: knowledge of composition and rhetoric pedagogies, understanding of relevant position statements of major literacy and language organizations (such as the MLA, NCTE, and CCCC), as well as curriculum and program development, evaluation of textbooks, evaluation of faculty, assessment, scheduling, counseling, and articulation.[1]

Despite the many parallels between WPA work at the community college and the 1992 Portland Resolution, written from a four-year institutional perspective, several significant characteristics distinguish two-year colleges. For one, the resolution identifies the scholarship inherent in the responsibilities for WPAs in most institutions—a point that has far less significance in a community college context. The identification is explicit because such scholarship may strengthen the tenure applications of junior faculty engaged in such work. The value

103

of this work does not need to be affirmed in the two-year college in the same way, though, since tenure is usually based on teaching and service.

Other distinctive characteristics that separate WPA work at two-year colleges from four-year colleges include: the predominance of composition courses among departmental offerings; the student body's presentation of diverse literacies, competencies, and educational needs and goals; and the faculty, including contingent faculty, who not only have very diverse educational backgrounds, but are the peers of the WPAs, since there are no teaching assistants or graduate students to teach the writing courses. These factors make collaborative decision-making and consensus building necessary processes, and at times thwart efforts to bring coherence and consistent assessment to the program.

Further, some of the responsibilities listed in the Portland Resolution either do not apply to community college WPA work, or are less of a priority than they are at four-year institutions. For example, the supervision of a writing program office does not pertain to these WPAs, since much of the writing program is the English department itself. For the same reason, coordination with developmental writing programs, as noted in the Resolution, does not pertain to community college WPAs, because developmental courses comprise a large portion of the courses offerings. Also, other points by the Resolution, such as the recommended preparation for WPA work that includes publishing and presenting at conferences, tends to be much less emphasized or nonexistent for WPAs at the community college. Nevertheless, the Portland Resolution outlines the major categories of WPA work that many individuals in the two-year institution will find useful.

The following outlines the most common responsibilities of the community college WPA. Some of the tasks parallel those at four-year institutions, including: developing a curriculum, facilitating articulation, scheduling class assignments, monitoring student enrollment, hiring contingent faculty, providing faculty development, managing a writing tutorial center, overseeing placement and assessment, managing budgets, representing writing faculty, and fielding needs and complaints from students and faculty. Several strategies exist for managing these responsibilities; the chapter closes with recommended strategies, such as maintaining an awareness of one's institution and its practices and policies, strengthening interpersonal skills, and perhaps most important, preparing oneself professionally and emotionally.

CURRICULAR DEVELOPMENT

Developing or coordinating the curriculum forms one of the major responsibilities of community college WPAs. Many aspects of curricular development center on the question of what qualifies student writing as "college level." Outcomes, course sequences, and instruction depend on how WPAs interpret this question. The range of student competencies, and the lack of research in the community college context, complicates criteria for college-level writing. Patrick Sullivan opens a discussion of these criteria in "What Is 'College-Level' Writing?" This 2003 article specifically locates the discussion within the context of the community college, and offers a general guideline for determining college-level writing, but acknowledges all of the contradictions within this institutional context. He describes the attempt of the Connecticut Coalition of English Teachers to create a definition of "college-level" student writing, but as Sullivan explains, "we found this task more daunting than we expected, and we found ourselves again and again returning to a variety of complex and in some cases heartbreaking questions related to teaching writing at open-admissions institutions" (374). Sullivan and his colleagues raise issues related to student writing that most writing instructors and WPAs in all institutions must consider, but they find the answers fraught with contradictions and complexities specific to the two-year college context. The issues the Coalition raised centered on the following questions:

- What makes a piece of writing "college-level"—as opposed to, say, high school level?
- Shouldn't a room full of college English teachers be able to come to some kind of consensus about what "college-level" writing is—even though they teach at a variety of schools around the state?
- If it is true that all politics are local, is it also true that standards related to "good writing" are local, too?
- Are variations in standards from teacher to teacher, campus to campus, and state to state something we ought to pay attention to or worry about? Or should we consider them insignificant, given the complexity of what we are teaching?

- We have an increasing number of students who come to us profoundly unprepared to do college-level reading, writing, and
thinking. Is it possible to teach these students to write at a "college level"? (374)

Despite the ambiguities these questions raise, Sullivan asserts a belief
in the possibility of "establishing a group of shared standards related
to 'college-level' work," but he writes "it will take the kind of patience,
careful listening, and sympathetic engagement with others that is essential for any act of successful communication" (384).

Sullivan suggests substituting the term "college-level writer" to
"college-level reader, writer, and thinker" for the purpose of evaluating
student preparedness for college work (384). He argues that "[g]ood
writing can only be the direct result of good reading and thinking,"
forming the foundation of student preparedness (384). He proposes
criteria for identifying college-level student work:

1. A student should write in response to an article, essay, or reading selection that contains at least some abstract content and
   might be chosen based on its appropriateness for a college-level
   course. The selection should not be a narrative and should not
   simply recount personal experience.

   Reading level or "readability" for this material might be determined by the approximate grade level it tests at on, say, the Fry
   Readability Graph, McLaughlin's SMOB Readability Formula,
   or the Raygor Readability Estimate. Some critics argue that the
   various readability tests can't accurately measure complexity of
   content (or "concept load") very well (see Nelson; Hittleman).
   My experience using these tests for work I assign in my own
   classes seems to indicate that sentence length, sophistication of
   vocabulary, and length of sentences is a good general indicator
   for determining what is appropriate for a college-level reader.

2. The writer's essay in response to this reading should demon-
   strate the following:
   - A willingness to evaluate ideas and issues carefully
   - Some skill at analysis and higher-level thinking
   - Some ability to shape and organize material effectively
   - The ability to integrate some of the material from the read-
     ing skillfully

- The ability to follow the standard rules of grammar, punctuation, and spelling. (385)

Sullivan's approach explicitly links writing to the processes of reading and thinking. He argues that assessing college-level writing through this framework may best suit the work of community college students: "But without at least attempting to design writing tasks that will allow us to evaluate our students for these kinds of skills, how can we speak, defend, or teach within a system that makes distinctions every day between developmental content and college-level content?" (385). Sullivan and his colleagues concluded that viewing student work holistically—as a synthesis of multiple, simultaneous cognitive processes—will strengthen the effectiveness of a writing program that prepares so many students to make the transition from developmental-level to college-level writing.

While Sullivan ultimately does not determine standard criteria for "college-level" writing (and reading and thinking), he points out that such an objective "may require the impossible—that we ignore or disregard the very powerful political and social realities that shape students' lives on individual campuses and in particular communities" (375). Nevertheless, he argues, opening a dialogue about what constitutes "college-level" writing is worthwhile if only because it enables instructors to engage assumptions surrounding writing instruction from within the institutions, the discipline, the state, and the nation (375). His argument underscores the challenges facing the community college WPA who seeks to develop a suitable program within an open access institution, but Sullivan also provides a viable starting point for creating a foundation for a curriculum—by viewing students through the interdependent processes of writing, reading, and thinking. Given that students arrive at the community college with a multiplicity of literacies and competencies—as well as educational deficiencies—approaching curricular development from this holistic assumption offers a broad scope for addressing the needs of a diverse student population.

The WPA Outcomes Statement for First-Year Composition reaffirms Sullivan's suggested criteria for evaluating student work, particularly in terms of linking writing to reading and thinking. The Outcomes Statement identifies the expectations for students completing first-year composition courses, and categorizes these expectations in terms of:

Rhetorical Knowledge;

Critical Thinking, Reading, and Writing;

Processes (for writing);

Knowledge of Conventions; and

Composing in Electronic Environments ("WPA Outcomes Statement")

These categorical outcomes may provide guidance to some community college writing programs. Malkiel Choseed, of Onondaga Community College, argues that the WPA Outcomes Statement offered a foundation from which his department could develop a viable writing program, particularly when the Outcomes Statement was "adapted to reflect the local context," enabling it to function as "a unifying force, laying the foundation for . . . building a cohesive writing program" (1). Onondaga Community College's Writing Program incorporates the principles inherent in the WPA Outcomes Statement, but makes alterations where necessary to accommodate the student population at the college. The following excerpt represents the nature of the adaptations the faculty made to the original WPA Outcomes Statement (see Appendix B) to meet the needs of the Onondaga Community College students:

Onondaga Community College Writing Program

Mission Statement and Outcomes

Outcomes based on and adapted from the Council of Writing Program Administrators (WPA), 2007, and consistent with the principles put forth in *Writing in the 21st Century: A Report from the National Council of Teachers of English*, 2009.

Mission Statement

The mission of Onondaga Community College's Writing Program is to expose students to the principles and practices of the writing process, thereby enabling them to lay a strong foundation for success in a liberal arts education and in their professional lives.

Introduction to Outcomes

> The act of writing is an extremely complex one that includes and depends on a variety of different, interlocking, simultaneous, multi-layered skills and principles. When faced with a writing task, we often just write. We do not necessarily reflect on the act of writing itself as we do it. This tendency is as true for seasoned professionals as it is for first year students. If we can develop a vocabulary for understanding writing and the ability to see it as a process, we can discuss it, make changes to it, and intervene when necessary in that process to change the outcome. . . . (Choseed 15)

The excerpts above reflect the emphasis the department placed on the goals for their particular students, who attend college in part to benefit "their particular lives." It also stresses the values the department shares and uses as the underpinnings of the program. For example, the introduction to the Outcomes Statement explicitly addresses two principles: the centrality of reflection in the writing process (by asserting the risks inherent in its absence), and the identification of the faculty with the students (seen in the use of the pronoun "we").

Although the five categories of the WPA Outcomes Statement remains intact for the outcomes statement of Onondaga Community College's Writing Program, one of the greatest distinctions is within the category of "Knowledge of Conventions." The WPA Outcomes Statement identifies the following objectives for first-year composition students:

- Learn common formats for different kinds of texts
- Develop knowledge of genre conventions ranging from structure and paragraphing to tone and mechanics
- Practice appropriate means of documenting their work
- Control such surface features as syntax, grammar, punctuation, and spelling.

The Onondaga Community College Writing Program, however, states the objectives under "Knowledge of Conventions" more explicitly:

- Use appropriate academic conventions regarding essay structure, paragraphing, and mechanics
- Use appropriate means of documenting work

- Recognize conventions in syntax, grammar, punctuation, and spelling and correct violations (or errors) in those conventions
- Demonstrate knowledge of literary conventions, terminology, and genres. (Choseed 16–17)

Choseed explains that such variations in his institution's writing program represent the multiplicity of pedagogical approaches within his department. He locates "a split between those who define the writing process as focused on editing and those who see it as focused on revision" (9). The program represents the synthesis of both general approaches to best address the diverse learning styles of that particular institution's incoming students. It also demonstrates how the CWPA outcomes statement may be adopted to meet the needs of the two-year college.

The outcomes statement is broad enough to extend to the community college curriculum, which usually includes developmental writing and composition courses, and sometimes ESL courses. Composition courses themselves can follow a two-course sequence for credit-bearing coursework. *The Writing Program Administrator's Resource: A Guide to Reflective Institutional Practice*, edited by Stuart Brown and Theresa Enos, offers several approaches to curricular development, and Susan McLeod's *Writing Program Administration* identifies a comprehensive overview of resources available for curricular development, including first-year composition, basic writing, ESL and Generation 1.5, articulation, and beyond first-year composition. Under the heading of "Curriculum Development," *The Bedford Bibliography for Teachers of Writing*, edited by Nedra Reynolds, Patricia Bizzell, and Bruce Herzberg, offers several categories for consideration and provides resources for further reading and development. The categories include: Course Development; Collaborative Learning; Essay and Personal Writing; Literature and Composition; Advanced Composition; Basic Writing; Gender, Race and Class; Cultural Studies; Teaching English as a Second Language; Technical Communication; and Business Communication. As community college WPAs sift through these and other resources, the distinct missions of their institutions remain a critical part of their reading. While evaluating resources, community college WPAs also consider the following questions:

- Do the values of this curricular approach match/support the core values of my college's writing program?

- Would this curricular approach meet the needs of most of our students?
- How does this curriculum build on the multiple literacies and competencies our students bring to the college?
- How well would this curriculum include/accommodate the diverse cultures presented by our students?
- How well would such a curricular approach satisfy all of the stakeholders invested in the writing program?

These questions enable the WPA to build a wide-reaching program for a diverse student population. The last question considers the diversity of the faculty and other constituents. Again, most WPAs initiate curricular change through collaboration and consensus building, particularly if generation gaps exist among the faculty. Such decision-making processes may facilitate discussion when some instructors express opposition to, or misunderstanding of, the proposed changes. The following example of a writing program outline represents a curriculum developed from collaboration, and explicitly articulates the faculty's commitment to individuality and self-determination:

English Studies Ad hoc Committee Outline of Program

Based on the past year's dialogue and exercises, the committee has outlined the following unifying principles and objectives for the development of English studies at the College. The outline below provides a foundation for addressing further and more specific issues, including student evaluation, assessment, assignment designing, and faculty development.

1. A Fluid, Self-Reflective program
The program is fluid and able to undergo continual reflection, assessment, and revision.

2. Bridges among Courses
Courses should share continuity of principles, even as there are distinctions among them. Bridges from one course to another are necessary so that students gain a sense of relevance and continuity with each enrollment.

3. Building Competencies
Continuity among courses is based on the building of competencies. In the appendices here, we have itemized additional competences or

specified those existing in the standard syllabuses. However, the basis for these competencies is the following:

   a.   Critical and creative thinking.

   b.   Composing with confidence, fluency, and the development of an individual voice.

   c.   Writing/composing extended essays/texts.

   d.   Engaging with writing as a process, with an emphasis on revision, including editing and incorporating appropriate criticism from peers and instructors.

   e.   Reading and writing in a globalized world.

   f.   Exposure to diverse texts, opinions, and cultural approaches.

   g.   Developing the ability to recognize a multiplicity of modes and genres and to compose within different genres, preparing students for written work in other disciplines and in their future lives, after WCC.

4.   Faculty Autonomy and Innovation

The strongest pedagogical principles that continue to emerge have been centered around faculty autonomy, freedom, innovation, and a deep desire to avoid an overdetermined program.

Therefore, we favor opportunities for faculty to develop approaches to teaching that simultaneously achieve the stated competencies, engage students and faculty intellectually, and retain the spirit of autonomy and innovation.

To this end, we support a variety of approaches, including those that engage or link courses outside the English discipline, as well as within the English discipline, thematically, pedagogically, or textually (i.e., linking an English course with a Business course or linking a Comp & Lit 1 and a Comp & Lit 2 course with a common theme, such as the environment or art).

5.   Assessment and Development

   a.   Regular meetings for assessment during the academic year, to look at evaluation, outcomes, grade norming, CL1/2 concerns, BW 1/2 concerns, readings in courses, final exam issues, electives, new forms of teaching (i.e. independent studies for BW). These meetings can be a continuation of the English Studies Ad hoc Committee's work and monthly schedule, for instance.

   b. Also, meetings that offer topics related to pedagogy for discussion. These meetings can be a forum for sharing assignments, syllabuses, texts, innovative approaches to courses, etc. The spirit of the discussion will be exploratory, enthusiastic, and supportive, with an emphasis on communication and collaboration. These meetings can alternate with assessment meetings.

6. Revising Standard Syllabuses

Through consensus, the committee has recommended several amended and/or enhanced competencies to the existing Standard Syllabuses for Composition and Literature 2, Composition and Literature 1, Basic Writing 2, and Basic Writing 1. The foundation of these amendments is articulated in #3 "Building Competencies" of this document, but the specifics have been itemized in the following appendices. [Not included here]

The committee recommends that a separate, smaller ad hoc committee(s) implement the additional competencies and the necessary corresponding revisions in the syllabuses, such as how such competencies are measured and how they support the New York State Gen Ed requirements.

7. Written Assignments

The committee supports the creation of assignments that adheres to the principles and objectives stated above. We recommend not limiting ourselves to prescriptive forms, in favor of creating assignments that encourage students to think critically and creatively and to bring originality to their work. ("English Studies")

In this example, committee members preserved faculty autonomy as a means to sustain the program's flexibility. It also demonstrates the end product of months of group discussions, seeking commonality among members' values, perceptions of student needs, and desired outcomes. In other words, the outline summarizes months of negotiations among very different faculty members, all who sought unity and coherence to a previously undefined "program."

Like the example above, Mary Slayter's account of establishing a writing curriculum at Rogue Community College (RCC) in Grants Pass, Oregon, provides another example of collaborative work. The questions faculty asked themselves during the course of curriculum development focused on the needs of the surrounding community and the educational goals of the students, including: "What classes did all these [vocational] programs need from departments like ours, which provided general education?"; and "What would [students] have to read and write in preparation for future academic work and careers, and how could we find out?" (18–19). They sought answers to these questions from everyone invested in the success of the college and the English courses. Slayton describes part of the process:

> The dean of instruction and the faculty established a variety of course offerings to meet the needs of prospective students, whether they intended to use RCC as a springboard to further academic training or to prepare themselves for careers in the community. . . . Local advisory committees representing different trades worked with faculty and administrators to decide which vocational programs would be most useful to the region and what classes should be offered. . . . (18)

Slayter's account includes the development of multiple programs in addition to an English-instruction program, but she points to the collaborative and inclusive process of discernment that occurred prior to the establishment of the programs. Typical of many community college WPA processes, the emphasis in the curriculum's design was on meeting the students' needs within the context of a local community. It assumes responsibility for coordinating with local stakeholders external to the college, such as industry, business, and legislators.

While the examples and texts above offer possible approaches to and multiple resources for curricular development, the community college WPA is wise to keep in mind McLeod's advice to all WPAs:

> [E]very curriculum is embedded in a particular site and context; an appropriate curriculum for one school and group of students may not be appropriate for another. Any curriculum must be guided by research and theories of learning and composing, have a philosophical coherence, and include good practices that are consistent with both theory and philosophy. (83)

In light of this advice, community college WPAs may find that research and surveys reflecting curricular issues and concerns within the two-year institution context best serve their needs.

WRITING ACROSS THE CURRICULUM

Because Writing Across the Curriculum programs offer the promise of interdisciplinary approaches to writing pedagogy, they hold a certain appeal to community colleges, given the diverse population and the emphasis on disciplines other than English. Since the 1970s, several community colleges have established or experimented with Writing Across the Curriculum (WAC) or Writing in the Disciplines (WID) programs. Leslie Roberts's 2008, "An Analysis of the National TYCA Research Initiative Survey Section IV: Writing Across the Curriculum and Writing Centers in Two-Year College English Programs," found that of 342 respondents, eighteen percent of the colleges had WAC/WID programs. One of the reasons Roberts explains for the somewhat surprisingly low number of these programs is due to the fact that WAC does not often effectively meet the various needs and educational goals of the diverse student body (140–41). She notes that over half of the respondents at colleges that offered a WAC program felt dissatisfied with it (146). The decrease in needed resources to sustain such programs accounted for part of the general dissatisfaction (Roberts 147). Yet some colleges have found success with such programs, such as Virginia's Tidewater Community College.

Mary McMullen-Light addresses why WAC programs flounder at community colleges, when such programs seem to reflect the same principles inherent in two-year institutions. She generalizes major sources of difficulty for WAC programs in these contexts:

> Though the cultures of WAC and of community colleges privilege consistent and similar values (i.e. inclusiveness, diversity, oriented to provide support, emphasis on learning), the structure and arrangement of community colleges do not typically accommodate independent WAC programs but rather promote the infusion of various new initiatives that emerge through other institutional agendas and don't require the same level of oversight a WAC program does. (McMullen-Light)

Clint Gardner locates the difficulties more simply in terms of "institutional support and institutional status." He explains:

> Many fields or disciplines may be represented at community colleges, but the focus on first and second year college students, and the emphasis on general (liberal) education, makes

generalist writing more prevalent than discipline-specific writing. Students are less-actively engaged in their prospective major fields of study, since the courses they take for their major are usually designated at the junior and senior level. (Gardner)

Despite the obstacles facing WAC programs in community college contexts, McMullen-Light argues they can be successful if they are "anchored" to college-wide initiatives and objectives, and if they are able to morph as needed to "adapt to the immediate contexts of their colleges as well as the broader contexts of higher education." McMullen-Light suggests the following strategies for establishing a WAC program in a two-year college:

   a. Allies: Make connections between leaders of the faculty and key administrators who can advocate for the WAC as needed; cultivate wide-reaching support for the program.

   b. Anchors: Connect the WAC program to the college's initiatives and goals.

   c. Place: Find a location for the WAC director where faculty can access his/her expertise or the collected resources (such as books, articles, etc.) that can support the exchange of ideas and dialogue about writing.

   d. Grants: Locate funds outside of the college to support the program.

   e. Identify and Exploit All Available Resources: Make connections to WAC directors at other community colleges and study their programs; sign up for professional listservs; visit the WAC Clearinghouse site (http://wac.colostate.edu/); attend professional conferences.

   f. Gather a Grassroots Group of Faculty with Significant Interest in WAC

   g. Invite interested and invested faculty from different disciplines to participate in the early development of the WAC program.

Further discussion of WAC programs in community colleges, including curricular design, teaching methodology, faculty development, and program assessment, can be found in *Writing across the Curriculum in*

Community Colleges, within the *New Directions for Community Colleges* series, edited by Linda C. Stanley and Joanna Ambron.

DEVELOPMENTAL WRITING

Developmental writing courses, most often non-credit bearing within the writing course sequence, constitute a significant portion of the writing curriculum at community colleges. Debate over including developmental studies in American higher education has continued in some form for the last four hundred years, and the two sides of the debate have varied little over the years, splitting between the preservation of standards to distinguish higher education from primary and secondary education, and the democratization of higher education. In a 2010 Lumina Report, Tara Parker, Leticia Tomas Bustillos, and Laurie Behringer explain the entrenched arguments:

> The history of remedial education can be envisioned as a system running on two parallel, yet seemingly divergent tracks. One track recognizes the critical function of higher education as the keeper of traditional norms and values of a scholarly endeavor whereas the other promotes democratic ideals of fairness and equality. (2)

For community college WPAs, such debates over developmental education are moot; however, they may at times confront resistance to developmental writing courses from the college's internal and external constituents. Regardless, developmental writing occupies a permanent place in the curriculum because of the numbers of students who require it.

Two important general resources offer a spectrum of information for implementing developmental writing courses within the composition sequence. One is *The Bedford Bibliography for Teachers of Basic Writing*, edited by Linda Adler-Kassner and Gregory R. Glau. Contributors provide annotated lists of resources under the following relevant categories: History and Theory; Basic Writing and Basic Writers; Pedagogical Issues; Curriculum Development, and an Administrative Focus. The bibliography offers resources to help answer crucial questions:

• Who are basic writers?

- What do (students called) basic writers do?
- What is "basic writing"?
- What are "alternative" models for basic writing programs?
- What is the state of basic writing?
- How can the best case possible be made for basic writing, and who should make it?
- What are relationships among writing, language, and culture? (vii)

Another significant general resource is the National Association for Developmental Education (NADE) that offers multiple resources on its website (www.nade.net) including general information, political advocacy, policy making, and conferences. NADE provides current information on trends and directions of developmental education.

Also, Dana Britt Lundell and Terence Collins's early work, "Toward a Theory of Developmental Education: The Centrality of 'Discourse,'" provides a meaningful framework for considering the needs of developmental students; they show specific consideration for students in community colleges, and are sensitivity to multiple cultures and socioeconomic classes. Through a literature survey, the authors identify misleading assumptions about developmental students based on the notion of deficiency. Their research indicates that the most prevalent assumptions in developmental education models "prioritize definitions and theories of students pitted against an imagined societal norm discounting their prior knowledge, strengths, and home cultures" (8). Their claim parallels the subtext in the work of Glynda Hull, Mike Rose, Kay Losey Fraser, and Marisa Castellano, seen in "Remediation as Social Context: Perspectives from an Analysis of Classroom." In this paper, Hull et al. point out the "long, troubling history in American education of perceiving and treating low-achieving children as if they were lesser in character and fundamental ability" (795). This perception has contributed to more dangerous assumptions, as the authors claim: "And with the advent of the IQ movement, the assessment of intelligence, as Stephen Jay Gould has observed, was pseudoscientifically reified into a unitary measure of cognitive—and human—worth" (795). In opposition to reductive generalizations, Lundell and Collins forge a theory of developmental education that uses James Paul Gee's notion of "Discourse" as a way to affirm the multiplicity of literacies and competencies developmental students bring to their studies. Lundell and Collins's theory lends itself very comfortably to the democratic vision of education shared by many community college WPAs, as they reject "popular conversations that place [developmental] students into simplistic, assessment-based categories" (7). They offer a viable alternative to thinking about developmental writing courses within the community college context that builds on students' competencies.

As an extension of Lundell and Collins's basic premise, LaRonna DeBrake's "Independent and Interdependent Remedial/Developmental Student Learners," takes the position that developmental classes should focus on the autonomous thought processes of such students and their self-directed/independent participation in group activities. This 2008 essay presents an ideological shift away from the assumption of student deficiency to student ability, and proposes the synthesis of independent and interdependent intellectual activities for developmental students within the classroom.

One area of developmental writing that continues to receive much attention is accelerated courses at the two-year college. "Acceleration" in developmental education is "the reorganization of instruction and curricula in ways that facilitate the completion of educational requirements in an expedited manner" (Edgecombe 4). One of the arguments for accelerated developmental courses holds that the conventional course sequence prevents students enrolled from reaching credit-bearing courses and achieving a degree (Edgecombe 1). Among the reasons for this failure to move beyond developmental courses are "competing work and family interests, discouragement, and differing self-assessments of ability"; research demonstrates that the chances of students completing their degrees increase the sooner they move toward enrolling in credit-bearing courses (Edgecombe 2–3). Senior Research Associate at the Community College Research Center at Teachers College, Columbia University, Nikki Edgecombe identifies three general models for developmental course acceleration, although institutions may have nuanced variations of these models. The models include: compressed courses, which accelerate a sixteen-week developmental course into a seven- or eight-week semester; paired courses that connect a developmental course to a credit-bearing, subject course; and curricular redesign that manifests in several ways, but often concentrates on limiting the developmental courses a student must enroll in (Edgecombe 8–10).

Edgecombe acknowledges that the promise of accelerated developmental courses requires further evidence to support its proliferation. She claims that recent research "suggests that there are a variety of models of course redesign and mainstreaming that community colleges can employ to enhance student outcomes" (35), but cautions against applying such an approach to all developmental students:

> Research also indicates that acceleration may not be the optimal approach for all students referred to developmental education. Although multiple pathways are available, practitioners have limited resources and imprecise information from assessment tests to direct students to courses or other interventions that will effectively address their academic and non-academic needs. (35–36)

Maria Scordaras reiterates Edgecombe's reservations, and points out: "Intensive writing courses may benefit stronger writers, but their usefulness for students at lower levels may be questionable" (278).

The Community College of Baltimore County, which developed the Accelerated Learning Project, sponsors what has become an annual conference on accelerated learning. The conference addresses all three areas of developmental study—writing, reading, and math—bringing a broad view to the complexity of the developmental student, as well as a range of possibilities for addressing developmental writing needs in individual institutions.

The important point here, as with general curricular development, is that the design and sequence of developmental writing courses logically follow the design and sequence of credit-bearing composition courses. However the courses are developed, they should reflect the principles of a writing program concomitant with the open-admissions policy of the institution, and be responsive to issues related to access and diverse student abilities.

READING

Under the umbrella of developmental studies, reading courses enroll significant numbers of students at the community college, and they can come under the purview of the WPA. A 2006 ACT study suggests that half of incoming students enter college prepared for reading at the college level (Bauer 41). Some writing programs link writing courses with reading courses. For example, Joanne Baird Giordano and Holly Hassel note that the University of Wisconsin College's (UWC) writing program (a program for its two-year college campuses) created a

Developmental Reading and Writing Coordinator position so that the individual could support the links between reading and writing the program sought to create. They found that "[d]esigning difficult assignments for basic skills courses (carefully scaffolding throughout the semester) to introduce students to college-level reading, writing, thinking, and learning helps bridge the gap between non-degree credit and degree-credit courses" (3). Several resources offer further general information on the development of reading courses, including: N.A. Stahl and H. Boylan's essay collection, *Teaching Developmental Reading: Historical, Theoretical, and Practical Background Readings*, and R. Routman's *Reading Essentials: the Specifics You Need to Teach Reading Well*. In addition, the *Reading Research Quarterly* provides current information on trends in this developmental discipline.

English as a Second Language (ESL) and Generation 1.5

Also related to curriculum design are the considerations of ESL (or L2) and Generation 1.5 students. Not all community college WPAs oversee the development of ESL courses, like reading courses, but they inevitably must coordinate and possibly consult with faculty members who do, because ESL students eventually enroll in composition courses. Similar to developmental writing courses, ESL courses should be consistent with the philosophy of the writing program. Alan Meyers's "Coming of Age in ESL: Memoirs of a Reluctant Pioneer" identifies programmatic and pedagogical challenges presented by the wide range of nonnative English speakers in the community college. He uses his experience at the City Colleges of Chicago as the basis of his discussion, where students from over one hundred countries enrolled and spoke more than seventy different languages. His account provides an early context for the historical development of ESL studies at the community college and raises issues based in cross-cultural communications and tolerance. Meyers points out that WPAs may encounter resistance to the inclusion of ESL courses, and he reminds his readers: "An enlightened, professional [ESL] program does not necessarily engender an enlightened legislature and central administration, especially with the frequent turnover among board members, chancellors, and vice chancellors" (88).

Like Lundell and Collins's theory of developmental student competencies, both Teaching English to Speakers of Other Languages
(TESOL) and the National Council of Teachers of English (NCTE)
propose similar positions on teaching English as a second language.
All three resources assert the centrality of the student competencies
and abilities brought to the classroom. The "Position Statement Prepared by the NCTE Committee on Issues in ESL and Bilingual Education" reaffirms the language of the TESOL position, which states
that "the linguistic and cultural resources the student brings to the
school are used as tools for learning in the content areas while at the
same time the students acquire proficiency needed in English to enable them to use it as a learning tool." Since Generation 1.5 students
(individuals who have lived in the United States for longer periods of
time and have earned high school diplomas) at times present similar
linguistic issues to ESL students, the NCTE and TESOL positions
can extend to address their concerns within the classroom. As noted
in Chapter Two, such students present unique concerns, separate from
those of recent immigrant ESL students, but their educational goals
can be similar—they may be preparing for credit-bearing composition
courses, or the successful completion of these courses is the primary
goal or step in the achievement of their educational plans. To support
the development of ESL courses that reflect the philosophy of the writing program, WPAs at community colleges may also refer to *Teaching
ESL Composition: Purpose, Process, and Practice*, by Dana Ferris and
John Hedgcock. This text provides a range of theoretical concerns and
practical applications for ESL course development. WPAs may also
refer to *Principles of Language Learning and Teaching*, by H. Douglas
Brown, a guide designed for teacher education that provides theoretical approaches to teaching second languages.

ARTICULATION

Articulation between the community colleges and other institutions
plays a role in the development of the writing program. The term
"articulation," as defined by Cohen and Brawer, indicates transfer of
a student's academic credits from one institution to another (356).
Richard Coley points out that in the past, articulation agreements between institutions automatically assumed "a one-way street with the
rules dictated by the four-year schools" and "mostly on a case-by-case

basis" (23). But Cohen and Brawer emphasize the nonlinear dimension of articulation today and outline its multiple processes:

> It covers students going from high school to college; from two-year colleges to universities and vice versa; double-reverse transfer students, who go from the two-year college to the university and then back again; and people seeking credit for experiential learning as a basis for college or university credit. The concept includes admission, exclusion, readmission, advising, counseling, planning, and course and credit evaluation. (356)

The community college WPA should be cognizant of all articulation dimensions, but spend much time in the areas of advising and course evaluation. Since nearly thirty percent of community college students transfer to a four-year institution, articulation knowledge is essential (see NCES table in Chapter One). And since many students transfer back and forth between different institutions, the WPA benefits from knowing how writing courses taken prior to the students' enrollment transfer to his or her institution. For instance, a community college may set criteria for accepting a transfer course in a particular subject as a passing grade of "C" or better, or a particular writing course in one college may or may not have a parallel in the WPA's institution. Connecting with the school's admission's office often facilitates understanding of transfer credits, since it may not be possible for the WPA to know every articulation agreement.

There is literature on articulation agreements that clarifies and supports these kinds of institutional relationships. Ann-Marie Hall's "Expanding the Community: A Comprehensive Look at Outreach and Articulation," identifies the range of programs that institutions foster articulation agreements with, and provides resources for additional information. Also, Christopher Burnham's "Reflection, Assessment, and Articulation: A Rhetoric of Writing Program Administration," clarifies the relationships among reflective practice and assessment and how they translate into articulation. Burnham's essay is especially helpful for verbalizing assessment specific to writing programs that may facilitate agreements between community colleges and four-year institutions. Both essays can be found in Stuart C. Brown and Theresa Enos's *The Writing Program Administrator's Resource: A Guide to Reflective Practice*.

In addition, community college WPAs often work with an academic affairs or similar office at their college as administrators negotiate articulation agreements with four-year institutions within the same state system, and also possibly private local colleges. General education courses form the basis for most articulation agreements, and states have intervened in several instances to facilitate such agreements (Coley 24). To facilitate articulation with other public institutions within the same state system, the WPA's knowledge of general education requirements is essential.

SCHEDULING COURSES

Scheduling courses forms one of the most common responsibilities of the community college WPA. Scheduling depends primarily on student enrollments in any given semester. In coordination with a division or a scheduling office, the WPA identifies how many writing courses—credit bearing and non-credit bearing courses—need to be scheduled based on past enrollments and current student needs. Prior to the beginning of a semester, WPAs also monitor the registration of students into writing courses. Following enrollments allows them to plan for additional courses and cancel under-enrolled sections. It also allows them to reassign open sections to instructors who have lost course assignments due to low enrollments, or to add sections if surging student enrollments require doing so.

In addition, the WPA should pay attention to economic trends, such as the effects of a recession or the rates of unemployment, as both tend to raise enrollments at public two-year institutions. College administrations watch such trends and usually communicate that information to WPAs, who must schedule courses accordingly. Regardless, monitoring economic trends and staying in communication with relevant administrators may afford WPAs foresight and preparation.

Scheduling classes may entail assigning rooms, a process which becomes complicated if the WPA must compete for precious few computer labs or computer-assisted classrooms. As the beginning of a semester nears, the management of course scheduling, enrollment management, and room assignment can become a last-minute balancing act, since the aspects of scheduling are interdependent. As Crowley argues, mandatory first-year composition at any institution, with its inextricable link to student enrollment, "makes planning nearly impossible" (119). The best ways to prepare for the process are to be organized; develop a sense of course times that usually have the highest enrollments; have backup plans for staffing, adding, or subtracting courses; and maintain good communication and relationships with everyone involved in the scheduling process, including supervisors (i.e. managers or deans), scheduling representatives, and instructors.

Preparation for each semester includes using an organizational system that facilitates the scheduling process. A spreadsheet, for example, provides a consistent way to plan and monitor courses from semester to semester, and enables the WPA to anticipate trends. It may also offer a way to recognize the availability of instructors more immediately than making dozens of calls at the last minute when a new course must be added. The following Excel spreadsheet demonstrates one possible organizational method, based on the English course schedule from Prairie State College, claiming 2,500 FTE. This sample omits online course listings, as they do not require room assignments. Depending on how the WPA wishes to organize the scheduling process, he or she may want to include online courses on the spreadsheet.

Spring 2011—English

	A	B	C	D	E	F
		English	098			
	Course	Section	Day	Time	Faculty	Rm
1	E98	01	MW	9–10:50	Inst. name	3138
2	E98	02	MW	10–11:50	Inst. name	4185
3	E98	03	TTh	9–10:20	Inst. name	4170
4	E98	04	TTh	12:30–2:30	Inst. name	4140
		English	099			
5	E99	01	MW	9:30–12:30	Inst. name	4185
6	E99	02	MW	11–1:50	Inst. name	3240
7	E99	03	TTh	11–1:50	Inst. name	3138
8	E99	04	TTh	7–9:50	Inst. name	4195
		English	100			
9	100	LS1	MW	4–4:50	Inst. name	3138

	A	B	C	D	E	F
10	100	LS1	TTh	12:30–1:20	Inst. name	3138
		English	101			
11	101	01	MW	8–9:15	Inst. name	3200
12	101	02	MW	9:30–10:45	Inst. name	3200
13	101	03	TTh	9:30–10:45	Inst. name	3200
14	101	04	W	7–9:50	Inst. name	3200
		English	102			
15	102	01	MWF	8–9:50	Inst. name	2508
16	102	02	MW	8–9:15	Inst. name	2509
17	102	03	T	4–6:50	Inst. name	2508
18	102	04	F	9–11:50	Inst. name	2507
		Literature	/Creative	Wtg		
19	111	01	TTh	9:30–10:45	Inst. name	4000
20	212	01	MW	11–12:15	Inst. name	4001
		Journalism				
21	J101	01	TR	9:30–10:45	Inst. name	4002

In addition to scheduling information, Excel spreadsheets can also include information on textbook requirements and assessment information for each course on additional pages.

HIRING CONTINGENT FACULTY

Many WPAs at the community college find themselves responsible for hiring contingent faculty. A clear sense of the objectives and core values of the writing program and/or the department/division can provide guidance through the hiring process for part-time as well as full-time instructors. Very often, the WPA hires contingent faculty without a search committee, unlike the process for hiring for a full-time position. However, the WPA should participate in as many full-time searches as possible, since new hires will certainly teach writing courses. Similar to full-time faculty searches, hiring new contingent faculty includes several steps: recruiting, hiring, training, and/or mentoring.

WPAs who hire contingent faculty need to be well acquainted with the parameters of their own authority and with the hiring policies of the college, all of which are available through a Human Resources (HR) office. They should understand how the institution contracts with part-time faculty and be able to articulate the terms of that contract. The college may have a HR representative responsible for contractual issues, but often contingent faculty members come to the WPA with questions and issues related to the terms of their employment, since he or she is usually the most accessible representative of the college they know. In fact, if an adjunct faculty member teaches in the evenings, on weekends, or off the main campus site, the WPA may be the *only* college representative he or she knows.

If WPAs have a hand in writing the job advertisement to recruit new writing instructors, they should include clear information about the kinds of applicants the program needs. For example, if attracting a diversity of applicants is a priority, then indicating this as a preference in the ad is important. Articulating the criteria for the position narrows applicants to a pool more reflective of the diversity and credentials desired. Also, job advertisements become legal documents of sorts—a statement of the expectations for the position. Veronica Pantoja, Nancy Tribbenesee, and Duane Roen note that: "We cannot overstate how important it is to write job ads carefully because once an ad is approved and published, it constitutes the legally binding criteria for evaluating applicants" (147). An example of a job announcement for a contingent faculty position in English follows:

> Community College of Allegheny County
>
> Position Information
> Position Title: Adjunct English
> Job Slot #: N/A
> Campus: College Wide
> Department: Adjunct Faculty
> Work location and additional information
> Salary Grade: N/A
> Job Close Date
> General Summary: The primary responsibilities of the faculty are to teach and develop the curriculum. To meet these

responsibilities, faculty must remain knowledgeable about advances in their disciplines, in learning theory, and in pedagogy. Faculty portfolios will include contributions and program development and show evidence of ongoing professional development.

Job Duties

1. The primary responsibilities of faculty are to teach and to develop the curriculum. Prepare and provide students with course outlines that support learning objectives set forth in the course syllabus. Develop and measure learning outcomes. Assess student performance and maintain grade records.
2. Create an effective learning environment through the use of a variety of instructional methods.
3. Collaborate in the development and continued assessment of learning outcomes for use in program reviews and curriculum revision.
4. Work with other program and/or discipline faculty to complete scheduled program reviews and to use the findings to revise the curriculum.
5. Participate in appropriate professional development activities to assure currency in both discipline knowledge and instructional methods.
6. Participate in department/discipline, division, campus, and college meetings and committees.
7. Participate in college projects, surveys, studies, and reports that relate to the discipline or program.
8. Collaborate in the development of program and/or discipline promotional materials.
9. Support the college's goals.
10. Perform other related duties as required or assigned.

Job Specifications: Master's degree in English, Linguistics, Composition, Rhetoric, or Literature OR an undergraduate degree in English with Master's in related field including at least 18 credits in English Literature, Composition, Literary Theory, or Writing. Some relevant teaching experience is required.

Applicants for teaching assignments are expected to have strong communication skills. Applicants are expected to have post-secondary teaching experiences; work experiences in the discipline to be taught; and knowledge of industry-related software and systems, including industry certifications, where appropriate. Degrees must be from an accredited institution.

Hours: Varies ("Adjunct English")

Not all adjunct job announcements are as detailed as this one, but clearly the English department of the Community College of Allegheny County contributed to developing the ad. Very specifically, the department outlined a position for part-time instructors who wish to be involved in the curriculum and who demonstrate knowledge of current theory and pedagogy. Some community colleges have several layers of approval before a job advertisement becomes public, and these layers can exclude, or minimally include, the input of the WPA. Since state and local governments regulate these positions, minimum requirements for applicants might necessarily appear lower than what is acceptable to the English Department or division, where the writing program is housed, because the ad reflects the rank of the state or countylevel employee, depending on local legislation. The following job announcement for contingent faculty provides an example of a job posting that had no input from the departments it advertises for, but instead is generated from a Human Resources office:

Adjunct Faculty

Openings for Summer and Fall 2011 semesters. Specify day/evening/weekend availability

Credit adjuncts (Master's and one-year related experience required unless otherwise indicated on website): Anthropology, Biology, Chemistry, Computer Information Systems, Computer Security and Forensics, Economics, EMS, English, English as a Second Language, Finance (Personal Finance), Food Service (Culinary Art, Dietetic Technician), Geography, History, Human Services/Social Work, Mathematics (Algebra including Algebra with Trigonometry and developmental courses in Pre-Algebra and Beginning Algebra, Contemporary Mathematics, Pre-Calculus, Statistics), Medical Billing

and Coding, Nursing, Philosophy, Psychology, Reading and
Study Skills, Sociology. ("Adjunct Faculty")

In the example above, the county has determined the minimum requirements for the rank of Adjunct Faculty, so the degree and teaching
experience appear inclusive of all disciplines.

Pantoja and her colleagues' point is particularly important when
the job announcement is vague and the WPA must understand his or
her legal obligations in light of the local, governmental job requirements. For example, if a college desires a minimum degree requirement of a Master's degree, the requirement might be represented in
the advertisement only as a preference, not an actual requirement, to
correspond to governmental criteria for a particular rank within its
system, regardless of the college's needs. Bureaucracy inadvertently
broadens the pool and increases time spent recruiting. With a defined
mission of the writing program, the task of sorting through applicant
credentials, however wide the candidate pool, becomes easier. Such
an example serves as a warning, though: The more specific the job
advertisement, the better the applicants (in general) can fulfill the job
requirements. The more narrowly defined announcement may also
present challenges and attract few applicants. The control the WPA
has over the development and publishing of a job advertisement varies from college to college, and depends on the levels of approval the
ad must go through before publication. The more input he or she has,
however, the easier the process becomes.

Related to the specific issue of recruiting diverse applicants is the
importance of receiving training in affirmative action, if needed, or
in becoming a member of affirmative action and Equal Opportunity
committees. These opportunities benefit the WPA by providing essential knowledge and education for recruiting and hiring a diverse,
contingent faculty. Pantoja, Tribbenesee, and Roen make this point
as well, claiming that attending training provided by such on-campus
committees is valuable (147). Trainings offer education in current interviewing standards and practices, and enable participants to understand how to conduct interviews within affirmative action guidelines.
Further, training explains the rights and the boundaries within the
faculty/institution relationship.

FACULTY DEVELOPMENT

Even as WPAs may follow the hiring procedures of their institutions, the instructors they hire can demonstrate varying comprehension of writing pedagogy theory and practice; therefore, another common responsibility of the WPA is to facilitate faculty development. Sometimes enrollments surge as the beginning of the semester nears, and he or she must hire contingent faculty "last minute." As a result, "the reality remains that we often have to 'take a chance on unknown teachers'" (Brown, qtd. in Klausman 245). Therefore, training and evaluation are essential to supporting adjunct and full-time instructors alike. Faculty development can also boost morale by asserting a commitment to faculty, and belief in their intelligence and capabilities.

Several community colleges provide faculty development as integral parts of a writing initiative or WAC program. Funded by a Title V grant, The Writing Initiative at Passaic County Community College has begun to reform writing intensive general education courses. Faculty development functions as a central element of this effort, and as of November 2010, the program claimed forty-three instructors trained in the areas of writing, critical thinking, information literacy, and writing techonologies ("Faculty Development"). Earlier, in 1999, LaGuardia Community College launched a faculty development effort to support a writing in the disciplines program; it received funding from CUNY in 2000 as part of an institution-wide effort to implement WAC. Since then, the college claims to have had four hundred full- and part-time instructors receive training, making "the institutional commitment to writing-intensive pedagogy . . . a central component of the strategic vision of the College" ("Writing in the Disciplines"). Faculty development culminates in the production of portfolios and videos documenting the implementation of WID principles in instructors' pedagogy ("Writing in the Disciplines"). In another example, Caldwell Community College and Technical Institute has implemented *Enhancing Writing—Write On!*, a program dedicated to faculty development in support of its WAC program. As part of an institutional Quality Enhancement Plan, the faculty development initiative culminated from the results of a professional development survey the college administered in 2005, identifying areas of development, including assessment tools and the dissemination of expertise ("Professional Development").

Unfortunately, many two-year institutions have little funding for faculty development. The lack of funding for faculty development for part-time instructors in particular affects writing pedagogy, including sharing best practices in the classroom, current pedagogical approaches, and cross-cultural awareness. In light of the disproportionate ratios of full-time to part-time instructors, this omission has serious consequences. As Ana Maria Preto-Bay and Kristine Hansen argue, two-year colleges implicitly deny their reliance on contingent faculty, and thus neglect their development as an oversight:

> Such institutions may not even have formal teacher development programs, either because they assume that their full-time teachers already know how to teach composition or because they lack the funds, time, and expertise to offer development to adjunct faculty who staff their courses. The fact that a large percentage of adjunct faculty are former graduate students leads to the further assumptions that they would teach as they were trained to when they were graduate students and that their training likely did not include teaching multicultural and linguistically diverse students. (44)

Preto-Bay and Hansen draw attention to several assumptions that justify withholding faculty development to adjunct instructors, but Klausman argues that WPAs should not assume that everyone who comes to teach at the two-year college knows how to teach and evaluate students, among the other tasks instructors must perform (245). Further, Preto-Bay and Hansen's suggestion that "their training likely did not include teaching multicultural and linguistically diverse students" (44) points to an additional challenge in the community college system—and perhaps for most institutions of higher education.[3] The more faculty who lack cross-cultural awareness, the greater the risk is for faculty perpetuating a national educational system already fraught with inequities. The WPA, then, has an obligation—socially, economically, and educationally—to provide faculty development for a range of relevant issues and topics.

With little or no funding, many community college WPAs find creative ways to provide faculty development trainings. One of the greatest challenges for the WPA is establishing reasonable uniformity among the writing courses. For this reason, as well as the fact that most community college faculty have a broad range of teaching and educational experiences, the WPA must work to address faculty development needs, including pedagogical approaches to evaluation "norming" or uniform criteria for grading, learning and physical disabilities, ESL or L2 needs, student behavioral issues, and multicultural sensitivity, among other topics. But even if the WPA manages to provide faculty training, if he or she is working with a large contingent faculty, the issue of attendance will need to be addressed. He or she does not have the luxury of mandating training, as one in a research institution might with graduate student instructors. Furthermore, adjunct instructors often shuttle between teaching jobs at different institutions, so their schedules may not permit attendance. Even though the desire to attend training may exist, given many contingent faculty work at different locations and institutions, often the breadth of their knowledge of the curriculum is limited simply because they are unable to spend enough time at the college to broaden it (Schell 185). Therefore, the WPA may find that informal training—hallway conversations, for instance—offers an effective way to transmit information. Because of teaching and committee schedules, and contingent faculty members' commitments to multiple campuses, individual work is necessary. According to Klausman:

> Non-mandatory meetings, as nearly all are at my college since we cannot pay adjuncts to attend, are rarely attended by the less engaged. So the WPA in the two-year college must work on a personal, individualized basis. This clearly marks the two-year college WPA as different from the university WPA who often oversees an assembly of TAs: the faculty we nominally oversee are not graduate students and not technically "under" us at all. We must work with our faculty to establish common goals and then work to achieve them. As "change agents," we must be colleagues, catalysts, and leaders simultaneously, a difficult balancing act. (244)

On the other hand, if the WPA is able to organize regular meetings for faculty development, this system may accomplish more than broadening faculty knowledge; it may foster community among the large group of part-time instructors, who are often excluded from campus-related activities or travel between two or more institutions, and therefore not especially connected to any of them.

WRITING CENTERS

Another responsibility of many, but certainly not all, WPAs is the management of a writing tutorial center, a mainstay of community college campuses. Reynolds suggests that two-year college faculty have been "pioneers in the development of writing centers, locales where they have addressed the needs not just of underprepared students, but also in all disciplines across their institutions" (8). The expectation for the writing center's accessibility parallels the expectation placed on composition courses in a certain sense. Tutors, like writing faculty, come with a range of educational experiences. WPAs will need to provide training for effective tutorial approaches for a diverse student population that needs assistance with various stages of writing (generating ideas, drafting, self-editing, etc.). With a focus on the needs of ESL, or L2, students, Howard Tinberg underscores the need for tutor training at a two-year college: "[C]ertainly writing center tutors ought to be trained to read the writing of L2 students effectively" (69). Tinberg's point extends beyond the needs of L2 students: Tutors can benefit from training that addresses variety of student writing needs.

Like staffing writing classes with competent adjunct faculty, hiring competent tutors is a similar endeavor, in terms of recruiting, hiring, and training. It also requires knowledge of how to manage a budget—a point addressed later in this chapter. Two valuable resources offer information specifically geared toward the administration of writing centers within the community college context. One is Ellen Mohr's *Inside the Community College Writing Center: Ten Guiding Principles*, which covers all relevant areas of this work, including: recruiting and training tutors, writing a mission statement, and developing political sensitivity within the institution. A second resource is the website of the International Writing Centers Association (www.writingcenters. org), offering a full range of information for administrators of writing centers, covers topics such as peer tutoring, conference information, relevant bibliographies, and includes discussion forums and resources specific to writing centers in community colleges.

Last, if the WPA does not direct the writing center, he or she will likely work closely with the individual who does. That situation still could mean that the WPA provides support and/or training of its tutors, in addition to keeping communication open between the writing center and the writing faculty. Whether the WPA runs the writing center or not, he or she will have regular contact with it or with an academic skills support office at the community college.

PLACEMENT

Student placement into appropriate writing courses forms a central responsibility for community college WPAs. As Daniel Royer and Roger Gilles claim, "Most writing program administrators . . . accept the need for placement as a given and indeed as a major part of the job" (264). In some instances, placement of incoming students is done separately from the English department, and housed in a different office, often connected to an academic skills center. Regardless of the location, the community college WPA—and in most cases, his or her department—is involved with various aspects of the placement process, including developing a placement evaluation, a rubric or criteria for evaluation, evaluating and adopting a technology-based assessment tool, hiring and training staff/faculty to assess placement results, and/or developing periodic assessment of the placement process itself. Having a clear sense of the validity and reliability of the methodology for placement, working with placement faculty/staff, and staying abreast of assessment instruments helps the WPA coordinate placement efforts as part of the larger whole of the writing program.

The method for student placement depends on the institution, the students, and the core values and objectives of the writing program. Susanmarie Harrington adds: "Placement decisions, among the most local of all assessment decisions, must necessarily be balanced against local constraints including budgetary allocations, turnaround requirements, and student backgrounds" (11). Each of these elements contributes to selecting the appropriate assessment method. Generally, placement assessment is not identical to exit assessments for students completing writing courses, although this condition is not always the case in every community college. As Royer and Gilles suggest, "Placement should force us to ask how well our students are finding their way into appropriate courses and succeeding in ways that meet at least our minimal expectations and also the students' own subjective purposes staked out in advance" (271). Further, they argue that placement should be future-directed, in other words, "a judgment about what someone could do, might be able to do, not a judgment about what they have already done" (268). The writing program provides a framework for developing student placement methodologies.

Methods for placement in the community college range. In "An Analysis of the National TYCA Research Initiative Survey, Section II" (2008), Patrick Sullivan points out that seventy-six percent of community colleges require placement for incoming students (15).[4] He provides the following statistics, representing the respondents' use of particular methods in this context: [5]

Assessment Type	% of Use
Standardized tests without a writing sample	48%
Standardized tests with a writing sample	33%
(such as ACT or SAT)	33%
Multiple criteria (for example, transcripts,	29%
placement in reading, math, etc.)	7%
In-house placement instruments	3%
Writing sample only	2%
Portfolio	
No placement procedure or program in place	

Notably, no category exists for directed self-placement. Sullivan points out that none of the methods for placement inspire unanimous satisfaction. Of the total respondents, fifty-eight percent report a general satisfaction over placement practices at their colleges. The researchers attribute the reasons for the reported dissatisfaction to the variety of placement methods and the absence of best practices. The variety within the category of standardized testing stretched widely, including Compass, Asset, Accuplacer, Access, SAT, Nelson Denny, ACT, THEA, TASP, TAKS, TAAS, CPT, and GORT-4. Institutions demonstrated an equal range among the alternate forms of placement practices (11–12).

Whether or not the WPA is directly responsible for administering placement assessment, he or she will necessarily be involved in its development. A main objective for the WPA becomes aligning the placement assessment with the core values and objectives of the writing program itself.

ASSESSMENT

Related to placement, assessment of student outcomes is equally integral to the WPA's work. The measurement of student competencies enables the WPA, the department/division, the institution, the state, and the accrediting agency to assess how much students are learning, as well as the effectiveness of the whole program. Furthermore, assessment plays an important role in articulation agreements with four-year institutions. WPAs should familiarize themselves with state mandates, including general education requirements. They also need to be acquainted with scheduled curricular assessments conducted from within the institution for the state and the accreditation agency.

Assessment, though, is not only a tool for meeting the requirements of interested outside agencies. Measuring student outcomes can directly benefit the writing program and the students. Daphne Desser puts it this way:

> I believe that grouping students by mandatory assessment, when it is done well and with sensitivity to the students involved, results in more effective curriculum design and classroom teaching that is more suited to the individual students' needs. (112)

However, Cohen and Brawer make clear that assessment methodologies conducted for assessing a student's performance within a course necessarily may—and should—look different from methodologies that assess the curriculum, a point returned to in Chapter Four (404–46).

"An Analysis of the National TYCA Research Initiative Survey II" provides statistics regarding the use of assessment methodology and the different kinds of methodologies utilized in the community college context. Sullivan indicates the range of approaches to competency and/or exit assessments, from development to transfer, in the sequence of composition courses: [6]

Method Percentage

No exit or competency assessment required: 52%
Timed essay exam: 23%
Traditional portfolio: 15%
Writing sample (not timed): 12%
Standardized tests with a writing sample (for example, ACT): 8%

Multiple criteria (transcripts, placement in other courses, etc.): 5%
Standardized tests without a writing sample: 5%
　　Electronic portfolio 2% (17)

The stages for student outcome assessment in writing courses also ranged:

Required competency or exit assessment Percentage in composition sequence

For students transitioning from developmental to transfer English: 46%
No exit or competency assessment required: 45%
For students completing transfer-level composition requirements: 17%
For students transitioning from ESL to mainstream composition programs: 15%
Other 5% (Sullivan 17)

Cohen and Brawer claim that assessment by way of testing can help individual students during their careers at the two-year institution, but it does not always work the same way for collecting other kinds of information:

> Testing individuals, which is familiar to all educators, is done to motivate students, set goals, design and modify media, and estimate learning attained through various interventions. Using the same process to assess group attainment distorts it, especially when it becomes the basis for judging the worth of a program. Because testing individuals to determine their progress is so familiar, it militates against educators using methods that are considerably more reliable and valid for estimating group progress. (405)

Several resources offer valuable insights into assessment practices. Among them is *Standards for the Assessment of Reading and Writing*, prepared by the Joint Task Force on Assessment of the International Reading Association and the National Council of Teachers of English. This document defines assessment through the lens of inquiry, framing assessment practices as "the exploration of how the educational environment and the participants in the educational community support the process of students as they learn to become independent and collaborative thinkers and problem solvers" (2). In this light, assessment assumes a relationship between the environment and student learning, and foregrounds the notion of diverse approaches to problem solving. "Quality assessment," the document claims:

Hinges on the process of setting up conditions so that the classroom, the school, and the community become centers of inquiry where students, teachers, and other members of the school community investigate their own learning, both individually and collaboratively. The onus on assessment does not fall disproportionately upon students and teachers. . . . Different members of the school community have different but interacting interests, roles, and responsibilities, and assessment is the medium that allows all to explore what they have learned and whether they have met their responsibilities to the school community. (3)

Standards includes primary and secondary institutions within its discussion of assessment, but given these institutions' relationship with surrounding communities, the parallels to community colleges and their assessment concerns are similar. For further discussion of WPA concerns and definitions regarding assessment, Chris Gallagher's "What Do WPAs Need to Know about Writing Assessment?: An Immodest Proposal" offers several propositions for consideration, including: WPA awareness of assessment history, knowledge of current assessment research and theory, understanding basic assessment concepts, the formulation of policies in support of teaching and learning, and responsibility for differences among culture and language, among others (34–38).

BUDGETS

Some community college WPAs also manage a budget. The budgets of community college writing programs tend to be minimal, if existent at all, a circumstance that forces many to become creative and resourceful. If they do oversee a budget, they may be responsible for a range of additional budgetary items, such as supplies and training, and very often, "budget management" takes the form of making budget requests. Last, even if no writing program budget exists, WPAs may be involved in grant writing to support the developmental writing and other writing initiatives.

WPAs often learn budget management on the job. Chris Anson suggests that "every WPA must become a self-taught budget expert in a specific context, gaining the critical expertise required for responsible fiscal management" (234). The extent to which WPAs understand how much funding is available and how to access it enables them to make effective use of resource funds and make persuasive arguments for additional financial support, as needed. Making a general point about WPAs in all institutions, Anson explains that this kind of awareness has not always come easily to WPAs:

> Because most budget decisions were made for them, they worked under a kind of allowance system within their departments, trying hard not to make too many photocopies or request extra tutorial hours in the writing center, but not really knowing what funding was available to them, where it came from, or how it could be used for different needs. (235)

However, the knowledge of funding—how much, where it comes from, what it covers—is crucial for the management of the writing program. When seeking additional funding, community college WPAs should consult strategic reports and link the writing program's goals to the strategic goals of the college. Furthermore, as Douglas Hesse advises, WPAs should generate their own strategic reports, formalizing the budgetary process and making it transparent. He suggests that they "should analyze the campus climate and schedule strategic reports on some periodic basis. Additionally, a program newsletter or annual report conveys a sense that the program is well-managed" (45). While Hesse addresses WPAs in four-year institutions here, his point easily extends to WPAs in two-year institutions with writing program budgets. Such a report can serve as documentation of the efficiency and success of a writing program, but also as support for requesting further funding, as needed.

The following sample spreadsheet represents one way of organizing a budget. The department chair organizes budgetary items categorically by stipends, special projects, and regular budget lines.

	A	B	C	D
1	**ENGLISH**	**DEPARTMENT**	BUDGET—	**FY 2011**
2	Stipends & special projects	FY 11		
3	ENG 101 assessment	$24,300	$300 assessment stipends	

	A	B	C	D
4	Adjunct Orientation	$975	$22 stipends for 22 adjuncts for orienta-tion & fac. development	
5	College Bowl	$1,638	3 hours @ FY 11 rate of $546 for contact hours 4–7, paid as stipend	
6	Portfolio Coordinator	$1,450	$600 per semester, $250 for summer	
7	COMPASS Prep workshop	$430	$43 stipend per 2hour ses-sion, includes prep time; 10 sessions or fewer	
8	Other fac. dev	$440	$22 stipends paid to 20 adjuncts at one extra fac. dev meeting	
9	Total	$29,233		
10	**Regular budget** Lines	FY10	FY11	
11	Regular FT Salary	$626,645		Change to reflect new placements on salary sched-ule, missing FT salary for half year at least in FY 2011

	A	B	C	D
12	Regular PT Salary	$334,250	$350,503	Change: Add $16,253 from various stipends above, including 60% of 101 assessment stipends
13	FT Overload	$97,064	$110,044	Change: add $11,970 from various stipends above (12% increase)
14	Ben-BCBS PPO	$75,806		
15	Ben-BCBS HMO	$11,326		
16	Ben-LTD	$790		
17	Ben-Life	$706		
18	Misc Outside Contracts	$350	$350	No change
19	Instructional Supplies	$500	$700	Change: add $200 to reflect additional supplies consumed during enrollment boost
20	Printing	$3,000	$3,000	No change
21	Publications and dues	$500	$500	No change
22	Hospitality	$500	$500	No change
23	**Totals**	**$1,151,437**	**$465,597**	

Because this budget provides information for a whole department, it perhaps offers more categories than are necessary for some writing programs. It models a systematic approach that can be scaled down to meet the needs of any budget, and includes several items essential to composition courses—courses that comprise most of the course offerings of this community college English department, including: assessment, adjunct items, faculty development, and salaries.

REPRESENTING WRITING FACULTY

A less formal responsibility of many community college WPAs is their institutional identification as spokespeople for writing faculty. They represent composition faculty to faculty in other disciplines and to administration in the contexts of committees, departments, and divisions. Hesse advises all WPAs to "have a place at the table," in other words, to be included in important dialogues related to the writing program (46). To do so, he suggests becoming a member of relevant committees. Such college-wide and departmental committees might include: assessment, curriculum, developmental studies, academic skills, disabilities, libraries, admissions, placement, diversity, affirmative action, and—certainly, if it exists—the academic or faculty senate. While there are seemingly infinite numbers of committees in the two-year college, the WPA should choose to participate in committee work that benefits the program.

Both Victoria Holmsten and Kristine Hansen have written about the essential "go-between" nature of the work of WPAs. Holmsten claims that "WPAs in community colleges work with both administrators and colleagues who may not understand the work of the WPA and it becomes part of our job to communicate this to them" (429–30). Giordano and Hassel report the following challenges they encountered with administrators during the process of revising the writing program at UWC:

- Getting local administrators to understand that teaching under-prepared students requires more (not less) expertise, experience, and graduate training compared to teaching degree-credit English courses
- Introducing instructors and campus administrators to new and unfamiliar approaches to remedial reading and writing
- Helping administrators understand the importance of providing students with multiple types of support programs to meet diverse learning needs (instead of just a single basic writing course) (2–3)

Especially with administrators, WPAs may function as translators, explaining needs, goals, and achievements of the writing program.

The ability to convey this information to administrators is especially urgent when funding or other support is needed. Hansen points out another crucial reason for this kind of "translation." She suggests that the WPA is often the only individual who knows adjunct faculty well enough to advocate for them with the administration,

> because to provosts, vice-presidents, deans, and sometimes even department heads, part-time teachers of composition are usually faceless, nameless individuals, line items on budget and fact sheets. . . . I am not suggesting that central administrators are heartless; rather, in the absence of face-to-face encounters with the other, the ethical demand is absent. (37)

The WPA has an opportunity to try to make adjunct faculty members' work as consistent, tolerable, and equitable as possible—an attempt, perhaps, to reconcile (at least partly) the inherent contradiction between the public two-year institution's democratic initiative and its exploitative dependence on part-time faculty.

As a go-between, the WPA needs a clear sense of the college and the writing program's place within it. Klausman argues that knowledge of the politics at work is essential, particularly for the establishment a new program: "A WPA at a two-year college that seeks to create a program from classes necessarily has to have a sense of where and how a writing program fits into his or her particular college community, where the lines of force are, so to speak" (239).[7] Tinsberg's notion of being "between places" speaks to the WPA's necessary awareness of the boundaries between the writing program and the department/division, or the writing program and the college—as well as what the program can accomplish under the circumstances. To fulfill the role of translator/advocate, John Schilb advises drawing upon the WPA's rhetorical skills as a teacher of composition. Although Schilb deliberately addresses WPAs who must negotiate with literature faculty in four-year institutions, his advice applies to community college WPAs, who must negotiate and communicate with administrators and faculty in other disciplines. He writes:

> Unofficially, we become "directors of composition/literature relations," for we more than anyone have to figure out ways of making the two subjects coexist. . . . It involves, to use a classic rhetoric enterprise, the WPA's sense of *kairos*. Of course, to bring up such a term at all is to acknowledge that relating

the two subjects is fundamentally a rhetorical enterprise, perpetually demanding the WPA be sensitive to situation and audience. (169)

Schilb advises a strong sensitivity to situation and audience—useful advice to any community college WPA, since the writing courses and program affect the work within virtually every other course on the campus.

RESPONDING TO COMPLAINTS AND NEEDS

Part of the work of the community college WPA, like that of WPAs at any institution, includes responding to student and faculty complaints and needs. Both constituents require the ability of the WPA to listen and respond appropriately, as well as to have knowledge of institutional and departmental resources and policies.

Students often come to the WPA with a myriad of issues in need of attention, some of which are more appropriately addressed by their own writing instructors or counselors (if they exist). Other issues include exceptions or waivers for required courses, conflicts with scheduled exams, or errors in placement assignments or final course grades—to name a few. Additionally, students may present problems they have with their instructors (such as a personal conflict), and in these instances, the WPA should be acquainted with the institutional process and the bargaining agreement (if one exists) before addressing students' complaints. For example, if the institution and the union have a due process agreement for handling student complaints against a faculty member, the WPA must abide by it, since such problems can escalate into legal issues. Also, if a student presents other personal issues, such as domestic violence or unwanted pregnancy, the WPA should have a list of resources on campus—and perhaps off campus (for example, if no counseling department exists on campus)—to offer the student.

In addition to knowledge of institutional policies and practices, knowledge of legal boundaries is essential. As a related issue to student complaints, parent complaints and inquiries into students' work and performance also arise. The WPA must be familiar with the guidelines of the Family Educational Rights and Privacy Act (FERPA) that prohibit discussion of adult student records with family members without explicit consent from the student.

Faculty also present the WPA with various administrative and personnel needs. Faculty emergencies, such as the inability to complete a course due to medical or family reasons may come up, or the WPA may need to find coverage for a final exam if an instructor must be absent. In these scenarios, backup plans can often be helpful, in addition to a short list of reliable faculty who can help in last-minute situations. Faculty may also present the WPA with personal conflicts with students or with other faculty members. Again, knowledge of the institution's processes and policies, and the college's ombudsperson, are essential.

Handling interpersonal issues and personal conflicts is an aspect of the work that some consider "invisible." Holmsten points out the distinction between what her writing program work entails and what her colleagues think it entails. On the one hand, her responsibilities are heavily administrative, but on the other, she writes:

> My colleagues in the English department have a slightly different take on my responsibilities. They see me as coordinator for departmental needs and backup for the support work they need to carry on with their very full teaching schedules. To them, I am also a liaison to the dean and other administrators. My colleagues expect me to call necessary meetings, deal with any disagreements with other faculty members and students, and make sure they get the teaching schedules they have requested. (437)

Yet hours—possibly days or weeks, in some situations—disappear while the WPA resolves various personal conflicts among faculty and students. Still, having a sense of what to anticipate year to year, semester to semester, and day to day, can make WPA work manageable, even if colleagues only acknowledge the yet unresolved conflicts and problems. Using Lynn Bloom's term, Crowley reiterates the notion of the WPA as "the Velcro professor": "All negative effects of the requirement stick to her though she gets little credit or reward for holding it all together" (227). Keeping a record of problems that were resolved successfully, and notations of things learned when they did not resolve so well, may help minimize the overall impact of criticism that problems sometimes invite.

Managing It All

Community college WPAs complete all of these duties with little or no course release time. While for many the work is a "labor of love," administering a writing program requires a wide range of professional, educational, organizational, and interpersonal skills and abilities. There are several strategies WPAs use to balance the details and the broad concerns of the program's administration with their own needs as individual faculty members. Strategies range from managing the specifics, such as developing policies, to protecting oneself from burnout, such as engaging with intellectual activities and organizations outside of the college. While the following suggestions offer a few strategies, WPAs must have a sense of their own personal boundaries and abilities to take a balanced approach to work that is often anything but balanced.

On a programmatic level, documenting all curricular decisions and changes enables the WPA to have a record as he or she encounters or revisits various situations during the course of an academic year. Developing policies in written form can provide consistent criteria and standards, as well as equitable responses to specific issues, problems, or situations. As noted previously, producing strategic reports also provides support and structure to the WPA's work (Hesse 44). Likewise, WPAs should keep a record of all of their responsibilities and successes. In part, such a record helps support an application for promotion or an argument for release time, but it also may help deflect criticism. Additionally, documenting policies, strategic reports, and responsibilities makes the individual's accountability transparent, but such documentation also provides a history to ensure consistency from situation to situation, as well as from an outgoing to an incoming WPA.

On a personal level, WPAs engage their emotional intelligence in their work with students, faculty, and administration. In a description of her own job requirements, Holmsten identifies a list of necessary tasks and abilities that are mostly emotionally based:

> If pressed for job requirements for a community college WPA, I would begin with this list: ability to listen and be nice to people; ability to multitask; tolerance for handling necessary grunt work, like collating and stapling, when necessary; ability to listen; strong sense of humor; willingness to take on tasks in larger institutional context that may not seem re-

> motely connected to the writing program; ability to listen; ability to collaborate and share power/authority/influence as required by situation; bearing patience and learning not to take it personally; ability to listen; flexibility in daily work schedules and in tolerance of shifting job requirements; ability to listen. (438)

The first requirement, she notes, is the "ability to listen and be nice to people"—an ability based in emotional intelligence, and notably not an organizational or necessarily administrative skill. In fact, the majority of Holmsten's list focuses on emotional intelligence, including good humor, patience, not taking things personally, flexibility, and as she stresses repeatedly, listening ability. Like the writing program itself, the WPA fits into a place in the institution; making a successful transition into that place depends wholly on "listening" for it and then shaping it within the college context to suit his or her own needs and abilities.

The WPA may also work to develop an especially good rapport with adjunct instructors, a skill that includes remembering details, responding to their needs promptly (such as procuring campus email accounts, adjunct office space, etc.), inviting them to department meetings (or opening up meetings to include them) and informal get-togethers, and finally, acknowledging the good work they do as often as possible. In fact, WPAs find that making connections to the instructors—part-time and full-time—parallels the work they do to discover the needs of students. Both audiences require listening and emotional intelligence.

In short, energy—lots of it—is essential to the success of the community college WPA. However, protecting oneself from burnout is equally essential: "Finally but foremost WPAs need to take care of themselves. Administrative work can be stressful; some stress is energizing, but too much can be debilitating" (McLeod 104). Saving energy for teaching is especially important, since classroom experience and practice are the most important sources for staying in touch with students. Usually, WPAs arrive at the community college as instructors first; the appreciation and abilities they bring to their teaching are essential to maintaining enthusiasm and energy for other duties. In addition, WPAs may regenerate, so to speak, with engagement in national and disciplinary conversations, as these provide a sense of community with those in similar positions. Such dialogues are found within the journals and conferences of organizations such as the Council of Writing Program Administrators (CWPA), the Conference on College Composition and Communication (CCCC), the National Council on Teaching English (NCTE), the Two-Year College English Association (TYCA), and the Modern Language Association Committee on Community Colleges (MLA CCC).

The work of the community college WPA is as grounded in pedagogy and administration as it is in interpersonal skills and self-knowledge. Emotional intelligence will sometimes serve the WPA better than a strong understanding of writing placement criteria. People are at the heart of every writing program—students, faculty, and administrators each contribute in specific and important ways. Ultimately, the WPA's job is to coordinate those contributions to support the success of everyone invested in student writing.

4 WPA Work in the New Era of Community Colleges

The 2009 announcement of the Obama Administration's commitment to community colleges considerably raised the profile of the two-year institution. The national attention, coupled with rising enrollment numbers, has placed the community college in an optimal position to gain further support in the twenty-first century. The previous chapter outlined the general responsibilities of community college WPAs. Much of this work parallels their counterparts in four-year institutions. In many ways, these responsibilities represent what John Dewey refers to as the elements of an institution's "original motive, which is limited and more immediately practical" than "the measure of the worth of any social institution, economic, domestic, political, legal, religious"; in other words, "its effect in enlarging and improving experiences" (6). The *other* work of the community college WPA is in the second half of Dewey's statement. During this current era of rapid change, the WPA's responsibilities extend well beyond the simple objective of coordinating writing instruction, toward the objective of "enlarging and improving experience." Yet, in spite of the nationwide attention community colleges have received, recent years have brought challenges to these lofty objectives with massive budget cuts, union conflicts, and deep concerns about "underprepared" students to discussions about public education. The two-year institution has met the twenty-first century within a national context fraught with contradictions: opposition and conflict amid federal commitment and philanthropic aid, and changing student bodies with multiple literacies amid conventional approaches to assessment and traditional ways of considering knowledge. Within this context, WPAs must consider ways to build and/or support a viable writing program, as well as how to define an institutional role for themselves.

Until now, this book has presented the community college context as one mainly identified with its inherent student diversity. The needs of an ever-changing student population determine the approach to addressing them and supporting the values and objectives of the writing program. But this "narrowly" defined context, in reality, includes a broad base of educational, social, and political concerns that the use of the term "student diversity" may seem to oversimplify. To aptly develop a writing program, WPAs must engage these concerns within an institution that shifts as much as its student body. To work in a community college, in other words, is to be in continual flux. To return to Tinsberg: "[T]o teach at a community college is to be 'in translation' or between places" (1). The notion of inhabiting a space "between places" points to the threshold of change where the WPA continuously engages all aspects of the writing program—from forces outside the institution, such as legislation and community funding, to those within the institution, such as literacy needs and developmental studies, among many other considerations and influences.

The most immediate educational, social, and political concerns currently emerge from a few predominant locations: the Obama Administration's, and subsequent philanthropic economic commitments, to community colleges; the field of developmental studies as a rapidly developing area of study and economic support; further development of plurality and inclusivity on college campuses; and not least of all, the multiple literacies students present in today's classrooms. In light of these broad-reaching concerns, community college WPAs must strategize how to carry out their daily responsibilities within an internally complex and individually defined institution.

Within this educational, social, and political landscape, they must be able to recognize the needs of a complex, dynamic student body, integrate the multiple literacies and competencies students bring to their studies, address the possibilities of multimodal composing, and stay abreast of current trends in writing pedagogy. Since no two community college writing programs are identical, the way one WPA manages to reconcile all of the dynamic aspects of the program in one institution, within the current educational, social, and political environment, may not be successful for a WPA in another. The effectiveness of the writing program depends on how WPAs shape their own roles in the college and envision a viable program; how they encounter and assess the program or courses that already exist; and how they understand and participate in the politics at work on multiple levels: the department or division, the institution, the surrounding community or state government, and the national educational policies and legislation. Given these considerations, this chapter explores the "other" responsibilities of WPAs in terms of their contributions to "enlarging and improving experiences"—in other words, how they must conceive of their programs and their own professional roles within the ever-changing and political context of the community college.

AMERICAN GRADUATION INITIATIVE

The year 2009 saw the community college emerge into the national spotlight. Since its inception in 1901, the institution only received comparable attention during its primary years of expansion in the 1960s and 1970s (Plinske and Packard). Given the strained economic situation in the United States, in 2009, the Obama Administration identified the public two-year college as a central institution in efforts to boost the nation's economy. If there had ever been a question about the politics surrounding the community college, President Obama's American Graduation Initiative confirmed it. While initial figures were significantly lowered from the proposal, competitive funding remains available through federal grants and subsequent philanthropic giving. The administration's original proposal was prepared to support community colleges with considerable funding. The American Graduate Initiative proposed twelve billion dollars to be spent over a decade to improve programs and facilities at two-year colleges. The administration intended the initiative to support the broader goal that enabled "the United States to have the world's highest proportion of college graduates by 2020" (Hebel). Drawing parallels to President Roosevelt's 1944 GI Bill, the Obama Administration sought to "rebuild crumbling community-college facilities; increase the number of two-year students who graduate and transfer to four-year colleges; improve remedial education; forge stronger ties between colleges and employers; and create inexpensive, open-source courses for students to take online" (Gonzalez, "Historic"). Not long after the President's announcement of the American Graduation Initiative, many of the possible benefits of the proposal had been derailed during negotiations among legislators over massive changes in student aid and the health care system. Although legislators reduced the initial twelve billion dollars proposed by the administration, they salvaged two billion dollars (distributed over four years) to support a competitive grant program that would enable community colleges to "create, expand, and restructure job-training programs" (Gonzalez, "2-Year"). Coupled with efforts supported by the Labor Department, the program intends to enable citizens to enroll in college and prepare for entering or reentering the job market. A year later, the administration held a first-of-its-kind White House Summit on Community Colleges on October 5, 2010, where representatives from colleges, business, and philanthropies had an opportunity to dialogue about the current state of community colleges and the role they might play in the development of the nation (Gonzalez, "Historic").

Despite the reduction of the initial program's proposed funding, and the resultant limitations on its goal-reaching abilities, several important dialogue threads emerged in terms of retention and remediation. These have led to the development of significant programs across the United States. In terms of access, the Obama Administration succeeded by raising Pell Grant awards and making the federal student financial aid form more accessible. Developmental education became a central thread within the proposal, as President Obama linked the rise in the number of graduates to increased attention to developmental studies (Parker, Bustillos, and Behringer 6). However, President Obama continued to speak to the necessity of increasing retention as well as access: "Over a third of America's college students, and over half our minority students, don't earn a degree, even after six years. . . . So, we don't just need to open the doors of college to more Americans, we need to make sure they stick with it through graduation" (Gonzalez, "In Texas"). As a result, and as one of the early objectives of the American Graduation Initiative, remediation became a focal point of many subsequent discussions. In its original form, the proposal explicitly identified developmental studies as an area of concentration, with nine billion dollars to support grant programs intended to help community colleges and states "to test promising programs and practices, including those designed to improve student learning and training, increase completion rates, and better track student progress" (Hebel).

While much of this proposed allocation did not materialize, the interest in supporting developmental studies at the community college has continued. Several philanthropic organizations provide funding with an emphasis on supporting developmental education. The

Bill and Melinda Gates Foundation concentrated efforts on funding grants for community colleges. It imposed its own goal of raising double "the proportion of low-income Americans who earn a postsecondary credential by age 26" (Ashburn). It has granted over $178 million in funding, sponsoring projects such as Achieving the Dream, which "is built on the idea of creating a 'culture of evidence' to raise the performance of community-college students" (Ashburn). The programs sponsored by the Foundation's funding have benefited colleges like Highline Community College, which created new opportunities for students interested in jobs that require knowledge of mathematics. Nonprofit programs have also received funding, such as North Carolina's MDC, which received $16.5 million to improve developmental studies (Ashburn). As of March 2011, the Foundation made pledges totaling $110 million dollars with the specific intention of improving developmental programs at public two-year colleges (Foderaro). Other foundations, including Carnegie, have joined the Bill and Melinda Gates Foundation with similar contributions to developmental education. Several have partnered to provide funding to community college initiatives. The Aspen Institute, The Joyce Foundation, the Lumina Foundation, and the philanthropic foundations of Bank of American and JPMorgan Chase, joined together to offer the Aspen Prize for Community College Excellence. This award grants one million dollars to "recognize outstanding performers and rising stars that deliver exceptional results in student-completion rates and work-force success" (Gonzalez, "Historic"). Parallel to the goals of the Obama Administration, The Gates foundation and the Lumina Foundation are jointly committed to the goal of raising the number of college graduates in the United States by 2025, which is very close to the President Obama's proposed year of 2020 (Ashburn).

Despite the noble enterprises of these charitable organizations, criticism of private funding of public institutions has emerged. As in the past, the potential for a conflict of interest exists: "Mixed feelings about philanthropists and their causes is nothing new. When Andrew Carnegie began building his libraries, more than a century ago, a debate raged between librarians and philanthropists over the proper design of the structures" (Ashburn). As a result of recent philanthropic support, assessment has emerged as an area of contention. The Obama Administration has emphasized its desire to assist in the assessment of student outcomes, and the Bill and Melinda Gates Foundation likewise supports collecting more information for the purposes of accountability and better student results (Ashburn). However, such efforts are reminiscent of previous, divisive assessment initiatives, such as those proposed by the Bush administration, including the creation of a "unit record" tracking system:

> The debate over that [the unit record systems] pitted some college associations, which were concerned about student privacy, against researchers and advocates who argued such data were necessary to adequately diagnose the state of higher education. . . . The Gates foundation was not involved in those debates, but they are a backdrop for its support of more data, accountability—and, hopefully, better student outcomes. Grantees, like the Data Quality Campaign, are leading that push. (Ashburn)

While Congress never passed a nationwide tracking system, the push for more student information and assessment reminds those outside and within higher education of the early debates.

Remaining cognizant of such arguments, community college WPAs still should be aware of grant opportunities through several of these philanthropic foundations, especially if they wish to improve developmental writing at their institutions. Visiting the websites of philanthropic organizations committed to higher education, such as the Bill and Melinda Gates Foundation, The Carnegie Foundation, and the Lumina Foundation, among others, provide more information.

In addition, Title III grants offer additional funding for further development. Distinct from the American Graduate Initiative proposal, these grants take the form of discretionary or competitive grants provided by the U.S. Department of Education and, according to the ED.gov website, support the following kinds of initiatives:

> Funds may be used for planning, faculty development, and establishing endowment funds. Administrative management and the development and improvement of academic programs also are supported. Other projects include joint use of instructional facilities, construction and maintenance, and student services programs designed to improve academic success, including innovative, customized, instruction courses designed to help retain students and move the students rapidly into core courses and through program completion, which may

include remedial education and English language instruction. ("Title III")

Title III grants explicitly support developmental studies and literacy instruction, two areas that community college WPAs work within daily. Further, Institutions of Higher Education (IHE) eligible to apply for Title III grants include community colleges, but an institution must apply for its designation of eligibility before applying for a grant. Whether WPAs seek federal or private funding, they should engage their institution's external affairs professional—particularly a grant writer, when possible—before applying for grants.

Financial support available from the U.S. Department of Education, the federal government, and philanthropic organizations points to the emergence of the community college in the new era. With the realization of so many students enrolling in this institution, the Obama Administration, philanthropists, and lawmakers have committed new efforts to support and complete their studies. For WPAs beginning to develop writing programs, now is an ideal time to think about the broad range of funding opportunities, particularly those designated for two-year colleges, low-income students, and developmental studies.

Regardless of whether WPAs apply for funding or not, they may not escape the political nature of the community college. The twenty-first century ushered in the new age of the two-year college, and the sheer numbers of students enrolling now make it a formidable institution, despite its difficult reputation as an inferior institution of higher education. Within this complex educational, social, and political context, the WPA must be able to navigate the complex waters of internal and external politics.

THE PRESENT AND FUTURE OF DEVELOPMENTAL STUDIES

One of these political areas has been the emergence of developmental studies as an expansive area of educational reform, support, and criticism. Few days pass before a major newspaper or online sources publish an article about the current successes and complaints of developmental education. As evidenced by the attention from the Obama Administration and philanthropic organizations, developmental studies in the community college is here to stay, and has emerged as a central concern for WPAs, instructors, and administrators. With increasing enrollment has come increasing numbers of developmental students. Previously, Chapters One and Three outlined the needs of developmental students and the basic tenets of developmental writing at the two-year college. As an emergent area of study on its own, developmental education, and developmental writing in particular, requires WPAs to be cognizant of the rapidly moving currents and trends within the field. One immediate way to join the dialogue is to access the Conference on Basic Writing listserv (CBW-L), where developmental writing instructors ask questions and share information relevant to developmental writing instruction and its administration.

Evident of the broadening dialogue on developmental education, the University of Texas at Austin Center for Community College Student Engagement (CCCSE) made several recommendations for developing remediation in its report on developmental students in the twenty-first century. Unsurprisingly, all of the recommendations center on strengthening the relationships between students and faculty. To this end, the CCCSE advocates that in spite of lessened emphasis on faculty development during these strained economic times,

> We must focus on hiring and developing faculty members who enjoy working with students even more than they enjoy their discipline, who are convinced that students are capable of learning, and who have the skills to engage students actively in the learning process. In so doing, we will increase the odds that our faculty and staff are well prepared to "make magic" in community college classrooms. (2)

The CCCSE identifies four central strategies for faculty development: supporting student engagement in the classroom, integrating student support within the classroom experience, broadening faculty development that emphasizes student engagement, and focusing the institution's policies on creating learning conditions (8).

The CCCSE report reiterates what many WPAs who work with developmental writing students already know: Action is required now, when so many students enter the community college underprepared— when up to sixty-five percent of students enrolled in a two-year institution require developmental courses (Foderaro). The CCCSE repeats a familiar call to arms:

> It is time for community colleges to start imagining what is possible. It is time to challenge the notion that some students

will not succeed. It is time to relinquish our resistance to *require*. It is time to raise not just our students' aspirations but to raise our own. (20)

As a parallel to President Obama's emphasis on retention, the CCCSE argues that "access to college is just not enough" (20). The report lays out several objectives for improving developmental education in the twenty-first century:

- Reconceptualize the classroom;
- Build a culture of evidence;
- Conduct courageous conversations (this point refers to using information to reveal unpopular truths about the institution);
- Maintain standards while affirming that all students can learn;
- Look for leadership across the campus;
- Revise academic policies;
- Engage unions;
- Provide strategically targeted professional development for all faculty; and
- Design institutional policies that foster student success. (20–21)

The CCCSE maintains that these goals represent a solid foundation for expanding developmental education in the community college, and ranges from adjusting classroom practice to creating a cultural change in the institution.

While the CCCSE report embodies a broad view of developmental education, inclusive of all three areas of writing, reading, and math, it offers WPAs a new context for developmental writing, as well as possible strategies for improvement and partnership within the institution. In "Development of Writing Programs at Multi-Campus, Two-Year Institutions: Aligning Basic Skills Courses with First-Year Writing Programs," a report produced by Joanne Baird Giordano and Holly Hassel of the University of Wisconsin Colleges (UWC), strategies include partnerships among disciplines. In this 2011 report, the writers trace the revisions of the UWC non-credit Academic Literacy Skills Program, demonstrating the application of several CCCSE recommendations:

Revised Academic Literacy Skills Program

A redesigned, non-degree credit program that does the following:

- Houses all remedial programs in the English Department except for basic math and discipline-specific tutorials
- Aligns remedial reading, writing, ESL, composition tutorial, and learning skills courses with the first-year writing program
- Creates a Developmental Reading and Writing Coordinator position to oversee the curriculum and provide both campuses and instructors with support in developing courses and local programs
- Reflects the learning needs of the students enrolled in the institution in relation to the demands of the general education curriculum
- Introduces students to college-level reading, writing, and critical thinking (not workbook style exercises)
- Prepares students to achieve the learning outcomes for the first-year writing program
- Offers a set curriculum (with course guides and learning outcomes) that campuses can adapt to meet locally situated needs
- Creates online teaching resources for instructors to help them develop courses in ways that match the student populations served on a specific campus, the learning needs of individual students in a classroom, and an instructor's teaching interests and strengths
- Provides campuses with guidelines for hiring instructors. (1)

Giordano and Hassel report from an institution with a specific organizational structure: the University of Wisconsin Colleges exist as thirteen individual two-year campuses that share one English department, all within the University of Wisconsin System. These campuses are distinct from Wisconsin's technical college system; however, many of the recommendations identified by CCCSE manifest in the revised system at UWC, particularly in regards to the emphasis on faculty relationships with students and also faculty development.

Giordano and Hassel also report on several strategies that proved instrumental in the successful revision of the developmental writing program. The writers break their findings into two categories of successful strategies: those on the institutional level, and those within the curriculum, quoted here in some length.

Strategies that Worked: Institutional Issues

- Starting with small pilot program on one campus and gradually expanding it to other campuses in the statewide institution in ways that meet the needs of each specific campus
- Working across functional units to involve instructors, administrators, and advisors in the process of creating local programs for underprepared and at-risk students
- Hiring basic writing instructors who are also qualified to teach degree-credit courses; providing them with regular opportunities to teach introductory composition and the core transfer-level writing course
- Creating a developmental reading and writing coordinator position from within the English Department (instead of through another institutional functional unit or as part of a separate department)
- Distinguishing between general academic literacy courses (taught by instructors with expertise in teaching college reading, writing, and English language skills) and tutorial courses that support learning in specific courses (taught by instructors with graduate degrees in those disciplines)
- Carefully assessing student's academic profiles to create a program that reflects the student populations that the institution serves
- Building on the strengths of the contingent faculty who teach basic skills courses (rather than assuming that they are novices who are not capable of adapting the curriculum to meet the needs of their own students)
- Refining the placement process with a multiple measures approach to assessing the college readiness and matching individual students with an appropriate set of first-year courses; adapting this process to campuses according to locally available resources, staffing, and programs
- Creating basic skills course placement guidelines that are flexible enough for campuses to adapt them in local ways based on the learning needs of their students and available resources
- Training advisors at both the institutional and campus levels

Strategies that Worked: Curriculum Development

- Using the first-year writing program learning outcomes as a starting point for redesigning and improving basic skills courses; focusing on what instructors expect student to do as readers and writers in degree-credit courses
- Aligning basic reading and writing courses with the first-year writing program; scaffolding instruction in ways that introduce students to the skills that instructors expect them to use in degree-credit writing courses and first-year general education classes
- Moving away from the approach to basic writing found in most textbooks and redesigning courses to fit institutional needs (in this case, the expectation that students will enroll in degree-credit English within one semester)
- Introducing essay writing and critical reading in non-degree credit courses
- Using the learning outcomes for first-year composition as a starting point for developing shared learning outcomes for each developmental course
- Redesigning existing courses to reflect the changing needs of students, the statewide institution, and local campuses
- Creating a writing course for multilingual students that is part of the first-year writing program and that fulfills the basic writing prerequisite for English 101 (taught by instructors with degrees in TESOL and experience in higher education)
- Providing instructors who teach basic skills courses and degree-credit English with opportunities to provide feedback on the curriculum (2)

The UWC Academic Literacy Skills Program provides a model for centralizing and developing non-credit writing courses within the broader context of academic skills development. The report's findings parallel the CCCSE's recommendations, especially in terms of coordinating coursework for developmental students. The authors demonstrate success in reconceptualizing the classroom and explicitly rejecting familiar textbook methodologies. They also sustain the belief that "all students can learn," as noted in the expectation that students *will* enroll in credit courses. In addition, they point out that several changes at the levels of the institution, policy, and curriculum had to occur for the program's success. Like the CCCSE's report, Giordano and Hassel emphasize faculty development as a central element in the program.

The CCCSE and Giordano and Hassel represent two similar approaches to improving developmental education, and specifically writing, in the community college. Certainly there are others, but what these two reports take into consideration is the mutability of the community college and the necessity for creating dynamic programs to meet the needs of the students. Other approaches, notably the Community College of Baltimore County's (CCBC) Accelerated Learning Program (ALP), emphasize the success of enrolling students in accelerated courses as opposed to traditional developmental writing courses. Such an approach can be effective for certain types of students, as noted in Chapter Three (Edgecombe 4–6). All of these programs point to the recent—and necessary—attention on improving developmental studies at the community college in the twenty-first century. The WPA at the two-year institution will inevitably engage in dialogues about developmental writing, and will need to find ways of adapting writing courses to suit the specific needs of the students enrolled at his or her college.

PLURALITY AND INCLUSIVITY

As indicated by the language in the American Graduate Initiative, the Obama Administration, lawmakers, and educators link developmental education with diversity and class issues (Musil 3–4). While developmental students are not nearly always students of color, students with nontraditional backgrounds, or students with low incomes, the imaginary and factual links between these categories require anyone invested in the community college to address the complexity of diversity on the college campus. However, as Caryn McTighe Musil points out, fostering diversity awareness at the nation's institutions of higher education is a complex endeavor. The American Association of Colleges and Universities recognizes that

> The most advanced diversity efforts now define diversity as both an end, in and of itself, and also a means for the institution to reach its own highest aspirations and meet its multiple obligations to students and society. . . . Overall, diversity is more commonly seen as the responsibility of the whole com-

munity rather than the purview of a single office or person. (4)

While popular discourse about educational access and developmental studies may forge the improvement of developmental education, diversity initiatives represent a "remaining challenge for the coming decade" (Musil 7). In the "new global century," Musil suggests that new "educational pathways" must manifest "a broad knowledge of and curiosity about the history, cultural traditions, and productivity of humanity both here and abroad" (7). She argues that diversity education may provide a way to profoundly instill this knowledge.

"Diversity," as well as the terms "pluralism," "multiculturalism," and "global citizen" (Beckham 10), represent the necessary direction of higher education. In a global economy, educators—particularly those at community colleges—cannot ignore the urgency of making institutions as inclusive as possible. In "Ties That Bind: Perpetuations of Racial Comfort and Discomfort at the Community College," Douglas Price, Adrienne Hyle, and Kitty Jordan write, "In terms of racial comfort and discomfort, higher education is precariously positioned to be a change agent or a perpetuator of the status quo" (3). Implied in their assertion is that institutions of higher education must choose; inactivity or passivity sustains "the status quo." Their findings, from a study of a mostly white community college campus, show that black students at this campus, and perhaps in other predominantly white community colleges, indicate higher levels of racial discomfort than their white peers. The authors thus delineate the decision for members of this college: "The choice is to either deconstruct racial discomfort and reconstruct positive race relations (through increased understanding and awareness of others who differ racially) or perpetuate the racial tensions that students bring with them" (4). If not addressed, the potential for "feed[ing] them back into the larger society, reinforcing the conditions that caused this discomfort in the first place," continues to manifest (Price, Hyle, and Jordan 4).

Because of their positions as intermediaries and leaders, WPAs can be instrumental in raising levels of inclusivity at their colleges. In "Diversity at the Crossroads: Mapping Our Work in the Years Ahead," Edgar F. Beckham urges educators:

> We have already discovered and created strategies and methodologies for pursuing diversity education in the classroom.

> They include, among others, the use of personal narrative to
> encourage students to invest themselves in their own learning,
> the establishment of dialogue groups that serve as safe venues
> for exploration and encounter, and the invocation of spiritual
> values to encourage students to see beyond the limits of the
> assumptions they receive from home traditions. We need to
> redouble our efforts to make these strategies and methodolo-
> gies more visible and more useful. And we can do so by in-
> creasing our emphasis on diversity as an educational resource.
> (16)

Beckham calls on educators to increase efforts at instilling diversity education, suggesting, of course, that wherever a college locates
its progression on issues of diversity, there is more work to be done.
Community college WPAs need to be mindful of this as the twenty-
first century progresses. While assessing diversity education in curricula was once identified by the number of required courses students
had to take, it is more common to infuse diversity issues into a curriculum, or for students to major or minor in a "diversity" area (AACU
31). WPAs should be vigilant for opportunities to infuse the writing
program with initiatives of diversity education. Opportunities to create learning communities, or to link courses, may present themselves.
Also, they should be cognizant of faculty development opportunities
as they measure the needs of their institution. In any way most appropriate to an individual institution, WPAs should stay abreast of
new developments in diversity education and look for ways to manifest them in their programs. As Tavis Smiley has written, "Diversity is
more than a hopeful goal; it is an imperative" (165).

MULTIPLE LITERACIES IN A NEW GLOBAL CONTEXT

In the "new global century," the demographic diversity of community
college students parallels the diverse ways they communicate. With
the continual influx of new technologies and new media, communication methods in society continue to expand. Within this context,
the WPA is always at the center of a writing program that must continually transform itself if it intends to transform its students. Raines's
1990 observations of the continual challenge of the changing student
population remain true:

> Since the community-college movement began its rapid
> growth in the 1960s, we have been challenged by constant
> change. While we always have prepared the traditional col-
> lege student to transfer to a baccalaureate school, we also have
> developed our abilities and resources to meet the needs of
> other groups. . . . These heterogeneous populations long have
> prompted our interdependency on the entire teaching com-
> munity and on resources outside our institutions. We con-
> tinue to find our greatest challenges and strengths in diversity.
> (159)

Raines points to the link between a diverse student population and
an institution in continual change. She also points out the need to
rely on, and dialogue with, colleagues beyond the walls of the institution—in her words, the "entire teaching community." She underscores
the importance of engaging diverse ideas from outside the college as
the WPA engages the program within the college. She emphasizes that
"the greatest challenges and strengths" are found in the college's own
diversity, a theory suggesting that the students themselves, with their
multiple literacies and competencies, have much to teach their WPAs
and their institutions.

A signifier of the new global era, students' literacies and competencies emerge in myriad of ways, including nonlinear texts and online
forms, such as blogs, text messages, email, chat rooms, avatars, wikis,
and many others. Even if they are not bilingual (although many community college students are), students now most often come to college
multi-literate:[1] they are the beneficiaries of the technological age. Technology has quickly transformed, and continues to transform, the ways
people communicate with each other, and, as a result, how the English
discipline considers what is meant by "text." As Kathleen Blake Yancey
has said, "literacy today is in the midst of a tectonic change. Even inside of school, never before have writing and composition generated
such diversity in definition" (298). Similarly, the "NCTE Definition
of 21st Century Literacies" links the evolutions of society and technology to the evolutions of literacy; consequently, the definition identifies
the following needs of modern-day readers and writers:

- Develop proficiency with the tools of technology
- Build relationships with others to pose and solve problems collaboratively and cross-culturally

- Design and share information for global communities to meet a variety of purposes
- Manage, analyze, and synthesize multiple streams of simultaneous information
- Create, critique, analyze, and evaluate multi-media texts
- Attend to the ethical responsibilities required by these complex environments ("NCTE Definition 21st Century Literacies")

Several assumptions emerge in the NCTE list of literacy needs, including the centrality of technology, the privileging of a collaborative approach to problem-solving, the multiplicity of purposes for writing, the multiplicity of information sources, the relevance of multimedia texts, and the integrality of an ethical responsibility within this new context of literacy. Implicit in each of these assumptions are the interdependent relationships among society, technology, and literacy, and the acknowledgement of a diverse society. In short, NCTE embraces the tectonic shift Yancey describes, a shift which has transformed communication within and outside the writing classroom—whether that classroom is in a room or online. There, multiple literacies, multimodal composing, and collaboration are the norms and expectations, whereas this certainly was not the case ten to fifteen years ago. Furthermore, the principles embedded within NCTE's list are already at work in the community college setting, where WPAs and instructors engage daily with innovative teaching that utilizes technology. Furthermore, cross-cultural and collaborative problem-solving processes have long been enlisted, and the ethical questions related to literacy instruction have engaged faculty for decades.

While the scope of this discussion cannot identify the entire spectrum of emergent literacies in society and the classroom today, the WPA in the community college must be (and most likely already is) cognizant of the continual evolution/revolution occurring. Because technology changes quickly, subsequently adding or revising methods of communication, current journals, such as *Writing Program Administration, Teaching English in the Two-Year College,* and *College Composition and Communication,* and especially web resources, such as CompPile.org and listservs such as the WPA listserv, offer up-to-date information and active dialogues on related issues. Importantly, WPAs have much to contribute to these dialogues, given their daily encounters with change and diversity. Within their own institutions, the key for WPAs is not simply to have the awareness that multiple literacies exist in the community college context, but to discern which ones exist predominantly or are emerging among the students in their programs. An even greater challenge, though, is addressing them in a way that meets the objectives of the writing program, and that benefits the students and helps them build on the competences and knowledge they already have.

Shaping the Identity of the WPA and Envisioning the Writing Program

In *The Activist WPA*, Linda Adler-Kassner argues that all WPAs are positioned to create change—in their institutions and beyond, particularly given today's technological climate. She makes the case for their collective ability to change the predominant, inaccurate "stories" about students, literacy, and education. She points out that Barbara Cambridge and Ben McClelland made similar claims that the role of the WPA offers individuals the opportunity to "orchestrate [a] broad strategic vision, develop [a] shared administrative and organized infrastructure, and create the cultural glue which can create synergies" (qtd. in Adler-Kassner 7). McLeod also asserts that one of the roles of the WPA is as a "change agent," who "[works] to change curricula and pedagogy to line up with what we know about learning theory" (17–18). The centrality of composition studies in the community college context strengthens the ability of the WPA to create change on a grand scale.

For these WPAs, the capacity for transformation comes with unique sociopolitical and ethical responsibilities. Referring to WPA history, Jeanne Gunner emphasizes the sociopolitical stakes for the WPA in any institution, but her point is poignantly applied to WPAs in the two-year institutional context:

> Knowledge of WPA history is a means to institutional critique, a method of understanding the ways in which writing program administrators and writing programs have historically been implicated in social structures that divide, direct, give access, deny access, replicate inequities, and use language in ways that construct ideologies which have material consequences. (275)

The political history of the community college influences how WPAs act as agents of change. The two predominant sociopolitical views of the community college argued for the institution either as part of a "great democratic initiative," or as part of an effort to reinforce the American caste system. The community college WPA stands where a choice emerges: either he or she will be an actor, cognizant of creating access for many to whom education has been denied or difficult to access in the past; or he or she can support a system of inequities, reinforcing the limitations on class mobility. Perhaps, more often than WPAs in four-year institutions, those in the two-year college feel their sociopolitical—and ethical—responsibilities acutely: The writing program affects community college students in immediate ways—and at times, devastating ways—such as when the failure of a developmental writing class results in the expulsion from a certificate program or the denial of entrance into a professional program. Whereas, at a four-year school, when students are placed on academic probation, one option is to enroll in a community college to improve grades, adjust to college life, and prepare for readmission at the original or another four-year school. At the community college, many students do not have an affordable, second option. If students are on academic probation, the option is to figure out how to succeed at the same institution. Klausman emphasizes that for community college WPAs, then, "the consequences of our actions . . . are concrete: they affect to some degree the real, lived experience of thousands of students. We must balance, therefore, the real and the imagined, the practical and the theoretical, the particular and the general" (242–43). Since professional certificates and programs, as well as associate degrees, offer preparation and certification for improved career opportunities and improved financial opportunities for many students, WPAs function indirectly as socioeconomic gatekeepers. How they view the mission of the community college, and subsequently shape their roles and work within the two-year institution, shapes the program, thus affecting students' educational experiences, and as Klausman implies, their lives.

At the community college, the role of the WPA is sometimes more loosely defined than it is at a four-year institution, in part due to the relative newness of the two-year college. Another reason is the absence of hierarchy among the faculty. Working with peers who teach similar courses, these WPAs generally have more freedom to envision their role and the program than their counterparts at four-year institutions.

The capacity the WPA conceptualizes for him or herself is, of course, a personal, ethical choice, but one that has direct bearing on the shape of the writing program and on the students. Yet, the decision is informed by having as much knowledge about the students in the institution, as well as knowledge of the community college's history and self-knowledge, as possible. As Holmsten writes: "The complications of our institutions require us to lead complicated, and constantly shifting lives, in order to require us to respond to the needs of our communities and to construct our roles as WPAs in our local contexts" (436).

Community college WPAs commonly accept the democratic vision of the institution—as articulated by Cohen and Brawer—as the basis for their roles within the writing program. Like many instructors teaching at the college, their sympathies lie with the students and with supporting their access to educational opportunities. Consequently, many WPAs view themselves as agents of change at the curricular and sociopolitical levels. They recognize that their professional identity affects the design of the program, including writing instruction, and the views of student literacies and knowledge. In the new, global era, WPAs cannot avoid engaging in disciplinary discussions about multiple literacies and multimodal composing practices, that is, if they have committed their professional roles to enabling access to educational opportunities.

Further, the programs they design benefit from "maintaining change as a dynamic condition" (Brady 31). Regardless of the details of the program, community colleges experience so much change with each cohort of students and the conditions surrounding the college that the program itself should manifest enough flexibility to enable it to change accordingly. Generalizing about all writing programs, Laura Brady argues:

> Faculty members come and go, and institutional factors—such as budget lines, enrollment totals, and policy statements—also shift. The change that was collaborative and innovative just a few years ago is what keeps systems dynamic. The key, as [Shelley] Reid and others point out, is to keep change purposeful rather than exhaustingly unpredictable. (31)

Brady reminds readers of Reid's parallel between the dynamic writing program and the revision process instructors teach composition students. Reid argues that "changing and its benefits are hardly new ideas to writing teachers. We recommend change to our students almost as often as we breathe. . . . Moreover, we frequently ask students to change their writing style or approach for the sake of becoming more flexible writers" (qtd. in Brady 31). Similarly, Brady suggests WPAs approach developing the writing program, outlining five possible strategies to affect particular kinds of change:

1. Changing to Improve Organization and Focus
2. Changing to Expand and Amplify
3. Changing to Create a New Audience
4. Changing the Program's Purpose
5. Changing the Administrative Persona (32–33)

Each strategy proposes different pathways to create changes within the program. The key inherent in each is the reflection on, and the recognition of, the need for change—the heart of a dynamic program. While Brady's five strategies do not complete an exhaustive list of possibilities, community college WPAs consider these and other possibilities in designing a program to meet the changing needs of the students and the institution, particularly in this global era.

No matter how WPAs go about creating a dynamic program, Sullivan's earlier question about what kinds of student writing qualify as "college level" inevitably arises. In view of the new global condition, criteria shifts to a context of multiplicity. In other words, the emergence of new technologies, multiple literacies, and diverse competencies force WPAs to take into account not just what constitutes "college-level writing," but also what constitutes "good writing." Certainly, as Adler-Kassner claims, "Definitions of 'good writing' are context dependent" (13). Internet communication technology (ICT) and other forms of electronic composing, as well as online library databases, Wikipedia, Google, listservs, and so many other research tools, all contribute to the continual evolution of the criteria of good writing. They also contribute to the development of student writers/composers, who often demonstrate different composing habits than their counterparts of twenty years ago. Lisa Bickmore and Ron Christiansen argue that for educators, "To move in this direction—the direction of invention and transformation rather than conservation, of designing a curriculum for a new kind of social human—runs counter to a powerful tendency of disciplinary activity, which is to maintain its jurisdictional powers" (231). Thus, WPAs and instructors, both at the community college and at the four-year institution, face an opportunity or an impediment, depending on their individual responses to change. For the community college WPA, there seems to be little opportunity for ignoring the newly emergent "kind of social human" in the twenty-first century; his or her "jurisdictional powers" create the possibility for such students to exercise their similarly newly emergent literacies. Bickmore and Christiansen rightly point out that the encounter with students who are more competent in emergent, technologically-based literacies than their instructor runs opposite to traditional expectations of the hierarchical teacher-student relationship. This encounter may mean "[c]oming face to face with nonlinear texts—even awkward or strange looking ones—[which] can both rejuvenate our teaching and force us to reshape our notions of assessment" (Bickmore and Christiansen 231). It may also mean, as they suggest, that once instructors (and by extension, WPAs) begin engaging students within the multiple realms of composition, and where students are perhaps most comfortable and proficient, "we confront almost immediately what we don't know about the places where writing circulates, and the intricate rhetorical options writers navigate in those places" (237). The essayistic literacies traditionally taught in composition courses often ignore the rhetorical contexts outside of the classroom, so instructors must engage in new pedagogical approaches better suited to today's literacy climate.

Because composition courses, previously literature courses, have become the primary site for "certifying students in the literacies and cultures of the academy," they also have become a primary location for the change in how the academy engages ICT and the subsequent developing literacies of incoming students (Schroeder). James Ray Watkins draws the point out further, arguing that the discipline of English must be responsive to emergent literacies and new rhetorical conditions:

> Indeed, as the rise of social networking illustrates, any revision of English studies has to be both dynamic and profoundly adaptive. Whatever else a wiki may be, it is not a book; a blog may be essayistic, but it is not an essay; and while e-mail may belong to an epistolary genre, it is not a letter. Moreover, as computers and broadband becomes as ubiquitous—at least in the West—as telephones and television, the dynamics of access are shifting yet again. (115)

For Watkins and Schroeder, this cultural/historical moment in literacy links new communicative technologies to the rise in access to information and education. Unlike the telephone and television, though, these new technologies enable composition of various texts, using a variety of literacies. Adler-Kassner arrives at a similar conclusion by pointing to the widespread use of emergent, communicative technologies that threaten the authority of higher education to set exclusive standards for literacy:

> And just as dominant cultural groups reacted to the development of [nineteenth and twentieth century] media (by using them for the purpose of spreading their own messages, or by protesting against them, or by removing themselves from the arenas where those media were widely used), so the same is happening today, as is demonstrated in comments about how these media must interfere in negative ways with the development of students' critical intelligences. (165)[3]

The confrontation of the new and the unknown—by some or all instructors teaching writing—must be addressed by the WPA, who can support the encounter with faculty development sessions and even simple, open discussions about the nature of such encounters.

The call to community college WPAs for a high level of responsiveness—addressing the unknown, in many cases, and then integrating it into the writing program—is especially strong, given the centrality of the nontraditional student to the mission of the two-year institution. Enabling students access to further educational opportunities absolutely includes a consideration of—and indeed, an open mind about—the literacies and competencies students bring to writing courses, and a willingness to re-evaluate the program and make changes where needed. In fact, it requires a willingness to re-evaluate how the program itself is evaluated or assessed. While an individual WPA—or a writing program committee—might be converted to the belief in multiple, emergent literacies, not all community college writing faculty and administrators may feel necessarily convinced or open, particularly since such literacies challenge traditional notions of language instruction and instructor authority, as noted by Bickmore and Christiansen. Even in an institution that continually reinvents itself in many ways to meet the needs of the changing cohorts of students, challenges to basic, traditional assumptions about language instruction can exist and thus are met with resistance. Therefore, WPAs may want to consider faculty development that enables all writing instructors to recognize the legitimacy of emergent literacies and new modes of instruction. However the WPA chooses to address the multiplicity of student literacies and composing methods, he or she must always return to the philosophy of the writing program, uphold the principles of open admissions and access, and develop the vision of his or her professional role as a change agent.

PEDAGOGY

Finding a single pedagogical approach that addresses the diverse student population and its multiple literacies can be a formidable, even impossible, challenge. This challenge is in large part due to the high level of academic freedom community college faculty enjoy. Taylor, Nist, and Raines all comment on the autonomy of instructors; the freedom most instructors have in terms of syllabus development and textbook adoption is one indicator of this autonomy (Taylor 123). Still, WPAs can share research and innovative pedagogical approaches through faculty development sessions. They will want to keep up to date with relevant journals, as noted earlier, and may find guidance in pedagogies that privilege context-based writing that allows students to apply writing instruction to their work in other disciplines, such as found in Anne Beaufort's *College Writing and Beyond: A New Framework for University Writing Instruction*, and as discussed in Tinberg's *Border Talk: Writing and Knowing in the Two-Year College*. Further, Reynolds and Holladay-Hicks's *The Profesion of English in the Two-Year College* offers several essays that address pedagogical approaches in community college writing classrooms, including those that consider technological and cultural literacy. While these texts and others provide guidelines for applying pedagogical approaches, WPAs should not feel restricted to these methodologies. Only they know their context best, and may develop site-specific or hybrid approaches enabling instructors the necessary flexibility. Further, in light of rapidly changing ICT, many published texts become somewhat outdated or inapplicable after a brief period of time. However the WPA addresses pedagogical issues in the writing program, he or she will inevitably consider the students' needs, the curricular vision and design, the ethos of the program, and the results of the program's assessment. If good writing is context-specific, as Adler-Kassner claims, so is "good" pedagogy.

PROGRAM ASSESSMENT

Program assessment plays an essential role developing a writing program and a WPA's role, and when properly done, it strengthens the case for programmatic or curricular change. Catherine A. Palomba and Trudy W. Banta's *Assessment Essentials: Planning, Implementing, and Improving Assessment in Higher Education* defines the purpose of program assessment as to "[help] determine whether students can integrate learning from individual courses into a coherent whole. It is interested in the cumulative effects of the educational process" (5–6).

Program assessment, like student outcomes assessment, offers relevant feedback to WPAs and departments about the effectiveness of courses and other aspects of the writing program. It should be directed by the WPA, faculty, and/or administrators engaged in the writing program. In addition, its methodology should reflect the ethos of the program. NCTE's position statement on writing assessment reiterates this point, emphasizing commonality among participants:

> Programs and departments should see themselves as communities of professionals whose assessment activities reveal common values, provide opportunities for inquiry and debate about unsettled issues, and communicate measures of effectiveness to those inside and outside the program. Members of the community are in the best position to guide decisions about what assessments will best inform that community. ("Writing Assessment")

Not only can assessment at this level provide information about how the program meets the needs of a multi-literate, diverse student population, but it also can reflect the principles that shape the philosophy of the program. Assessment can clarify the program's ethos and, if necessary, identify areas for development, where practice aligns with philosophy. Maurice Scharton links assessment to inherent values:

> The history of assessment is rife with technically based political movements, each promoting its dream of the ideal technique that will satisfy and unify everyone. Yet one person's dream is always another's nightmare. We have no godlike

vantage point beyond our own perspectives from which to perceive or construct the ideal assessment. We measure the validity of a test against our subjective sense of how well the results square with our values. If an assessment does anything, it helps us to recognize that we have values, an investment in one belief system. (54)

The challenge of program assessment at the community college is in determining the appropriate measurement methodology, a decision complicated by the fact that many students do not enroll with the goal of completing a program's course of study, a certificate, or a degree. Many students take classes when they can or want to, leave, and possibly return at a later time, thwarting many attempts to identify cohorts of students who move through a sequence of courses and are still around to participate in assessment. For programs such as the community college writing program that offers courses in sequence, the approach to assessment may sometimes depend on student records, including transcripts, coursework, and capstone courses (Bers 44–45).

Most program-level assessments at the community college rely on one or more of the following approaches that Trudy Bers identifies. Some are certainly more effective than others:[4]

- Capstone courses: a final course in a disciplinary sequence where students demonstrate their cumulative knowledge of a subject
- Testing: the administration of a standardized test[5]
- Satisfaction surveys: self-identified assessments of learning
- Portfolio assessment: in hard copy or e-copy, portfolio submissions of student work are measured against program objectives
- Narratives: based in dialogue, students tell the "story" of their learning to faculty who listen and ask questions.
- Successful transfer: the tracking of student transfers to four-year institutions. The National Student Clearinghouse Enrollment Search program provides information for 91% of all postsecondary education students in the country. (47–48)

Several of these approaches are beneficial when used in coordination with other approaches, in particular testing (although this is the least favored method), surveys, and narratives. Edward White, in *Developing a Successful College Writing Program*, supports a multifaceted approach to program assessment (204), and Cohen and Brawer recommend multiple matrix sampling instead of testing to assess the value of a program (405). Cohen and Brawer particularly recommend the cross-sectional model that draws upon any relevant configuration of the most common methods, such as those Bers lists. They note that program assessment is quite effective when there is a cohort of students participating in a program from the beginning to a measurable end; however, when students drop in and out, the cross-sectional model offers the best results, because this model "skirts the problem of student retention and the difficulty of follow-up because it generates new cohorts each time it is administered" (Cohen and Brawer 406). Further models for programmatic assessment can be found at the CWPA's website, in addition to consultant-evaluator opportunities, which McLeod recommends as "the single most valuable program evaluation tool available to WPAs" (97).

In the event that programmatic change—however small or large—occurs as the result of assessment or another impetus, the WPA will more than likely engage in politics on several possible levels: among faculty, administrators, other colleges, and the local community and state. Writing assessment, White, William Lutz, and Sandra Kamusikir write, "is unavoidably a political act" (1). CWPA advises employing communication strategies in the context of program assessment, suggesting that the politics surrounding assessment necessitates dialogue and understanding among all involved parties:

> Designing and implementing good assessments is just one part of the work, however. Another involves helping stakeholders—whether colleagues in the program or department, campus administrators, community members, parents, or legislators—understand what it means to engage in *valid, reliable, and discipline-appropriate assessement that is used to improve teaching and learning.* ("Communication Strategies")

At the legislative level, community colleges must frequently advocate for an assessment measurement that is appropriate to community colleges. Performance reporting—a shift from outcomes assessment—has become the preferred methodology in higher education. However, since the 1990s, state-level criteria for performance studied in twenty-nine states, and has "largely ignore[d] the diverse clientele and the specific purposes of community colleges" (Burke and Minassians 53). Instead, states' evaluative criteria were based on expectations for four-year institutions. For community college WPAs, this model means they must keep abreast of statewide expectations, and either advocate alongside state representatives, or request that other college representatives—including local legislators—advocate on behalf of the community college writing program. Program assessment, whether for internal or external data collection, is fraught with politics, and the more the WPA knows about who is involved, what the investment in writing assessment is, and what strategies can support the program within this context, the more effective the WPA will be at advocating for the program.

POLITICS

Politics does not only surround assessment, but in fact penetrates nearly every aspect of WPA work—just as the support of the presidential administration and the lack of support from many lawmakers indicated in 2009. Hesse underscores the link between the political work of the WPA and the necessity of good communication, writing, "For a good deal of their work, WPAs simply must be politicians—and of course, rhetoricians" (41). Politics in any institution is unavoidable, and understanding the political environment and developing an effective approach enables the WPA to navigate what can be, at times, difficult political terrain.

Hesse offers two political premises for WPAs: one, expertise does not necessarily persuade invested parties who do not share the expertise, and two, political antes are highest when resources are concerned. He claims that "the most meaningful political decisions generally involve competition for resources: time, space, and money. This is clearest in terms of class size, faculty lines, salaries, computers, offices, and so on, but even curricular decisions have profound resource dimensions" (42). While Hesse refers to four-year institutions specifically, his observations apply equally to two-year institutions, where nonspecialists can be involved in curricular development, and where resources can be particularly scarce. The WPA must engage his or her rhetorical skills to ensure understanding and support for the program, but also to procure necessary resources as much as possible.

In his essay, "Politics and the WPA: Traveling Through and Past Realms of Experience," Hesse outlines advice to the WPA engaged in politics in his or her program and department, including: knowing the "system," developing policies and writing them down, constructing "an effective ethos," and writing strategic reports, as mentioned earlier (42–45). Further, at the level of institutional politics, he advises involvement in college-level committees relevant to the writing program (48). Participation in such committees enables the WPA to work with, and thus make connections to, colleagues in other disciplines— a link which may be necessary when proposing policies that affect the college at large. On the level of higher education and the public realm, Hesse emphasizes involvement in disciplinary and professional organizations. He names the American Association for Higher Education (AAHE), the American Council on Education (ACE), and the American Association of College and Universities (AAC & U) (54). Particularly relevant for community college WPAs is the American Association of Community Colleges (AACC) and the Two-Year College English Association (TYCA) (and its affiliation with NCTE). Understanding national trends and forming coalitions through meetings and online resources, Hesse argues, provides "a forum not only for sharing program ideas but also for sharing information and developing political strategies" (55).

Adler-Kassner provides political strategies for WPAs, drawing from progressive, grassroots activist practices. She emphasizes the rhetorical work WPAs must do in political negotiations over programmatic change, and in particular, stresses the need to reframe familiar "stories"assumptions that shape attitudes toward college writing. She identifies seven viable steps common to grassroots political movements:

- Identifying an issue and a goal for change
- Identifying what we know, and what we need to know, to achieve the goal
- Developing a message
- Identifying audiences for that message
- Crafting specific messages for specific purposes/audiences
- Creating an overall plan to circulate our messages among those audiences
- Assessing our work (130–31)

Adler-Kassner's seven steps offer a highly organized option for engaging in political negotiations for WPAs at two-year institutions. Like Hesse, Adler-Kassner emphasizes the need for a strategy that includes a rhetorical dimension. For WPAs at the community college, having a sense for how the politics work at their own institutions is as important as how they decide upon their roles within them. Knowing what the objectives are, who the players are, and existing alliances form central components of any strategy employed to create changes to the writing program and the curriculum.

Politics begin and end this chapter. President Obama's 2009 call to raise the nation's number of college graduates marked the era of the community college as the democratic educational institution for the twenty-first century. The arguments and negotiations of legislators reduced the original support proposed by the American Graduation Initiative, but the federal government and philanthropic organizations still provide funding in support of the President's vision and the community college's central role in fulfilling it. Now more than ever, community college WPAs find themselves at the threshold of enormous change, where educational, social, and political forces demand more from the institution—and in this age of multiple literacies—especially from its writing programs.

5 Conclusion: Community College WPAs as Educational Leaders

In the new global era, community college WPAs find themselves in positions to make significant contributions to national and disciplinary dialogues on literacy in higher education. The parallels between the principals of NCTE's "Definition of 21st Century Literacies" and writing instruction and program administration in the two-year institution suggest an optimal moment for the WPAs' participation in these dialogues. Given their work with nearly half of all undergraduates in the nation, an enormously diverse student population far more representative of the typical American undergraduate than previously assumed, their experience and knowledge can help shift conventional assumptions about institutional hierarchies and student literacy and intelligence.

Not only do community college WPAs have a plethora of experiential knowledge to share with their disciplines, but they also have a professional obligation to share. Peter Mortensen suggests the primacy of all WPAs to national discussions on writing, WPA work, and student learning:

> In our journals and at our conferences, one finds repeated again and again the assertion that our work—our teaching, researching, and theorizing—can clarify and even improve the prospects of literacy in democratic culture. If we really believe this, we must then acknowledge our obligation to air that work in the most expansive, inclusive forums imaginable. (qtd. in Adler-Kassner 80)

Mortensen's point applies most directly to WPAs at the community college. More than ever before, the knowledge and understanding of these professionals is vital to the mission of improving "the prospects of literacy in democratic culture." Their literacy work with the many college students who enroll places them at the vanguard of higher education in the twenty-first century. Reynolds argues that community college faculty can make significant, specific contributions to the English discipline *particularly* because of classroom interactions with diverse student populations:

> They have been at the forefront of teaching at all levels to diverse populations. Their knowledge about literacy production and transmission is especially valuable. Their expertise in dealing with nontraditional students, with multicultural audiences, with all the attendant issues of gender, race, class, and ethnicity can be the source of valuable and useful information to all of higher education as student populations in all settings grow more diverse and more nontraditional. (11)

The current trends in higher education, as Reynolds claims, call for the unique experience of community college instructors and WPAs. Until recently, research on composition and WPA work in the two-year college context—if it were done at all—was mostly generated by researchers at four-year institutions, such as Columbia University Teachers College's Community College Research Center, Cornell University's Institute for Community College Development, and the Center for Community College Student Engagement at the University of Texas at Austin. As valuable as much of that research has been, experiential knowledge and research on community college WPAs and compositionists themselves are irreplaceable. Further, they have a responsibility to their own students to assert the authority of their knowledge, thus reframing common misconceptions of community colleges as inferior institutions.

Still, the educational hierarchy that resulted in the establishment of the community college by leaders of prominent four-year institutions will not voluntarily dismantle itself. Certainly, the recent national attention and the mutual interest shown by colleagues in four-year institutions helped raise the profile of community colleges. Members of both institutions are beginning to recognize the need to exchange ideas and information among WPAs and faculty members. In 2010, MLA President Sidonie Smith asserted the prominent role community colleges play on the stage of today's higher education:

> Community Colleges open a crucial pipeline to the BA, MA, and PhD programs that four-year colleges and universities

> offer in literatures and languages. With expertise in address-
> ing the aspirations and needs of immigrants, first-generation
> students, and underrepresented populations as well as return-
> ing adults, including veterans, community college faculty
> members are critical partners of four-year college and univer-
> sity faculty members. (2)

Consequently, Smith invites the MLA to increase its membership from
two-year colleges (2). Of course, one way to continue strengthening
the institution's profile is for its instructors and WPAs to initiate conversations with their counterparts at four-year institutions. Educators
such as Tinberg, Raines, Nist, and Taylor have also called for further collaboration and dialogue between the two types of institutions.
Open dialogue among diverse institutions, Taylor suggests, enables
best practices to emerge more readily: "[C]ollaborative research about
two-year college WPA work could show us a more detailed picture
of the diversity of writing program administration while also letting
us see the effectiveness, weaknesses, and strengths of various WPA
models" (133). Community college WPAs can engage in national and
disciplinary dialogues through conference attendance, association
memberships, and scholarly writing. All of these activities necessitate a
reduced course load, additional sabbatical time, and increased faculty
development funding—consistent obstacles for some. Fortunately,
community college WPAs have a unique sociocultural moment in
American higher education to aid their efforts to enter national dialogues and offer their educational insights and knowledge in greater
numbers. With recent national attention on the two-year institution,
they can and should join these dialogues as often as possible.

Like any social movement, reframing literacy discussions and re-
working the image of the community college requires focused leaders and effective strategies. Also like a social movement, much is at
stake: With millions of students enrolling each year, WPAs cannot
afford to ignore the cultural moment. In his 2002 study, "Why David
Sometimes Wins: Strategic Capacity in Social Movements," Marshall
Ganz argues that the reason some "underdogs" succeed in affecting
massive social change is due to the combination of leadership and
circumstance:

> Opportunities occur at moments when actors' resources ac-
> quire more value because of changes in the environmental

> context. Actors do not suddenly acquire more resources or de-
> vise a new strategy, but find that resources they already have
> give them more leverage in achieving their goals. A full gra-
> nary, for example, acquires greater value in a famine, creating
> opportunity for its owner. . . . This is one reason timing is
> such an important element of strategy. (5)

This cultural moment for community college WPAs is the culmination of several important forces. The slow recovery of the recent
global economic crisis, and the Obama Administration's call to raise
the number of college graduates, along with the allotment of funding
earmarked for community college grants and philanthropic initiatives,
have placed public two-year institution educators in a central position
to shift conventional perspectives on higher education and literacy.
This position hinges on the intersections between the rise in enrollment rates and an increase in access to emergent communication technologies. NCES indicates that by 2019, undergraduate enrollment is
expected to rise to nineteen million, from 13.2 million in 2000. At the
two-year college alone, enrollment is expected to rise to 8.2 million,
and has already risen to seven million from 5.9 million between 2000
and 2008 ("Undergraduate Enrollment"). The increasing diversity of
all undergraduates nationwide, argues James Ray Watkins, in *A Taste
for Language*, will affect a collective resistance to the dominance of
traditional academic discourse within institutions of higher education,
particularly the discourse found in composition classrooms:

> Traditionally, of course, English studies have sought, in effect,
> to transform the language of non-white, non-middle-class
> students, instilling in them the habits of the white middle-
> class professional. A contemporary student body, increasingly
> non-white and politically aware, [as] Schroeder suggests, will
> be less inclined to accept this arrangement. (114)

Watkins bases his claim on Christopher Schroeder's argument, where
Schroeder asserts that the "crisis of literacy," a crisis of students failing
conventional literacy expectations, as perceived by political representatives and cultural critics, is actually a crisis of legitimacy resulting from
an enrollment boom (see *A Test in Leadership*, Spellings Commission,
2006). Schroeder points out that what he calls a "crisis of legitimacy,"
and others call a crisis of literacy, historically has been linked to rises
in undergraduate enrollments, as in the past, during the 1870s, 1910s,

1940s, 1970s, and now, since the latter part of the 1990s.[1] He claims that the current crisis of legitimacy results from an emerging discrepancy between the cultural values taught in the writing classroom and those of the society. Echoing Bickmore and Christiansen, Watkins adds to Schroeder's argument that the increase and expansion of communication technologies has widened this discrepancy:

> The rise of these technologies, in other words, has only deepened the rift between the work (of reading and writing) done outside of the academy and the educational priorities within. This rift, again, was founded on a traditional paradigm of English studies shaped by a strict disciplinary hierarchy in which the formal aesthetic, defined as the non-useful, was prioritized over the popular ethos. (113)

Both Watkins and Schroeder locate the emergent discrepancy of cultural values, as Schroeder frames it, "the decentralized literacies of the academy mask[ing] the cultural values that these literacies authorize," as the point of crisis, complicated by new composing technologies and increased enrollment.

Adler-Kassner similarly perceives the crisis of literacy/legitimacy that Watkins and Schroeder identify, but she addresses it through the matrix of public policy and advocacy. She strongly advocates for the WPAs' necessary role in shaping dialogues—and by extension, public policy—about student literacy. And she links the emergence of communication technologies to this same culminating moment in national education, in which public policy was legislated based on the assumed failure of educational institutions to provide literacy instruction properly.[2] She cites *A Test of Leadership*, the final report produced by the Bush Administration's Spellings Commission, faulting English instructors with a perceived failure in national student literacy: "The point made in the report's preface is reiterated throughout: threats to achievement of the [democratice] promise—and the betrayal of education's fundamental mission—come from inside" (62–63). Adler-Kassner argues that the report and similar public criticism of public education are part of an educational argument that ignores social context and relies on the authoritarian presumptions of past literacy instruction—including the propagation of inflexible literacy standards. Through this lens, she explains, "students are failing. They don't know, they can't do, and things aren't good. It also suggests that teachers, by extension, are struggling; they aren't teaching students what they need to know" (166). Adler-Kassner, like Watkins and Schroeder, identifies this current cultural moment as one of intervention. She recognizes the threat new media technology presents to the status quo—or more precisely, the academy's control—of literacy and knowledge production, as in other historical moments of technological innovation. Similar to McLeod and others, she perceives the WPA as an agent of change, and she views WPAs as central to intervening efforts to reframe reductive thinking about student literacy and competencies.

The shifts in literacy and knowledge production have inevitably begun affecting the relationship between instructors and students. Referring to James E. Russell, Tinberg claims that the new era of technology has altered the role of the teacher-scholar as expert in the classroom. The success of the instructor, he claims, is based on his or her ability to navigate information as much demonstrating intellectual ability. Tinberg views this new role as indicative of the emergent, integrative role shaping English departments in general, but has already manifested in community college English departments ("Teaching English" 142). To help foster this role, the moment of intervention calls for experiential knowledge gained through writing program administration within the community college context. Working with a student population far more representative of the typical American undergraduate, WPAs in the two-year institution bring knowledge in the most urgent and rapidly developing areas of education: cross-cultural and class awareness, institutional access, and multiple student literacies. In these areas, community college WPAs are steeped more in practice than in theory. They are well acquainted with routine change and habitually reassessing the needs of a changing student population. This cumulative professional experience places WPAs at the two-year college in a position to speak to the changing needs of an increasingly diverse *American* undergraduate population, whose access to ICT has vastly distinguished them from past generations of students in terms of literacy and composing texts. These professionals lend their situated and experiential knowledge of diverse student populations, with multiple literacies to dismantle prescriptive, traditional assumptions about student literacy, and to shift criteria for "good writing" to include the cross-cultural considerations and multiple competencies of today's undergraduate students. Last, they bring their individual senses of the democratic and ethical dimensions attached to dialogues about educational standards as a reminder that literacy instruction directly relates to the quality of the lives of all students—indeed, all American citizens.

Through their sheer diversity, community college students thus challenge their WPAs and their instructors to meet them where they are intellectually in a program or in a classroom, to reject the status quo of class hierarchy and to enable them to achieve the goals—the dreams—they bring to community college, or start to develop once they get there. Doing so may mean for many WPAs and instructors further rejecting traditional notions of what "intelligence" or "valued knowledge" is. Importantly, their wealth of knowledge derives from both theory and experiential learning, not unlike many of their students. To resist conventional definitions of knowledge as the only authoritative measurement of intelligence fortifies the value of their own—and that of other students—experiential and situated knowledge. This may mean engaging with their four-year college counterparts and persuade them to rethink notions of the traditional student, and to reconsider how vital the community college is to the discipline of composition and their own work. It may mean finding more creative ways to build on the literacies and competencies students bring to the college so they can find their way to academic discourse (or their way out of it). It may mean one or more of these possibilities, but each of them centers on the students themselves.

The work and the sociopolitical responsibility of the community college WPA depends on his or her commitment and awareness of the students and their academic needs. This commitment and awareness extends to the understanding of, and service to, the surrounding community, society, and the global world—all contexts that students engage during and after their studies. In fact, the future of the institution depends on this awareness: "While its place in the history of American education is assured, the future success of the community college system will depend on how well it adapts to the changing needs of society" (Coley 3).

While several national organizations such as the CCCC, the CWPA, and to a certain extent, the MLA, have conscientiously included community college instructors and WPAs in student literacy and instruction dialogues, the participation of community college faculty in these venues is still very often marginal. Given this moment of intervention, community college WPAs do not necessarily have to wait for invitations to join such venues. The national debate over public education is already happening; recent enrollment surges and the current presidential administration have called community colleges into the mix. At a time when two-year institutions have been awarded twenty-seven percent of federal money spent on higher education, despite enrolling nearly half of all college students, the time for action is now (Gonzalez, "Community Colleges"). Ganz argues that the way a "David" can achieve revolution depends on shifts in the surrounding environment and the resourcefulness of the movement's leaders:

> Changing environments generate opportunities and resources, but the significance of those opportunities or resources—and even what constitutes them—emerges from the hearts, heads, and hands of the actors who develop the means of putting them to work. People can generate the power to resolve grievances not only if those with power decide to use it on their behalf, but also if they can develop the capacity to outthink and outlast their opponents—a matter of leadership and organization. As an "actor-centered" approach, analysis of strategic capacity suggests ways to design leadership teams and structure organizations that increase the chances of devising effective strategies to deal with the challenges of organizing, innovation, and social change today. As students of "street smarts" have long understood, resourcefulness can sometimes compensate for a lack of resources. (26)

Low funding and low regard for the community college externally cannot serve as reasons to avoid national literacy debates. Community college educators, like Tinberg, have pointed to public two-year institutions leading in the shifting modes of instruction and learning ("Teaching English" 144). Now the question community college WPAs must decide is not if they want to engage, but *how* they want to engage in educational dialogues, nationally and within their discipline. Their experience and knowledge legitimizes their contributions, and their students—indeed *all* undergraduate students—require and deserve their WPAs' insights, innovation, and advocacy.

6 Continuing the Conversation: A Selective List for Further Reading

WRITING PROGRAM ADMINISTRATION

Adler-Kassner, Linda. *The Activist WPA*. Logan: Utah State UP, 2008. Print.

Employing grassroots activist strategies for promoting progressive causes, Adler-Kassner maps out how WPAs and compositionists can reshape pervasive narratives that limit perceptions of student literacy. She links reshaping literacy narratives to influencing public educational policy, and by doing so, identifies broader contexts for WPAs to play pivotal roles beyond the realm of their own institution.

Brown, Stuart C., and Theresa Enos, eds. *The Writing Program Administrator's Resource: A Guide to Reflective Institutional Practice*. Mahwah: Lawrence Erhlbaum, 2002. Print.

The essays in this collection provide a comprehensive view of WPA work. Of particular interest to community college WPAs is an essay by Victoria Holmsten that specifically addresses WPA work within the public two-year institutional context. Other essays include topics such as collaborative administration, placement, politics, legal issues, and adjunct concerns, among the more general WPA issues.

CompPile (http://comppile.org).

CompPile is a comprehensive, online resource listing publications relevant to composition, rhetoric, technical writing, and ESL in higher education. This website provides links to related organizations, such as CWPA (see below), WPA/NMA (Network for Media Action), and

CBW (Conference on Basic Writing). It also offers lists of bibliographies, books, and other publications relevant to WPA work in any context.

Council of Writing Program Administrators (www.wpacouncil.org).

The Council of Writing Program Administrators is a professional organization devoted to WPA work, research, and scholarly exchange. Its website provides forums for exchange, including access to the WPA listserv, and the organization offers annual conferences in addition to relevant resources, including program consultant services.

Klausman, Jeffrey. "Mapping the Terrain: The Two-Year College Program Administrator." *Teaching English in the Two-Year College* 35.3 (2008): 238–51. Print.

This article gives a general overview of WPA work at the community college and emphasizes the ways student diversity and the democratic principles implicit in an open-access institution shape writing program development in this context.

McLeod, Susan. *Writing Program Administration*. West Lafayette: Parlor Press, 2007. Print.

Writing Program Administration is a comprehensive source for general WPA work and research at four-year and two-year institutions. McLeod provides a thorough history of the development of English studies and WPA work in higher education, in addition to providing WPA resources ranging from the role of the WPA, accompanying responsibilities, and current issues and concerns.

Taylor, Tim. "Writing Program Administration at the Two-Year College: Ghosts in the Machine." *Writing Program Administration* 32.3 (2009): 120–39. Print.

This article provides a comparative statistical look at the development of writing programs, faculty, and WPAs at the two-year institution since Helon Howell Raines's 1990 study of the same. Taylor's comparison offers a current, comprehensive view of WPA work in the two-year institution.

Related Community College Information

Alford, Barry, and Keith Kroll, eds. *The Politics of Writing in the Two Year College*. Portsmouth, NH: Heineman, 2001. Print.

The essays in this collection offer perspectives on the politics at work in writing courses and programs at two-year institutions, with focuses ranging from working-class women, instructors' professional identities, contingent faculty, critical literacy and technical training, assessment, and technology.

Cohen, Arthur M., and Florence B. Brawer. *The American Community College*. 5th ed. San Francisco: Jossey-Bass, 2008. Print.

The American Community College offers an authoritative, comprehensive history and current assessment of the community college. Cohen and Brawer map the development of the community college within the social, political, and educational landscapes of the United States since the turn of the twentieth century. Because the volume provides a comprehensive view of the two-year institution, including data and information about all disciplines, programs, certificates, and services provided by the college, the text offers the WPA a broad contextual view of the two-year institution.

Holladay, Sylvia A. "Order Out of Chaos: Voices from the Community College." *Composition in the Twenty-First Century: Crisis and Change.* Ed. Lynn Z. Bloom, Donald A. Daiker, and Edward M. White. Carbondale: Southern Illinois UP, 1996, 29–38. Print.

This essay provides a detailed exploration of the complex lives of many community college students and the implications for composition studies at the college, particularly in terms of class issues and emotional trauma.

Raines, Helon Howell. "Is There a Writing Program in This College? Two Hundred and Thirty-Six Two-Year Schools Respond." *College Composition and Communication* 41.2 (1990): 151–65. Print.

An early, definitive study, this article addresses the conditions of English studies, writing programs, faculty, WPAs, and students at the community college. Raines emphasizes the effects of a diverse student population on the development of writing programs in this context.

Reynolds, Mark, and Sylvia Holladay-Hicks, eds. *The Profession of English in the Two-Year College*. Portsmouth, NH: Heinemann, 2005. Print.

This collection provides informative essays that address professional issues for faculty at two-year institutions, from professional roles to curriculum and professional development.

CURRICULUM AND PEDAGOGY

Beaufort, Anne. *College Writing and Beyond: A New Framework for University Writing Instruction*. Logan, UT: Utah State UP, 2007. Print.

In this text, Beaufort argues for teaching composition in response to contexts that influence the situations of writing. Of particular interest to community college educators is her comparative study of a student's work in first-year composition, in history, in engineering, and after college, since she posits her argument upon the notions of disciplinary writing. She emphasizes the interdisciplinary transfer of learning, a concept of relevance within the two-year institutional context.

Miller, Susan, ed. *The Norton Book of Composition Studies*. New York: Norton, 2009. Print.

This anthology of significant research on composition studies over the course of the last fifty years provides a comprehensive view of the discipline. Categorical topics range from the history of composition studies to its development as a discipline to composition theories to cross-cultural concerns to global perspectives, among others. Contributions include work by theorists and educators such as Janet Emig, Chaim Perelman, Nancy Sommers, Sharon Crowley, Mina Shaughnessy, Patricia Bizzell, George Hillocks, Mike Rose, Kurt Spellmeyer, Lynn Z. Bloom, Peter Elbow, Douglas Hesse, and James Paul Gee.

"The NCTE Definition of 21st Century Literacies." *NCTE.org*. NCTE. 18 Feb. 2008. Web.

This position statement, available on the NCTE website (www.ncte. org), provides a modern-day expectation for student literacies, inclusive of technology-based proficiencies and multimedia texts.

Reynolds, Nedra, Patricia Bizzell, and Bruce Herzberg. *The Bedford Bibliography for Teachers of Writing.* 6th ed. Boston: Bedford/St. Martin's, 2004. Print.

This bibliography provides a comprehensive list of resources for teaching writing, including topics such as history, theory, process, literacy, argument, style, grammar, usage, curriculum development, and writing programs.

Rose, Mike. *The Mind at Work.* New York: Viking, 2004. Print.

The Mind at Work explores the binary of the hand/mind within the contexts of working-class occupations. The text examines the intellectual processes inherent in several professions, and compares them to Western ideals of intelligence. *The Mind at Work* provides a useful context to WPAs in community colleges who engage with nontraditional students that present a range of literacies and knowledge. It places a high value on the intelligence many of these students bring to the classroom.

Stanley, Linda C., and Joanna Ambron, eds. *Writing Across the Curriculum in Community Colleges.* San Franscisco: Jossey-Bass, 1991. Print.

While nearly twenty years old, the essays in this collection present a range of perspectives and practices of WAC in community colleges, including the history of WAC programs in the two-year institution, as well as pedagogy, curriculum, assignments, and assessment.

Sullivan, Patrick. "What Is 'College-Level' Writing?" *Teaching English in the Two-Year College* (2003): 374–90. Print.

Sullivan's article establishes a framework for discussions of college-level writing within the community college context. He raises questions about standards and identifies challenges to the creation of uniform standards in the two-year institution.

Tinberg, Howard. *Border Talk: Writing and Knowing in the Two-Year College.* Urbana: NCTE, 1997. Print.

An ethnographic account that includes collaborative work among interdisciplinary writing tutorial colleagues, this study offers a discussion on the expectations for student writing in the community college context. It also focuses on the tensions between the specialized knowledge of instructors within a general studies curriculum, while raising questions about college-level writing and writing pedagogy.

Tinberg, Howard, and Jean-Paul Nadeau. *The Community College Writer: Exceeding Expectations.* Carbondale: Southern Illinois UP, 2010. Print.

Based on the study of students in their own institution, Bristol Community College, the authors of *The Community College Writer* discuss expectations for student writers in the community college context, aiming to broaden writing program discussions in two-year and four-year institutions.

Watkins, James Ray. *A Taste for Language: Literacy, Class, and English Studies.* Carbondale: Southern Illinois UP, 2009. Print.

Within the autobiographical context of the author, this text explores the historical and cultural relationships between English studies and the American class system. It explores assumptions about higher education and class, and argues for literacy instruction appropriate and well-suited to an increasingly multi-literate (and increasing) undergraduate population.

Developmental Writing Issues

Adler-Kassner, Linda, Gregory R. Glau, eds. *The Bedford Bibliography for Teachers of Basic Writing.* Boston: Bedford/St. Martin's, 2002. Print.

This bibliography offers a comprehensive list of resources for community college WPAs and teachers of developmental writing. Resource subjects are organized under the following categories: History and Theory; Pedagogical Issues; Curriculum Development; and Administrative Focus. The texts and resources listed here provide a foundation for including developmental writing courses within a writing program or within a program of their own.

Conference on Basic Writing (http://orgs.tamu-commerce.edu/CBW/ASU)

A Special Interest Group of the CCCCs, the Conference on Basic Writing (CBW) offers educators discussions and resources on pedagogy, curriculum, administration, and the social concerns related to basic writing. Its website provides links to a CBW listserv, online resources, conference information, basic writing programs, additional reading, and the *Journal of Basic Writing.*

Lundell, Dana Britt, and Terence Collins. "Toward a Theory of Developmental Education: The Centrality of 'Discourse.'" *The Expanding Role of Developmental Education.* Ed. Jeanne L. Higbee and Patricia Dwinell. Morrow: NADE, 1999. Print.

Within a collection of essays that addresses all areas of developmental instruction, this article posits James Paul Gee's notion of "Discourse" as the framework for a theory of developmental education that is still useful, particularly in the community college today. In Lundell and Collins's view, Discourse lends itself to a perspective of developmental students who bring intelligence and competence to their studies, a move away from conventional assumptions about these students as "deficient."

Rose, Mike. *Lives on the Boundary: A Moving Account of the Struggles and Achievements of America's Educationally Underprepared.* New York: Penguin, 2005. Print.

This text looks beyond labels such as "remedial," "illiterate," and "intellectually deficient" assigned to many developmental students, and offers viable approaches to initiating such students into academic discourse.

ESL Issues

Brown, H. Douglas. *Principles of Language Learning and Teaching.* 5th ed. New York: Pearson, 2011. Print.

Brown's text offers an accessible overview of current trends in the pedagogy of second language learning. He explores the psychological, sociological, and educational forces that shape language acquisition and teaching.

Kirklighter, Christina, Diana Cárderas, and Susan Wolff Murphy, eds. *Teaching Writing with Latino/a Students.* Albany: State U of New York P, 2007.

The collection of essays in *Teaching Writing with Latino/a Students* offers several perspectives on pedagogy and teaching Latino/a students. Of particular note are essays that provide statistics and definitions for working with this particularly diverse ethnic population. Additionally, work by scholars such as Michelle Hall Kells points to the rising number of bilingual students and the resultant, destabilized intellectual elitism found in many institutions of higher education.

"Position Statement Prepared by the NCTE Committee on Issues in ESL and Bilingual Education." *NCTE.org.* NCTE. 1981. Web.

This position statement provides historical background for English and bilingual instruction. It outlines relevant pedagogical and political issues and identifies a position very similar to TESOL's statement, asserting: "the linguistic and cultural resources the student brings to the school are used as tools for learning in the content areas while at the same time the students acquire proficiency needed in English to enable them to use it as a learning tool." Both NCTE and TESOL assert that utilizing a student's proficiencies that he or she already exhibits is essential to ESL instruction. The position statement can be found at www.ncte.org.

ASSESSMENT

Serban, Andreea M., and Jack Friedlander, eds. *Developing and Implementing Assessment of Student Learning Outcome: New Directions for Community Colleges.* San Francisco: Jossey-Bass, 2004. Print.

While this collection of essays deals with a range of disciplinary concerns and assessment, as an overview of the assessment of student outcomes, it provides practical and theoretical insights for this work within the community college context, such as how to engage faculty and students in assessment activities, implementing program and institutional assessment, addressing accreditation reviews, and assessing online education.

White, Edward, William D. Lutz, and Sandra Kamusikiri, eds. *Assessment of Writing: Politics, Policies, and Practices.* New York: MLA, 1996. Print.

While mostly geared toward professionals in four-year institutions, the essays in this collection address the politics—implicit and explicit—in assessment work, addressing related topics such as political and legal concerns, issues of validity and reliability, writing assessment models, equity issues, and the future of assessment.

"Writing Assessment: A Position Statement." CCCC Position Statement. *NCTE.org.* NCTE. 2000. Web.

This position statement provides practical recommendations for assessment and applications for classrooms, placement, proficiency, programs, and school admission.

CLASS AND THE COMMUNITY COLLEGE

Dougherty, Kevin J. *The Contradictory College: The Conflicting Origins, Impacts, and Futures of the Community College.* Albany: State U of New York P, 1994. Print.

Dougherty's text focuses on nuanced, class-based perspectives on the community college and its development. He outlines the contradictions in the institution's establishment, as well as its mission and its role in future years.

Sullivan, Patrick. "Cultural Narratives about Success and the Material Conditions of Class at the Community College." *Teaching English at the Two-Year College* 33.2 (2005): 142–60. Print.

This article argues for increased instructor sensitivity to class-based issues students present in the community college writing classroom. In particular, Sullivan identifies distinctions between the assumptions of a middle-class faculty and the reality of many of their working-class students.

Diversity Education

Banks, James A. *Cultural Diversity and Education: Foundations, Curriculum, and Teaching.* New York: Allyn & Bacon, 2005. Print.

A textbook aimed at education students, *Cultural Diversity and Education* identifies the foundations of "pluralistic education." Banks provides teaching approaches and methodologies for creating culturally competent programs.

Journal of Diversity in Higher Education.

A quarterly publication, *Journal of Diversity in Higher Education* provides studies and theoretical work in diversity education, in addition to methodologies for instilling effective diversity practices.

Smith, Daryl G. *Diversity's Promise for Higher Education: Making It Work.* Baltimore: Johns Hopkins University Press, 2009. Print.

Smith argues that institutions must move toward new measurements of how they meet diversity needs. She compares diversity to technology as a topic of concern that must be integrated into teaching and research practice. This text offers methodologies to enable educational institutions to more effectively address their constituents' diversity needs.

Adult Learning

Adult Education Quarterly.

This journal focuses on adult and continuing education practices and theory. It offers a spectrum of diverse perspectives on adult learning, with a focus on innovation.

Merriam, Sharan B., Rosemary S. Caffarella, and Lisa M. Baumgartner. *Learning in Adulthood: A Comprehensive Guide.* 3rd ed. San Francisco: Jossey-Bass, 2007. Print.

Merriam, Caffarella, and Baumgartner's text offers newcomers to adult education a comprehensive overview of the theories, practices, issues, and concerns relevant to adult educators. With a focus on the social context of adult learning, the authors examine the significant theories of adult learning. They clarify distinctions between conventional educational approaches and innovative approaches to teaching this population of students.

Michaud, Michael J. "The 'Reverse Commute': Adult Students and the Transition from Professional to Academic Literacy. *Teaching English in the Two-Year College.* 38.3 (2011): 244–57.

With a case study of one adult student moving from the world of work to the world of academia, Michaud generalizes challenges and outcomes for writing instructors. His focus on one student enables a window into the lives of many adult students who enroll in community college.

Writing Centers

International Writing Centers Association (www.writingcenters.org).

This online resource, sponsored by the International Writing Centers Association (IWCA), provides a full range of information for writing center administrators, including: peer-tutoring, a writing center directory, conference information, bibliographies, discussion forums, workshop institutes, and most important, resources that specifically address issues at two-year college writing centers.

Mohr, Ellen G. *Inside the Community College Writing Center: Ten Guiding Principles.* Emmitsburg: IWCA, 2007. Print.

This text identifies ten principles that shape the work of the writing center administrator within the community college, including recruiting and training tutors, writing a mission statement, and political sensitivity within the institution, among others.

Appendix A: "The Portland Resolution:" Guidelines for Writing Program Administrator Positions

Adopted by the Council of Writing Program Administrators, 1992

Published in *WPA: Writing Program Administration* 16.1/2 (Fall/ Winter 1992): 88–94.

Christine Hult and the Portland Resolution Committee:

David Joliffe, Kathleen Kelly, Dana Mead, Charles Schuster

BACKGROUND

The theme of the 1990 Council of Writing Program Administrators Conference was "Status, Standards, and Quality: The Challenge of Wyoming." Christine Hult, editor of *WPA: Writing Program Administration,* presented a paper at the conference that essentially called for extending the challenge of the Wyoming Resolution— and the subsequent Conference of College Composition and Communication (CCCC's) "Statement of Principles and Standards for the Postsecondary Teaching of Writing"—to WPAs. In "On Being a Writing Program Administrator," she invited WPAs to begin a dialogue toward the formulation of a statement of professional standards by the WPA organization. Such a statement would outline prerequisites for effective administration of writing programs as well as equitable treatment of WPAs. At the pre-conference workshop, participants were working on similar document, which they dubbed the "Portland Resolution." A representative committee was commissioned by the

WPA Executive Committee to draft a document; their combined work was presented at the 1991 summer conference and also sent to WPA members in *WPA News* to solicit comments toward revision of the document. This final version of the Portland Resolution, accepted by the Executive Committee at their 1992 CCCC meeting, is intended to help both Writing Program Administrators and those with whom they work and to whom they report develop quality writing programs in their institutions.

GUIDELINES FOR WRITING PROGRAM ADMINISTRATOR POSITIONS

I. Working Conditions Necessary for Quality Writing Program Administration

Many WPAs at colleges and universities, and department or division chairs at community colleges, find themselves in untenable job situations, being asked to complete unrealistic expectations with little tangible recognition or remuneration, and with few resources. The CCCC statement points out the exploitation of writing teachers at all levels, including program administrators: "The teaching, research, and service contributions of tenure-line composition faculty are often misunderstood or undervalued. At some postsecondary institutions, such faculty members are given administrative duties without the authority needed to discharge them; at others, they are asked to meet publication standards without support for the kind of research that their discipline requires." The following guidelines are intended to improve working conditions for more effective administration of writing programs.

1. *Writing job descriptions for WPAs.* Each institution is responsible for providing clear job descriptions or role statements for its WPAs (See Part II below). Such descriptions should be flexible enough for WPAs and the institution—and open to negotiation, especially when hiring a new WPA or starting a new writing program. The institution is responsible for providing a clear formula for determining "equivalence" for a WPA: What responsibilities are equivalent to teaching a full load (as determined by that institution)? What release time will be given for administration and staff development? What administrative work will be counted as "scholarship" in tenure and promotion decisions?

In addition, WPA positions should be situated within a clearly defined administrative structure so that the WPA knows to whom he or she is responsible and whom he or she supervises. A WPA should not be assigned to direct a program against her or his will or without appropriate training in rhetoric and composition and commensurate workplace experience. If a WPA needs specialized training in any area outside the usual purview of rhetoric and composition studies, the institution must be prepared to provide for and fund that training.

2. *Evaluating WPAs.* The institution is responsible for setting forth informed guidelines for assessing the work of a WPA fairly and for determining how administrative work is to be compared to traditional definitions of teaching, research, and service in decisions involving salary increases, retention, promotion, and tenure. Assessment of a WPA should consider the important scholarly contribution each WPA makes by virtue of designing, developing, and implementing a writing program.

3. *Job security.* WPA positions should carry sufficient stability and continuity to allow for the development of sound educational programs and planning. The WPA should be a regular, full-time, tenured faculty member or a full-time administrator with a recognizable title that delineates the scope of the position (e.g., Director of Writing, Coordinator of Composition, Division or Department Chair). WPAs should have travel funds equivalent to those provided for other faculty and administrators and should receive a salary commensurate with their considerable responsibilities and workload (including summer stipends). Requirements for retention, promotion, and tenure should be clearly defined and should consider the unique administrative demands of the position.

4. *Access.* WPAs should have access to those individuals and units that influence their programs—English department chairs or heads, deans, the Faculty Senate, Humanities directors, budget officers, people in admissions and in the registrar's office, and those who have anything to do with hiring, class sizes, placement. WPAs should have ample opportunities and release time to work in close consultation with colleagues in related fields and departments—Writing Center Directors, freshman advisors and freshman affairs officers, basic skills or developmental writing faculty, English-as-a-Second-Language Specialists,

student counseling services, committees on student issues such as retention or admissions standards.

5. *Resources* and *Budget.* WPAs should have the power to request, receive, and allocate funds sufficient for the running of the program. Resources include, but should not be limited to, adequate work space, supplies, clerical support, research support, travel funds, and release time. WPAs should be provided with administrative support—e.g., clerical help, computer time, duplicating services—equal in quality to that available to other program directors and administrators.

II. Guidelines for Developing WPA Job Descriptions

Each institution should carefully consider the role statements or job descriptions for its WPAs. Depending upon the size and scope of the writing program, the amount of administrative work expected of each WPA will vary considerably. Typically, however, WPAs have been exploited in these positions: given unrealistic workload expectations with little credit for administrative work.

At large institutions with diverse programs staffed by numerous faculty or graduate assistants, several WPAs may be needed (e.g., Director and Associate Director of Writing, Writing Center Director, Basic Writing Director, Computer Writing Lab Director, Director for Writing Across the Curriculum, and so on). At smaller institutions with fewer faculty and less diverse programs, fewer writing program administrators may be needed. It is also desirable to provide advanced graduate students with administrative experience in the form of internships or assistantships to the WPAs.

The following outline suggests both the scope of preparation needed to be an effective WPA and the diverse duties that WPAs at various institutions may perform. This list is illustrative of the kinds of duties WPAs typically are engaged in: it is not descriptive of an "ideal" WPA. Nor do we wish to imply that each WPA should be assigned all of these duties. On the contrary, the workload of each WPA should be carefully negotiated with the administration annually in the form of a role statement or job description to which all parties can agree.

1. Preparation for a WPA should include knowledge of or experience with the following:

- teaching composition and rhetoric
- theories of writing and learning
- research methods, evaluation methods, and teaching methods
- language and literacy development
- Various MLA, NCTE, and CCCC guidelines and position statements
- local and national developments in writing instruction
- writing, publishing, and presenting at conferences

2. Desirable supplemental preparation may include knowledge of or experience with the following areas:

Business

- accounting
- business administration
- grant writing
- information systems and computers
- personnel management
- records management
- public relations

Education

- curriculum design
- English as a Second Language
- testing and evaluation
- psychology of learning
- developmental or basic writing

3. As a particular institution negotiates job descriptions with each WPA, the responsibilities of the WPAs may be selected from among the following comprehensive list:

Scholarship of Administration:

- remain cognizant of current developments in teaching, research, and scholarship in rhetoric, composition, and program administration

- pursue scholarship of teaching and curriculum design as part of the essential work of the WPA

Faculty Development and Other Teaching:

- teaching a for-credit graduate course in the teaching of writing
- designing or teaching faculty development seminars
- training tutors
- supervising teaching assistants and writing staff
- evaluating teaching performance: observing and evaluating TAs and adjunct faculty in class; reviewing syllabuses and course policy statements; reviewing comments on student essays and grading practices
- preparing workshops and materials, conducting workshops, and conducting follow-up meetings
- undergraduate writing, reading, language, teaching, courses, etc.

Writing Program Development:

- designing curricula and course syllabi
- standardizing and monitoring course content
- serving on or chairing departmental committees on writing
- initiating or overseeing WAC programs
- developing teaching resource materials/library
- interviewing and hiring new faculty and staff
- selecting and evaluating textbooks (which may include establishing and supervising a textbook committee; maintaining a liaison with the bookstore; ensuring that orders are properly placed)

Writing Assessment, Writing Program Assessment, and Accountability:

- coordinating assessment and placement of students in appropriate writing courses
- administering writing placement exams and diagnostics (this may include creating and testing an appropriate instrument, acting as second reader for instructors, notifying the Registrar and instructors of any change in placements)
- administering competency, equivalency or challenge exams
- creating, or having access to, a database of information on enrollments, faculty and student performance
- administering student evaluations of teachers

- evaluating data on student retention, grade distribution, grade inflation, enrollment trends
- reporting to supervisors, chairs, deans, etc.
- conducting program reviews and self-studies

Registration and Scheduling:

- determining numbers of sections to be offered
- evaluating enrollment trends
- staffing courses
- monitoring registration

Office Management:

- supervising writing program office and secretary and staff
- supervising maintenance of office equipment and supplies
- (managing computer lab & staff)*
- (managing writing center staff)*
  (*may be separate positions)

Counseling and Advising:

- arbitrating grade disputes and resolving teacher and student complaints, such as placement, plagiarism, grade appeals, scheduling problems (which may include acting as liaison with the appropriate office)
- writing letters of recommendation for graduate students, adjuncts,and tutors

Articulation:

- coordinating writing courses and instruction with other academic support services (e.g., study skills center)
- coordinating with English as a Second Language programs
- coordinating with remedial/developmental programs
- coordinating with high school (AP, CLEP, concurrent enrollment) programs
- coordinating with English Education programs
- revising and updating any publications of the writing program
- discussing the writing program with administrators, publishers' representatives, parents, prospective students

Appendix B: WPA Outcomes Statement for First-Year Composition

Adopted by the Council of Writing Program Administrators (WPA), April 2000; amended July 2008.

A version of this statement was published in *WPA: Writing Program Administration* 23.1/2 (fall/winter 1999): 59–66

INTRODUCTION

This statement describes the common knowledge, skills, and attitudes sought by first-year composition programs in American postsecondary education. To some extent, we seek to regularize what can be expected to be taught in first-year composition; to this end the document is not merely a compilation or summary of what currently takes place. Rather, the following statement articulates what composition teachers nationwide have learned from practice, research, and theory. This document intentionally defines only "outcomes," or types of results, and not "standards," or precise levels of achievement. The setting of standards should be left to specific institutions or specific groups of institutions.

Learning to write is a complex process, both individual and social, that takes place over time with continued practice and informed guidance. Therefore, it is important that teachers, administrators, and a concerned public do not imagine that these outcomes can be taught in reduced or simple ways. Helping students demonstrate these outcomes requires expert understanding of how students actually learn to write. For this reason we expect the primary audience for this document to be well-prepared college writing teachers and college writing program administrators. In some places, we have chosen to write in their professional language. Among such readers, terms such as "rhetorical" and "genre" convey a rich meaning that is not easily simplified. While we have also aimed at writing a document that the general public can understand, in limited cases we have aimed first at communicating effectively with expert writing teachers and writing program administrators.

These statements describe only what we expect to find at the end of first-year composition, at most schools a required general education course or sequence of courses. As writers move beyond first-year composition, their writing abilities do not merely improve. Rather, students' abilities not only diversify along disciplinary and professional lines but also move into whole new levels where expected outcomes expand, multiply, and diverge. For this reason, each statement of outcomes for first-year composition is followed by suggestions for further work that builds on these outcomes.

RHETORICAL KNOWLEDGE

By the end of first year composition, students should

- Focus on a purpose
- Respond to the needs of different audiences
- Respond appropriately to different kinds of rhetorical situations
- Use conventions of format and structure appropriate to the rhetorical situation
- Adopt appropriate voice, tone, and level of formality
- Understand how genres shape reading and writing
- Write in several genres

Faculty in all programs and departments can build on this preparation by helping students learn

- The main features of writing in their fields
- The main uses of writing in their fields
- The expectations of readers in their fields

CRITICAL THINKING, READING, AND WRITING

By the end of first year composition, students should

- Use writing and reading for inquiry, learning, thinking, and communicating
- Understand a writing assignment as a series of tasks, including finding, evaluating, analyzing, and synthesizing appropriate primary and secondary sources
- Integrate their own ideas with those of others
- Understand the relationships among language, knowledge, and power

Faculty in all programs and departments can build on this preparation by helping students learn

- The uses of writing as a critical thinking method
- The interactions among critical thinking, critical reading, and writing
- The relationships among language, knowledge, and power in their fields

PROCESSES

By the end of first year composition, students should

- Be aware that it usually takes multiple drafts to create and complete a successful text
- Develop flexible strategies for generating, revising, editing, and proof-reading
- Understand writing as an open process that permits writers to use later invention and re-thinking to revise their work
- Understand the collaborative and social aspects of writing processes
- Learn to critique their own and others' works
- Learn to balance the advantages of relying on others with the responsibility of doing their part
- Use a variety of technologies to address a range of audiences

Faculty in all programs and departments can build on this preparation by helping students learn

- To build final results in stages
- To review work-in-progress in collaborative peer groups for purposes other than editing

- To save extensive editing for later parts of the writing process
- To apply the technologies commonly used to research and communicate within their fields

KNOWLEDGE OF CONVENTIONS

By the end of first year composition, students should

- Learn common formats for different kinds of texts
- Develop knowledge of genre conventions ranging from structure and paragraphing to tone and mechanics
- Practice appropriate means of documenting their work
- Control such surface features as syntax, grammar, punctuation, and spelling.

Faculty in all programs and departments can build on this preparation by helping students learn

- The conventions of usage, specialized vocabulary, format, and documentation in their fields
- Strategies through which better control of conventions can be achieved

COMPOSING IN ELECTRONIC ENVIRONMENTS

As has become clear over the last twenty years, writing in the 21st-century involves the use of digital technologies for several purposes, from drafting to peer reviewing to editing. Therefore, although the *kinds* of composing processes and texts expected from students vary across programs and institutions, there are nonetheless common expectations.

By the end of first-year composition, students should:

- Use electronic environments for drafting, reviewing, revising, editing, and sharing texts
- Locate, evaluate, organize, and use research material collected from electronic sources, including scholarly library databases; other official databases (e.g., federal government databases); and informal electronic networks and internet sources

- Understand and exploit the differences in the rhetorical strategies and in the affordances available for both print and electronic composing processes and texts

Faculty in all programs and departments can build on this preparation by helping students learn

- How to engage in the electronic research and composing processes common in their fields
- How to disseminate texts in both print and electronic forms in their fields

Notes

Notes to Introduction

1. For the purposes of this book, the terms "community colleges," "two-year institution," and "two-year college" refer to public, two-year, not-for-profit institutions.

2. Statistics from the AACC does not separate the percentage of white students enrolled in community colleges across the nation.

3. For example, Howard Tinberg's influential *Border Talk: Writing and Knowing in the Two-Year College* explores the ways students write and think—and how they are taught to write and think—within several different disciplines at the community college.

4. The academy's general disinterest in community college work is lessening, as seen in the inclusion of panels based on community college work at recent annual conferences of the MLA and WPA Council. Also, some English graduate programs are now explicitly addressing work in the two-year institution context; for example, Master's students may earn a Certificate in Teaching English at the Two-Year College at DePaul University (Murphy, Aiossa, and Winter 350).

Notes to Chapter One

1. The AACC states that the average annual tuition for public community colleges is $2,361; by contrast, public four-year colleges average $6,185 a year.

2. Total enrollment, including non-credit bearing courses, is 11.5 million students.

3. The AACC does not identify statistics for white students, in the majority, enrolled in community colleges.

4. The AACC notes that over two million community college students were Pell grant recipients, but "[b]ecause of the low costs to attend community college, the amounts borrowed are lower for community college students than they are for their counterparts at four-year institutions (public and private)" ("Students at Community Colleges").

5. This point is addressed more fully in Chapters 3, 4, and 5.

6. In affluent communities, this claim is not always the case. In these locations, demographics can include working and middle classes, who may live in the surrounding community or county, but are not necessarily representative of all residents.

7. More international students are enrolled in Santa Monica College in California and Houston Community College in Texas than anywhere else in the United States (Cohen and Brawer 48).

8. While there are several resources that speak to class awareness in the classroom, work done by Patrick Sullivan, Mike Rose, and Howard Tinberg provides a strong foundation for such a discussion; see the Works Cited list at the end of this text.

9. Still, the capacity of community colleges to instruct developmental students, coupled with open admissions policies, provides many four-year institutions and state systems the justification to insist that *only* community colleges address developmental writing and other developmental courses. While over fifty percent of states regulate developmental education, several have created mandates that place such instruction solely into the hands of the public two-year college, categorically removing it from the four-year institution. Among these states are Florida, Missouri, South Carolina, and Arizona (Roueche and Roueche, qtd. in Cohen and Brawer 293).

10. If WPAs are not acquainted with developmental writing resources already, they may want to become familiar with the Conference on Basic Writing and the National Association for Developmental Education (NADE) as two possible resources.

11. It may be beneficial to invite a learning disabilities professional on campus—if one exists—to address writing faculty. General information, such as universal design (e.g., the visual appearance of writing assignments), may be instrumental to instructors. Also, as related point, knowledge of services available for physically disabled students may also be beneficial.

12 WPAs must ensure that all faculty—particular part-time faculty for whom institutional information is sometimes elusive—understand emergency-response procedures and policies.

Notes to Chapter Two

1. Shor's number of 1,200 community colleges represents the total two-year institutions in the United States, including public, private, and tribal colleges.

2. Class-related discussions permeate all aspects of community college work, including the level of faculty salaries. Comparing salaries of community college faculty and their counterparts at four-year colleges and universities reflects class concerns even within the academic hierarchy. Full-time (up to five courses per semester) community college faculty salaries usually depend on the community surrounding the public two-year school; however,

the average faculty salary in a suburban school is $59,960, and $46,534 in a rural school. Up until the 1980s, community college salaries mostly paralleled university salaries. By 2006–2007, community college faculty were paid twenty-nine percent less than their university peers. However, most community colleges award tenure between the second and third year of service, as opposed to the more standard seven years at a four-year institution (Cohen and Brawer 92–94).

3. The rising popularity of First-Year Experience (FYE) programs in community colleges has resulted in coordinating developmental and first-year composition courses with the purpose of increasing student retention.

4. The notion of English courses as offerings of a "service" department derives from common assumptions about writing as a skill and not a knowledge-generating activity. These assumptions shape how writing is often administered in the community college context, as well as in four-year institutions. Mike Rose argues: "Writing is not just a skill with which one can present or analyze knowledge. It is essential to the very existence of certain kinds of knowledge" (593). If the WPA holds this view, he or she may find conflict or tension in working with instructors outside (or possibly even within) his or her discipline. Including developmental writing in his discussion, Mike Rose argues that if we accept that "Writing is a skill or a tool rather than a discipline," then we run the risk of reductive thinking:

> This kind of thinking and talking is so common that we often fail to notice that it reveals a reductive, fundamentally behaviorist model of the development and use of written language, a problematic definition of writing, and an inaccurate assessment of student ability and need. This way of talking about writing abilities and instruction is woven throughout discussions of program and curriculum development, course credit, instructional evaluation, and resource allocation. And, in various ways, it keeps writing instruction at the periphery of the curriculum. (586–87)

Still, even in the community college context, many administrators and instructors take such a view of writing instruction, based on the assumption of its service to other disciplines, and not as a means of creating knowledge. The WPA needs to identify assumptions about writing, in addition to being self-reflective about his or her own assumptions, and address them, deciding on a working view of writing as an academic activity within the community college context, and how that view guides the development of the writing program, and by extension, the English department.

Notes to Chapter 3

1. Appendix A replicates the Portland Resolution in full.

2. Hereafter, the Council of Writing Program Administrators will be referred to and cited as CWPA.

3. Cross-cultural training is often provided in an educational institution by inviting an outside contractor or consultant. Several organizations provide institutional assessments and in-house trainings and developments. However, it is rare to see cross-cultural issues addressed as pedagogical issues in English or composition and rhetoric graduate programs, aside from the study of work by multicultural authors.

4. TYCA stands for Two-Year College English Association, which is affiliated with NCTE.

5. Sullivan notes that the percentages add up to over 100% because respondents were permitted to select "all that apply" rather than placement practices categories (9).This table is replicated from his report "An Analysis of the National TYCA Research Initiative Survey, Section II: Assessment Practices in Two-Year College English Programs," which appeared in *Teaching English in the Two-Year College* (2008); see Works Cited list for details

6. Sullivan notes again that the percentages add up over one hundred because respondents were permitted to select "all that apply" of placement practices categories (17).

7. Politics and programmatic changes are addressed more explicitly in Chapters Four and Five.

Notes to Chapter 4

1. It is also true that some community college students enroll with little or no technological skills; some must be taught how to use a computer for word processing purposes. Further, even if students know how to use computers, WPAs must be sensitive to the fact that some do not own computers and/or their work schedules prevent them from accessing computers at a college computer lab during open hours.

2. This point may seem obvious; however, WPAs should not take for granted that the training or educational experience they received in graduate school is transferable directly to community college work. Four-year institutions often have slightly more or greatly more homogenous student populations than two-year institutions; therefore, placement, assessment, and all other aspects of the writing program can differ from those in the community college.

3. Here, Adler-Kassner compares such technological innovations as the motion picture and the radio, as well as the railroad.

4. The following list of assessment approaches has been narrowed only to reflect practices in writing programs, though Bers provides a more com-

prehensive list than identified here, one that includes approaches for all disciplines at the community college.

5. Bers points out that standardized tests are "controversial" and require buy-in from the faculty, a condition which is dependent on the test's alignment with programmatic objectives. Furthermore, she writes, "[u]nless test results directly affect graduation or grade-point averages, students have little incentive to take them seriously" (47).

Notes to Chapter 5

1. Schroeder notes that the departmental establishment of the English discipline occurs around the first perceived literacy crisis of the 1870s, and also around the time of an enrollment surge.

2. Adler-Kassner's *The Activist WPA* and Mike Rose's *Why School?* both speak extensively to legislation and public policy based on the perception of failure. Both texts link the perception to political agendas, and propose strategies for an effective response that legitimizes student literacy and reaffirms educators' experiential knowledge and insights.

Works Cited

"Adjunct English Posting Details." *Community College of Allegheny County Jobs*. Community College of Allegheny County. 7 Jan. 2011. Web. 10 Jan. 2011.

"Adjunct Faculty." *Jobs/Human Resources*. Westchester Community College. 2011. Web. 20 June 2011.

Adler-Kassner, Linda. *The Activist WPA*. Logan: Utah State UP, 2008. Print.

—, and Gregory R. Glau, eds. *The Bedford Bibliography for Teachers of Basic Writing*. Boston: Bedford/St. Martin's, 2002. Print.

Alford, Barry. Introduction. *The Politics of Writing in the Two Year College*. Ed. Barry Alford and Keith Kroll. Portsmouth: Heineman, 2001. v-viii. Print.

Anson Chris M. "Figuring It Out: Writing Programs in the Context of University Budgets." Brown and Enos 233–52.

Ashburn, Elyse. "Gates's Millions: Can Big Bucks Turn Students into Graduates?" *The Chronicle of Higher Education*. 8 August 2010. Web. 20 October 2010.

Association of American Colleges and Universities. *More Reasons for Hope: Diversity Matters in Higher Education*. Washington: Association of American Colleges and Universities, 2009. Print.

Bailey, Thomas, Davis Jenkins, and Timothy Leinbach. *What We Know about Community College Low Income and Minority Student Outcomes: Descriptive Statistics from National Surveys. Community College Research Center*. Teachers College, Columbia University. January 2005. Web. 15 June 2010.

Bailey, Thomas R., Katherine L. Hughes, and David Thornton Moore. *Working Knowledge: Work-Based Learning and Education Reform*. New York: Routledge, 2004. Print.

Bartholomae, David. "Inventing the University." *When a Writer Can't Write: Studies in Writer's Block and Other Composing-Process Problems*. Ed. Mike Rose. 1985. Rpt. in Miller. *Norton*, 605–30. Print.

Bauer, Laurie. "Utilizing Reading Conferences in Developmental Reading Courses." *NADE Digest* 4.2 (2009): 41–48. Print.

Beckham, Edgar F. "Diversity at the Crossroads: Mapping Our Work in the Years Ahead." *More Reasons for Hope: Diversity Matters in Higher Edu-*

cation. Washington: Association of American Colleges and Universities, 2009. 9–17. Print.

Bers, Trudy H. "Assessment at the Program Level." Serban and Friedlander 43–52.

Bickmore, Lisa, and Ron Christiansen. "'Who Will Be the Inventors? Why Not Us': Multimodal Compositions in the Two-Year College Classroom." *Teaching English in the Two-Year College* 37.3 (2010): 230–42. Print.

Bloom, Lynn Z., Donald A. Daiker, and Edward M. White, eds. *Composition in the Twenty-First Century: Crisis and Change*. Carbondale: Southern Illinois UP, 1996. Print.

Brady, Laura. "A Greenhouse for Writing Program Change." *Writing Program Administration* 29.3 (2006): 27–43. Print.

Breznau, Anne. "Operationalized Democracy: Teaching English at the Community College." *ADE Bulletin*. 120 (1998). Web. 26 Jan. 2011.

Brown, Stuart C., and Theresa Enos, eds. *The Writing Program Administrator's Resource: A Guide to Reflective Institutional Practice*. Mahwah: Lawrence Erlbaum, 2002. Print.

Bullock, Richard, and John Trimbur, eds. *The Politics of Writing Instruction: Postsecondary*. Portsmouth: Heinemann, 1991. Print.

Burke, Joseph C., and Henrik P. Minassians. "Implications of State Performance Indicators for Community College Assessment." Serban and Friedlander 53–64.

Burnham, Christopher. "Reflection, Assessment, and Articulation: A Rhetoric of Writing Program Administration." Brown and Enos 303–14.

Center for Community College Student Engagement. *The Heart of Student Success: Teaching, Learning, and College Completion*. Austin: The University of Texas at Austin, Community College Leadership Program, 2010.

Choseed, Malkiel. "(Re)Creating a Writing Program: Instituting and Negotiating Change Using the WPA Outcomes Statement." WPA Work in Community College Contexts. MLA Annual Convention. Philadelphia. 28 Dec. 2009. Conference paper.

Coley, Richard J. "The American Community College Turns 100: A Look at its Students, Programs, and Prospects." Princeton: ETS, 2000. Print.

"Communications Strategies." *Assessment Gallery and Resources*. Council of Writing Program Administrators. 2009. Web. 2 July 2010.

"Community Colleges Past to Present." American Association of Community Colleges. 2010. Web. 13 July 2010.

Connors, Robert J. "The Abolition Debate in Composition: A Short History." Bloom and White 47–63.

Cohen, Arthur M., and Florence B. Brawer. *The American Community College*. 5th ed. San Francisco: Jossey-Bass, 2008. Print.

"Community College of Vermont Admissions." Community College of Vermont. 2010. Web. 2 June 2010.

Crowley, Sharon. "How the Professional Lives of WPAs Would Change if FYC Were Elective." Brown and Enos 219–30.

"Course Descriptions." Westchester Community College. Web. 26 Jan. 2011.

Dallas County Community College District. "Developmental Writing Faculty." *Inside Higher Education*. 31 Jan. 2011. Web. 31 Jan. 2011.

DeBraak, LaRonna. "Independent and Interdependent Remedial/Developmental Student Learners." *NADE Digest* 4.1 (2008): 11–18. Print.

Desser, Daphne. "Assessment as Political Definition: Who Speaks for the Underprepared?" Alford and Kroll 107–18.

Dewey, John. *Democracy and Education: an Introduction to the Philosophy of Education*. 1944. New York: Macmillan, 1961. Print.

"Doing More with Less: The Inequitable Funding of Community Colleges." American Association of Community Colleges. 8 September 2010. Web. 9 June 2011.

Dougherty, Kevin J. *The Contradictory College: The Conflicting Origins, Impacts, and Futures of the Community College*. Albany: State U of New York P, 1994. Print.

Edgecombe, Nikki. "Accelerating the Academic Achievement of Students Referred to Developmental Education." *Community College Resource Center*. Teachers College, Columbia University. Feb. 2011. Web. 21 Feb. 2011.

"Employment." Heartland Community College. Jan. 2011. Web. 10 Jan. 2011.

"Enrollment." *Community College Enrollment*. American Association of Community Colleges. 2011. Web. 8 June 2011.

"Faculty Development." *The Writing Initiative at PCCC*. Passaic County Community College. 23 Nov. 2010. Web. 15 Mar. 2011.

"Fast Facts." *About Community Colleges*. American Association of Community Colleges. 2011. Web. 8 June 2011.

Ferris, Dana R., and John S. Hedgcock. *Teaching ESL Composition Purpose, Process, and Practice*. Mahwah: Lawrence Erlbaum, 2005. Print.

Ferretti, Eileen. "Just a Little Higher Education: Teaching Working-Class Women on the Vocational Track." Alford and Kroll 1–18.

Florence-Darling Technical College Admissions. Florence-Darling Technical College. Web. 2 June 2010.

Foderaro, Lisa W. "CUNY Adjusts Amid Tide of Remedial Students." *The New York Times*. 3 March 2011. Web. 3 March 2011.

Fox, Tom. "From Freedom to Manners: African American Literacy Instruction in the 19th Century." *Composition Forum* 96.1 (1995): 1–12. Rpt. in Miller 119–28.

Gallagher, Chris W. "What Do WPAs Need to Know about Writing Assessment? An Immodest Proposal." *Writing Program Administration* 33.1–2 (2009): 29–45. Print.

Ganz, Marshall. "Why David Sometimes Wins: Strategic Capacity in Social Movements." 2002. Microsoft Word file.

Gardner, Clint. "Introduction to Writing Across the Curriculum at the Community Colleges: Beating the Odds." *Across the Disciplines*. 2010. Web. 30 Nov. 2010.

Giordano, Joanne Baird, and Holly Hassel. "Development of Writing Programs at Multi-Campus, Two-Year Institutions: Aligning Basic Skills Courses with First-Year Writing Programs." CCCC Annual Convention. Atlanta. 2011. Conference paper.

Gonzalez, Jennifer. "2-Year Colleges Get Details of $2-Billion Grant Program." *The Chronicle of Higher Education*. 20 Jan. 2011. Web. 21 Jan. 2011.

—. "Historic White House Summit to Put Community Colleges in the Spotlight." *The Chronicle of Higher Education*. 5 October 2010. Web. 20 October 2010.

—. "In Texas Speech, Obama Renews His Educational Goals for the Nation." *The Chronicle of Higher Education*. 9 August 2010. Web. 20 October 2010.

Gunner, Jeanne. "Collaborative Administration." Brown and Enos 253–62.

—. "Doomed to Repeat It?: A Needed Space for Critique in Historical Recovery."*Historical Studies of Writing Program Administration*. Ed. Barbara L'Eplattenier and Lisa Mastrangelo. West Lafayette: Parlor Press, 2004. 263–78. Print.

Hall, Anne-Marie. "Expanding the Community: A Comprehensive Look at Outreach and Articulation." Brown and Enos 315–30.

Hansen, Kristine. "Face to Face with Part-Timers: Ethics and the Professionalization of Writing Faculties." Janangelo and Hansen 23-45.

Harrington, Susanmarie. "Learning to Ride the Waves: Making Decisions about Placement Testing." *Writing Program Administration*. 28.3 (2005): 9–29. Print.

Hebel, Sara. "Obama to Propose Graduation Goal and $12-Billion in Programs for 2-Year Colleges." *The Chronicle of Higher Education*. 14 July 2009. Web. 20 October 2010.

Hesse, Douglas H. "Politics and the WPA: Traveling Through and Past Realms of Experience." Brown and Enos 41–58.

Hillocks, George, Jr. *Teaching Writing as Reflective Practice*. New York: Teachers College P, 1995. Print.

Holladay, Sylvia. A. "Order out of Chaos: Voices from the Community College." Bloom, Daiker, and White 29–38.

Holmsten, Victoria. "This Site Under Construction: Negotiating Space for WPA Work in the Community College." Brown and Enos 429–38.

Hull, Gynda, Mike Rose, Kay Losey Fraser, and Marisa Castellano. "Remediation as Social Construct: Perspectives from an Analysis of Classroom."

College Composition and Communication 42.3 (1991): 299–329. Rpt. in Miller 783–812.

Jenkins, Davis, and Thomas Bailey. "How Community Colleges Can Reach Obama's Goals." *Inside Higher Ed.* 13 Oct. 2009. Web. 15 Oct. 2009.

"Jobs." *Community College of Allegheny County Jobs.* Community College of Allegheny County. 10 Jan. 2011. Web. 15 Mar. 2011.

Joint Task Force on Assessment of the International Reading Association and the National Council of Teachers of English. *Standards for the Assessment of Reading and Writing.* Delaware: IRA & NCTE, 2010. Print.

Kells, Michelle Hall. "Lessons Learned at Hispanic-Serving Institutions." Foreword. Kirklighter, Cárdenas, and Murphy vii-xiv.

Kirklighter, Cristina, Susan Wolff Murphy, and Diana Cárdenas. Introduction. *Teaching Writing with Latino/a Students.* Eds. Cristina Kirklighter, Diana Cárdenas, and Susan Wolff Murphy. Albany: State U of New York P, 2007. 1–13. Print.

Klausman, Jeffrey. "Mapping the Terrain: The Two-Year College Program Administrator." *Teaching English in the Two-Year College* 35.3 (2008): 238–51. Print.

Kort, Melissa Sue. "Crossing the Great Divide: From the Two-Year College to the University and Back." *Teaching English in the Two-Year College* 21.3 (Oct. 1994): 177–82. Print.

Leaker, Cathy, and Heather Ostman. "Composing Knowledge: Writing, Rhetoric, and Reflection in Prior Learning Assessment." *College Composition and Communication* 61:4 (2010): 691–717. Print.

"LPTC Mission Statement." Little Priest Tribal College. Web. 7 Feb. 2011.

Lundell, Dana Britt, and Terence Collins. "Toward a Theory of Developmental Education: The Centrality of 'Discourse.'" *The Expanding Role of Developmental Education.* Ed. Jeanne L. Higbee and Patricia Dwinell. Morrow: NADE, 1999. 3–20. Print.

Lyons, Scott Richard. "Rhetorical Sovereignty: What Do American Indians Want from Writing?" *College Composition and Communication* 51.3 (2000): 447–68. Rpt. in Miller 1128–47.

Madden, Frank. "Crossing Borders: The Two-Year College." *College English* 61 (July 1999): 721–30. Print.

Marcotte, Dave E., et al. "The Returns of a Community College Education: Evidence from the National Education Longitudinal Study." Educational Evaluation and Policy Analysis. 27.2 (2005): 165-171. Print.

McLeod, Susan H. *Writing Program Administration.* West Lafayette: Parlor Press, 2007. Print.

McMullen-Light, Mary. "Great Expectations: The Culture of WAC and the Community College Context. *Across the Disciplines.* 2010. Web. 30 Nov. 2010.

McTighe Musil, Caryn. "The Evolution of Campus Diversity Work." *More Reasons for Hope: Diversity Matters in Higher Education*. Washington: Association of American Colleges and Universities, 2009. 1–7. Print.

Merriam, Sharan B., Rosemary S. Caffarella, and Lisa M. Baumgartner. *Learning in Adulthood: A Comprehensive Guide*. 3ʳᵈ ed. San Francisco: Jossey-Bass, 2007. Print.

Meyers, Alan. "Coming of Age in ESL: Memoirs of a Reluctant Pioneer." Reynolds and Holladay-Hicks 82–89.

Merrill, Yvonne, and Thomas P. Miller. "Making Learning Visible: A Rhetorical Stance on General Education." Brown and Enos 203–17.

Miller, Susan. "The Feminization of Composition." Bullock and Trimbur 39–53.

—, ed. *The Norton Book of Composition Studies*. New York: W.W. Norton & Co., 2009. Print.

Millward, Jody, Sandra Starkey, and David Starkey. "Teaching English in a California Two-Year Hispanic-Serving Institution." Kirklighter, Cárdenas, and Murphy 37–59.

"Mission Statement of San Antonio College." San Antonio College. 14 Oct. 2010. Web. 7 Feb. 2011.

MLA Committee on Community Colleges. *A Community College Teaching Career*. MLA. 2006. 6 Jan. 2011. Web.

Moltz, David. "Suggestions for the Summit." *Inside Higher Ed*. 16 Apr. 2010. Web. 6 May 2010.

"More about Springfield Technical Community College." Springfield Technical Community College. Web. 7 Feb. 2011.

Murphy, Sean P., Elizabeth Aiossa, and Mary Mugica Winter. "Preparing Future Faculty: Ten Years Later." *Teaching English in the Two-Year College* 37.4 (2010): 350–62. Print.

"The NCTE Definition of 21ˢᵗ Century Literacies." *NCTE Position Statement*. NCTE. 18 Feb. 2008. Web. 19 Mar. 2010.

Nist, Elizabeth A., and Helon H. Raines. "Two-Year Colleges: Explaining and Claiming Our Majority." Janangelo and Hansen 59–70.

"Our Mission." Columbus State Community College. Web. 7 Feb. 2011.

Palomar College 2010–2011 Catalog. Palomar Community College. Web. 7 Feb. 2011.

Palomba, Catherine A., and Trudy W. Banta, eds. *Assessment Essentials: Planning, Implementing, and Improving Assessment in Higher Education*. San Francisco: Jossey-Bass, 1999. Print.

Pantoja, Veronica, Nancy Tribbenesee, and Duane Roen. "Legal Considerations for Writing Program Administrators." Brown and Enos 137–53.

Parker, Tara L., Leticia Tomas Bustillos, and Laurie B. Behringer. *Getting Past Go: Remedial and Developmental Education Policy at a Crossroads*. Boston: U Mass Boston PrePare, 2010. Web. 12 Dec. 2010.

Parry, Marc, and Karin Fischer. "Obama's Ambitious Plan for Community Colleges Raises Hopes and Questions." Government. *The Chronicle of Higher Education.* 15 July 2009. Web. 20 October 2010.

Phelps, Louise Wetherbee. "Turtles All the Way Down: Educating Academic Leaders." Brown and Enos 3–39.

Plinske, Kathleen, and Walter J. Packard. "Trustees' Perceptions of the Desired Qualifications for the Next Generation of Community College Presidents." *Community College Review* 2010. Web. 13 July 2010.

Portland Resolution. Writing Program Administration 16.1/2 (1992): 88–89. Rpt. Council of Writing Program Administrators. Web. 10 Nov. 2010.

"Position Statement Prepared by the NCTE Committee on Issues in ESL and Bilingual Education." *NCTE Guideline.* NCTE. 1981. Web. 15 July 2010.

"Posting Details." *Prairie State College Employment Site.* Prairie State College. 14 Dec. 2010. Web. 18 Jan. 2011.

Power-Stubbs, Karen, and Jeff Sommers. "'Where We Are Is Who We Are': Location, Professional Identity, and the Two-Year College." Alford and Kroll 19–41.

Preto-Bay, Ana Maria, and Kristine Hansen. "Preparing for the Tipping Point: Designing Writing Programs to Meet the Needs of the Changing Population." *WPA: Writing Program Administration* 30.1–2 (2006): 37–57. Print.

"Professional Development." *Caldwell Community College & Technical Institute: Quality Enhancement Plan.* Caldwell Community College & Technical Institute. Web. 15 Mar. 2011.

Pusser, Brian, et al. *Returning to Learning: Adults' Success in College is Key to America's Future. Lumina Foundation.* March 2007. Web. 29 Jan. 2010.

Raines, Helon Howell. "Is There a Writing Program in This College? Two Hundred and Thirty-Six Two-Year Schools Respond." *College Composition and Communication* 41.2 (1990): 151–65. Print.

Reynolds, Mark. "Two-Year-College Teachers as Knowledge Makers." *The Profession of English in the Two-Year College.* Ed. Mark Reynolds and Sylvia Holladay-Hicks. Portsmouth, NH: Heinemann, 2005. 1- 15. Print.

—, and Sylvia Holladay-Hicks, eds. *The Profession of English in the Two Year College.* Portsmouth: Heinemann, 2005. Print.

Rifkin, Tronie. "Public Community College Faculty." American Association of Community Colleges. 2011. Web. 31 Jan. 2011.

Ritter, Kelly. "Before Mina Shaughnessy: Basic Writing at Yale, 1920–1960." *College Composition and Communication* 60.1 (2008): 12–45. Print.

Roberts, Leslie. "An Analysis of the National TYCA Research Initiative Survey Section IV: Writing Across the Curriculum and Writing Centers in Two-Year College English Programs." *Teaching English in the Two-Year College* 36.2 (2008): 138–52. Print.

Rose, Mike. *Lives on the Boundary: a Moving Account of the Struggles and Achievements of America's Educationally Underprepared.* New York: Penguin, 2005. Print.

—. *The Mind at Work.* New York: Viking, 2004. Print.

—. *Why School?* New York: The New Press, 2009. Print.

Royer, Daniel J., and Roger Gilles. "Placement Issues." Brown and Enos 263–74.

Scharton, Maurice. "Politics of Validity." *Assessment of Writing: Politics, Policies, and Practices.* Ed. Edward M. White, William D. Lutz, and Sandra Kamusikiri. New York: MLA, 1996. 53–75. Print.

Schell, Eileen E. "Part-Tim/Adjunct Issues: Working Toward Change." Brown and Enos 181–201.

Schilb, John. "The WPA and the Politics of LitComp." Brown and Enos 165–79.

Schroeder, Christopher. "Academic Literacies, Legitimacy Crises, and Electronic Cultures." *Journal of Literacy and Technology* 1.2 (2001): n. pag. Web. 8 July 2010.

Schwegler, Robert A. "The Politics of Reading Student Papers." Bullock and Trimbur 203–25.

Scordaras, Maria. "Just Not Enough Time: Accelerated Composition Courses and Struggling ESL Writers." *Teaching English in the Two-Year College* 36.3 (2009): 270–79. Print.

"Search Jobs." *Mountain View College.* Dallas County Community College District. 2010. Web. 18 Jan. 2011.

Serban, Andreea M., and Jack Friedlander, eds. *Developing and Implementing Assessment of Student Learning Outcomes.* San Francisco: Jossey-Bass, 2004. Print.

"Serving Communities." *Members.* Association of Canadian Community Colleges. 2010. Web. 9 June 2011.

Shafer, Gregory. "The Process of Change in a Community College Writing Program." *Teaching English in the Two-Year College* 29.1 (2001): 7–15. Print.

Shaughnessy, Mina P. *Errors and Expectations: A Guide for the Teacher of Basic Writing.* 1977. Rpt. in Miller 387–96.

Shor, Ira. Afterword, "The Community College: Still Cooling Out." Alford and Kroll. 132–36.

Slayter, Mary. "Creating Our College, Our Community, and Ourselves." Reynolds and Holladay-Hicks 16–26.

Slevin, James F. "Depoliticizing and Politicizing Composition Studies." Bullock and Trimbur 1–21.

Smiley, Tavis. *Fail Up.* New York: Smiley Books, 2011. Print.

"STCC Course Descriptions for English." Springfield Technical Community College. Web. 7 Feb. 2011.

"Students at Community Colleges." *American Association of Community Colleges.* 2009. Web. 8 Jan. 2009.

Sullivan, Patrick. "An Analysis of the National TYCA Research Initiative Survey, Section II: Assessment Practices in Two-Year College English Programs." *Teaching English in the Two-Year College* 36.1 (2008): 7–26. Print.

—. "Cultural Narratives about Success and the Material Conditions of Class at the Community College." *Teaching English in the Two-Year College* 33.2 (2005): 142–60. Print.

—. "What Is 'College-Level' Writing?" *Teaching English in the Two-Year Institution.* NCTE (May 2003): 374–90. Web. 15 July 2010.

Taylor, Tim. "Writing Program Administration at the Two-Year College: Ghosts in the Machine." *Writing Program Administration* 32.3 (2009): 120–39. Print.

"Title III Part A Programs." *ED.gov.* U.S. Department of Education. 9 March 2011. Web. 31 May 31, 2011.

Tinberg, Howard. "Are We Good Enough? Critical Literacy and the Working Class." *College English* 63.3 (2001): n. pag. Web. 5 Aug. 2006.

—. *Border Talk: Writing and Knowing in the Two-Year College.* Urbana: NCTE, 1997. Print.

—. "Examining Our Assumptions as Gatekeepers: A Two-Year College Perspective." *Administrative Problem-Solving for Writing Programs and Writing Centers: Scenarios in Effective Program Management.* Ed. Linda Myers-Breslin. Urbana: NCTE, 1999. 62–69. Print.

—. "Teaching English in Two-Year Colleges: A Review of Selected Studies." Reynolds and Holladay-Hicks 137–46.

Two-Year College English Association. *Research and Scholarship in the Two-Year College.* Two-Year College English Association, NCTE, 2004. Print.

"Undergraduate Enrollment." *Participation in Education.* National Center for Education Statistics. 2010. Web. 9 July 2010.

"Vision and Mission." Hillsborough Community College. Web. 7 February 2011.

Watkins, James Ray. *A Taste for Language: Literacy, Class, and English Studies.* Carbondale: Southern Illinois Press, 2009. Print.

Wall, Susan and Nicholas Coles. "Reading Basic Writing: Alternatives to a Pedagogy of Accommodation." Bullock and Trimbur 227–46.

White, Edward, William Lutz, and Sandra Kamuskiri, eds. *Assessment of Writing: Politics, Policies, Practices.* New York: MLA, 1996. Print.

White, Edward. "Teaching a Graduate Course in Writing Program Administration." Brown and Enos 101–12.

—. *Developing Successful College Writing Programs.* San Francisco: Jossey-Bass, 1999. Print.

"Wind River Tribal College Mission Statement." Wind River Tribal College. Web. 7 Feb. 2011.

Worthen, Helena. "The Problem of the Majority Contingent Faculty in the Community Colleges." Alford and Kroll 42–60.

"Writing in the Disciplines at LaGuardia Community College." LaGuardia Community College. 2010. Web. 15 Mar. 2011.

"WPA Outcomes Statement for First-Year Composition." Council of Writing Program Administrators. July 2008. Web. 15 July 2010.

"Writing Assessment: A Position Statement." *CCCC Position Statement.* NCTE. 2000. Web. 21 Apr. 2010.

Yancey, Kathleen Blake. "Made Not Only in Words: Composition in a New Key." *College Composition and Communication* 56.2 (2004): 297–334. Print.

—. *Reflection in the Writing Classroom.* Logan: Utah State UP, 1998. Print.

Index

Adjunct faculty, *see contingent faculty*

Adler-Kassner, Linda, 5, 16–17, 117, 167, 170, 172, 174, 178, 180, 184, 188, 193, 214–215

American Association of Community Colleges (AACC), 3, 93, 178

American Graduation Initiative, 152–153, 179

articulation, 15, 21, 103–104, 110, 122–123, 137

assessment, 10, 22, 36, 44–45, 49, 52, 60–61, 87, 98, 100–101, 103–104, 111–112, 118, 120, 123, 126, 128, 131, 135–139, 141–143, 150, 154–155, 171, 174–177, 190, 192, 195–196, 204, 213–214

average age of community college students, 25, 36

Brawer, Florence B., 13, 18, 20, 27, 41, 48, 54, 5859, 62, 64, 69–70, 81, 90, 94, 122, 137–138, 169, 175, 190, 212–213

Budgets, 4, 38, 104, 134, 139–142, 144, 150, 169, 201

Clinton, President William, 41

Cohen, Arthur M., 13, 18, 20, 27, 41, 48, 54, 58, 59, 62, 64, 69–70, 81, 90, 94, 122, 137–138, 169, 175, 190, 212–213

Community College of Vermont, 21

Conference on Basic Writing (CBW), 189, 194

Conference on College Composition and Communication (CCCC), 103, 149, 186, 196, 199–200, 203

contingent faculty, 10, 71, 94, 96–97, 104, 126–127, 129–134, 144, 160, 190, 204, 212

Council of Writing Program Administrators (CWPA), 91, 103, 108, 110, 149, 176, 186, 188–189, 199, 206, 214

curricular development, 105, 107, 110, 114, 120, 177

curriculum, 15, 21, 58–59, 70, 77, 86–87, 98, 103–105, 107, 110–111, 113–114, 117, 119, 121, 127–129, 133, 137, 143, 159–161, 164, 167, 170, 179, 191–194, 203–204, 213

decision-making processes, 57, 98, 102, 104, 111

Definition of 21st Century Literacies, NCTE, 6, 165, 180, 191

developmental students, 26, 48, 50, 51, 88, 93, 118–119, 120, 157, 161–162, 194, 212

developmental studies, 10, 49, 117, 120, 143, 151, 153, 156, 162–163 developmental writing, 23, 48, 49, 51, 72, 104, 110, 117, 119–121, 139, 155, 157–159, 162, 168, 193, 201, 212–213

diversity, 4, 10, 14, 20, 22–26, 54, 56, 61–62, 81, 85, 89, 111, 115, 127, 143, 151, 162–166, 182–183, 186, 189, 197

Dougherty, Kevin, 196

emergent literacies, 6, 166, 171–172

emotional intelligence, 51, 53, 147–148

emotional needs, 14, 52–53

English-as-Second Language (ESL), (L2), 8, 14, 35, 44, 79–80, 82, 93, 99, 110, 121, 133–134, 138, 159, 188, 194–195

enrollment, 5, 10, 11, 21, 35, 39–41, 44, 46, 48, 51, 53–54, 66, 67, 104, 111, 123–124, 142, 150, 157, 169, 183–184, 187, 205, 211, 215

ethnicity, 8, 14, 36, 48, 52, 54, 181

faculty development, 97–98, 100, 104, 111, 116, 131–133, 143, 155, 157, 159, 162, 164, 172–173, 182, 204

Florence-Darling Technical College, 21

Full-time equivalents (FTSEs), 77

full-time faculty, 71, 94, 127

Functionalist Advocates, 67

gender, 34, 36, 52, 68, 93, 181

Generation 1.5, 8, 35, 44, 110, 121

Graduate Equivalency Diploma (GED), 21, 27, 33

Harper, William Rainey, 65, 68

Harvard College, 70

Hispanic-Serving Institutions (HSI), 41

Instrumental Marxists, 68

Internet communication technology (ICT), 170, 171, 173, 185

Joliet, Illinois, 58

Jordan, David Starr, 68, 163

junior college, 3, 58, 65–66, 68

Klausman, Jeffrey, 11, 13, 71, 79–81, 97, 100, 131–133, 144, 168, 189

Lange, Alexis, 68

Latino students, 3, 41, 45

learning disabilities, 8, 14, 52, 212

Marxist views of the community college, 67

McLeod, Susan, 9, 13, 58, 66, 70, 77, 101, 110, 114, 148, 167, 176, 185, 189

Modern Language Association (MLA), 24, 66, 72, 77, 86, 88, 89, 95, 96, 98, 103, 149, 181–182, 186, 196, 203, 211

multiple literacies, 5, 10, 11, 111, 150, 151, 165, 166, 169, 170, 173, 179, 185

National Association for Developmental Education (NADE), 118, 194, 212

National Council of Teachers of English (NCTE), 6, 103, 122, 149, 165–166, 174, 178, 180, 191–192, 195, 196, 203, 214

Native American students, 3, 41–42

nontraditional student, 22, 26, 35–36, 86, 172, 181, 192

Obama Administration, 3, 5, 150–
154, 156, 158, 162, 179, 183
open admissions, 14, 20–23, 41,
42, 54, 57, 173, 212

pedagogy, 7, 8, 11, 71, 81, 85–87,
92–94, 96, 99, 110, 112–113,
115, 121, 128–129, 131, 133,
149, 151, 167, 171, 173,
192–195, 214
placement, 10, 49, 72, 104,
135–138, 143, 145, 149, 160,
188, 196, 201, 204–205, 214
politics, 10, 105, 144, 152, 156,
176–178, 188, 190, 196
portfolios, 128, 131, 137–138, 175
Portland Resolution, 91, 103–104,
199, 214
postsecondary education, 27, 154,
175, 200, 206
program assessment, 10, 116, 174,
175–176

race, 8, 14, 36, 48, 52, 54, 68, 93,
163, 181
reliability, as in assessment methods, 135, 196
religion, 8, 36, 45, 150
Rogue Community College (RCC),
113
Rose, Mike, 5, 47, 55, 118,
191–192, 194, 212–213, 215

Santa Barbara City College
(SBCC), 20
scheduling courses, 10
sexual orientation, 8, 36
Shor, Ira, 54, 68, 212

single parents, 25
standardized tests, 215

Tappan, Henry, 65, 68
*Teaching English in the Two-Year
College*, 6, 91, 166, 189, 192,
198, 214
Teaching English to Speakers of
Other Languages (TESOL), 82,
122, 161, 195
technology, 6, 8, 34, 37, 56, 62,
86–89, 165–166, 170, 185, 190,
197
The Contradictory College, 67, 196
Tidewater Community College, 33,
40, 115
Tinberg, Howard, 11, 48, 65,
78–79, 81, 92, 134, 173, 182,
185, 187, 192–193, 211–212
traditional student, 26, 39, 186
transfer students, 9, 22, 24, 32,
60–61, 68–69, 83, 122–123,
137–138, 152, 165, 175, 191
tribal community colleges, 41, 54

working students, 45–46
working-class students, 46–47, 196
WPA Outcomes Statement for
First-Year Composition, 107–
109, 206
Writing Across the Curriculum
(WAC), 115—116, 131, 192,
204
writing centers, 78, 86, 134, 140,
198, 205

Yancey, Kathleen Blake, 5, 165, 166

About the Author

Heather Ostman is Associate Professor and Assistant Chair of the SUNY Westchester Community College English Department, where she teaches courses in writing and literature. Before joining Westchester Community College, she served as the writing program coordinator at the Metropolitan Manhattan campus of SUNY Empire State College. Her work has appeared in essay collections and in journals such as *College Composition and Communication*, *Women's Studies*, *Prose Studies*, *Philological Quarterly*, and *New Writing*. She is the editor of *Kate Chopin in the Twenty-First Century: New Critical Essays* (2008) and serves as the President of the Kate Chopin International Society. She is also the recipient of the SUNY Chancellor's Award for Excellence in Scholarship and Creative Activities and the Westchester Community College Foundation Faculty Excellence Award in Scholarship. In 2012, she and her colleague Frank Madden were awarded a National Endowment for the Humanities Challenge Grant for Two-Year Colleges to establish and co-direct the SUNY Westchester Community College Humanities Institute, which provides curricula, events, and pedagogical training in the humanities with an emphasis on the immigrant experience in the United States.

Photograph of the author by Sally Linehan.

CPSIA information can be obtained at www.ICGtesting.com
Printed in the USA
BVOW04s0037291113

337567BV00002B/73/P